All
That
Hollywood
Allows

Gender & American Culture

Jackie Byars

All That Hollywood Allows

Re-reading
Gender in
1950s
Melodrama

The University of

North Carolina Press

Chapel Hill &

London

©1991 The University of North Carolina Press
All rights reserved

Library of Congress Cataloging-in-Publication Data
Byars, Jackie.
    All that Hollywood allows : re-reading gender in 1950s
melodrama / Jackie Byars.
        p.   cm.—(Gender & American culture)
    Includes bibliographical references and index.
    ISBN 0-8078-1953-0 (alk. paper).—
        ISBN 0-8078-4312-1 (pbk. : alk. paper)
    1. Sex roles in motion pictures. 2. Women in motion
pictures. 3. Melodrama in motion pictures. 4. Feminist
film criticism. 5. Motion pictures—Social aspects—United
States. 6. United States—Popular culture—History—
20th century. I. Title. II. Series.
PN1995.9.S47B9   1991
791.43'6538—dc20   90-46738
                    CIP

The paper in this book meets the guidelines for permanence
and durability of the Committee on Production Guidelines
for Book Longevity of the Council on Library Resources.

Manufactured in the United States of America
95 94 93 92 91
5 4 3 2 1

TO CARL

Contents

Acknowledgments

Rituals survive because they continue to be personally and socially valuable; the practice of acknowledging and thanking those people important to the development of a book project remains common because it allows us to express gratitude in a public and formal way that admits to the ultimately collaborative process of intellectual labor. There are many people I want to thank for various kinds of help I received as I developed this book. First, I would like to thank a few people who have been especially important to me, personally and intellectually, over the past few years, the period during which I wrote and rewrote this book. I have been privileged to share both ideas and good times with each of them, and to each of them I owe a great debt: Mary Layoun, Alda Blanco, Janice Radway, and Horace Newcomb.

Several people read early versions of this book and gave me invaluable intellectual, political, and personal help during the course of my early formulations, for which they have my gratitude. They are Jim Kinneavy, Doug Kellner, Horace Newcomb, Tom Schatz, and Gayatri Spivak. Other friends were particularly helpful and supportive during that period and have remained so; I want to thank Ellen Draper, Pat Singleton, and Kay Sloan.

I spent a year as an Andrew W. Mellon Postdoctoral Fellow at Bryn Mawr College, for which I particularly thank former Dean of Graduate Studies Barbara Kreutz; that time allowed me to reconceptualize the direction of my manuscript. My students at Bryn Mawr, especially Amy Villarejo, deserve credit for allowing me to think through my redirection as a part of their courses, as have my students in the Women's Studies Program and in the Department of Communication Arts at the University of Wisconsin-Madison; I want to thank, particularly, Chad Dell, Ann Leighton, and Jane Shattuc, and my former colleagues Lynn Spigel and Tom Streeter. In addition, Christine Gledhill's commentary on my work on melodrama was particularly reassuring at a time when my own faith was flagging. Similarly, Stuart Hall's faith in and commentary on my work enabled me to continue working in the face of adversity. And the University of North Carolina Press's conscientious readers offered rigorous critiques and suggestions that helped me to strengthen my arguments.

I also am grateful to those who have actually helped in the research for and the production of this book. Barbara Humphries and Emily Sieger, of the Library of Congress, were particularly helpful during two different periods of intense research. Chad Dell helped prepare the first full computerized draft of my manuscript while remaining faithful, competent, and almost always cheerful. I thank my editors at the University of North Carolina Press—Iris Tillman Hill, Kate Torrey, Sandra Eisdorfer—and my copyeditor, D. Teddy Diggs, for their patience and for their attention to my manuscript. Finally, my husband, Carl Michel, and Carla Pommert-Cherry—my student at Texas Christian University—gave generously of their time to help me through the final stages of preparing the manuscript.

Our loved ones are usually the ones who most deserve gratitude for the patience with which they surround and support our intellectual labor. I want to express my gratitude to my parents, Charline and Jesse Byars, and my parents-in-law, Jean and Mike Michel, for believing in me, and to my husband, Carl Michel, for living with me and with this book project, because, in the words of David Letterman, "We all know how painful that can be." I dedicate this book to him, with love.

Finally, I thank this book project for pulling me back to where I want to be and for allowing me to articulate that locale.

Saying What

Can't Be Said,

Reading What

Must Be Read:

Feminist Criticism,

Melodrama, and

Introduction

Film Studies

Criticism and Struggle

Constantly barraged by various and contradictory notions concerning sex and gender, we are all always engaged—explicitly or implicitly, consciously or unconsciously—in the struggle over the relation between sexual difference and gender definition. As increasing numbers of women enter the work force, especially in occupations previously defined as "masculine," and as governmental bodies debate legalizing "alternative families," questions like the following have become common: What is "natural" about being a woman? About being a man? Is there anything "natural" about gendered social roles? About family structure? These questions imply the rejection of traditional notions of sex and gender and of their relationship. They rely, instead, on non- or antiessentialist concepts of gender. They imply that gender and, indeed, "reality" are social constructions. They indicate the assumption that Heidi Hartman put so

I

succinctly: "Biology is always mediated by society."[1] Sex we're born with; gender we learn. Contemporary feminist theorists examine the manipulation and distribution of power in this mediation of biology, and feminist critics analyze representational texts, addressing questions concerning the manner in which social institutions—especially those of the arts and the mass media—exercise their power in the construction and enforcement of normative concepts and values concerning sexual difference and gender construction in and through their cultural products. As a theorist, I evaluate the bases for feminist textual analysis, addressing questions relating to the ongoing creation and re-creation of gender; as a critic, I read the struggle over the meanings of categories such as "female" and "feminine" and "male" and "masculine" in mass-produced, mass-consumed texts.

Contemporary feminism is by no means monolithic, and there are numerous approaches to feminist criticism, but as Tania Modleski has observed, feminism "has by now its pieties and routines."[2] Trying to remain on the academically privileged "cutting edge," feminist film theorists and critics have tended to assume dogmatically that certain theoretical advances are secure (beyond critique) while they have simultaneously adopted the latest continental theory. With this book, I address the results of this faddism and this reluctance to engage in theoretical fine-tuning. And although most feminist film theorists and critics to this point have approached their work from other directions, I find the recent theorizing of the notion "ideology" by scholars within the theoretical milieu known as "cultural studies" most productive and informative for my analyses of both film texts and critical approaches, and my approach is firmly embedded within that milieu and tradition. Within cultural studies, *culture* is taken to mean the process through which we circulate and struggle over the meanings of our social experience, social relations, and therefore, our *selves*. With other cultural studies analysts, mine is an antiessentialist approach, based on the assumption that, through their cultural practices, the members of a society create and manipulate their realities.[3] My task, with that of other cultural studies scholars who are centrally concerned with textual analysis, is the explication of power relations among textual elements that influence the meaning-making process; as a feminist, I have as a primary concern the construction and manipulation of gendered categories, with an eye toward developing strategies for intervention in that process. Talking and writing about texts actively involves critics in the production and circulation of meanings—that is, in the construction of culture; feminist theorists and critics generally acknowledge their intention to intervene in this meaning-making process as a challenge to the patriarchal institutions that oppress us all, women and men (however inequitably). Much of my focus is on struggle: the ideological struggles that go on as we produce and consume representations of gender in mainstream cultural texts—here, specifically, Hollywood films—and the struggles within feminist theory.

No readers, no critics should allow themselves the luxury of thinking their particular readings definitive; neither should critics shrink from the struggles necessary in building theory adequate to its explanatory purpose and productive of social change. I am concerned with the struggle among explanatory theories and the critics that use these theories, as they attempt to account for the relation between representation and gender, and I devote this examination of critical, theoretical, and representational texts—all participants in the ideological process in, by, and through which we create categories of "reality" such as "gender"—to the feminist project of intervention in meaning-making and theory building. Criticism and theory only stagnate when self-criticism is avoided, and feminist criticism is no exception. Learning from our failures is the product for which we hope as we engage in self-criticism; struggle can strengthen.

Early in the contemporary feminist movement, in 1970, Lillian Robinson delivered a warning to feminist literary critics, fearing that the field of feminist studies, in its attempt to become a respectable part of academe, "would become indistinguishable from that which it was designed to criticize." Her warning was and still is applicable to feminist scholarship in all areas; at the time, it was prescient:

> Feminist criticism, as its name implies, is criticism with a Cause, engaged criticism. But the critical model presented to us so far is merely engaged to be married. It is about to contract what can only be a *mésalliance* with bourgeois modes of thought and the critical categories they inform. To be effective, feminist criticism cannot become simply bourgeois criticism in drag. It must be ideological and moral criticism; it must be revolutionary.[4]

In fact, as Edward Said insists, all criticism—not just feminist criticism—should not reproduce oppression but should "think of itself as life-enhancing, and constitutively opposed to every form of tyranny, domination, and abuse; its social goals are noncoercive knowledge produced in the interests of human freedom"[5]—precisely the egalitarian goals of feminism and exactly what feminist criticism strives toward, for all of us.

If we are to avoid reproducing the very forms of power we seek to challenge, feminist theorists and critics *cannot* uncritically adopt the categories and modes of thought so directly responsible for women's (and therefore men's) oppression. We must realize that criticism is always a social and political activity. As Said noted, criticism is "always situated; it is skeptical, secular, reflectively open to its own failings. This is by no means to say that it is value free. Quite the contrary, for the inevitable trajectory of critical consciousness is to arrive at some acute sense of what political, social and human values are entailed in the reading, production, and transmission of every text."[6] Texts are sites for the struggle over meaning, the struggle central to the construction and reconstruction of culture, and interactions with texts—at every stage of their production, distribution, and consumption—must be understood as inherently political.

Fortunately, feminist scholarship proved to be more vigorous and broader in scope than Robinson, in 1970, had feared it would become, a fact she happily admits. Feminist scholarship has, in fact, thrived, but even so, Robinson acknowledges that her fears concerning its progress were justified in a great many—too many—cases.[7] In numerous fields, embracing the theories on which their disciplines are based has led feminists to paradoxically embrace theories that actually undermine women's emancipation. Robinson noted this tendency among feminist literary scholars who approached their work—indeed, their field—unskeptically. Surprisingly, they perceived and described ideas and documents as independent from the social, political, and economic conditions and people that produced them. Critics—especially feminist critics—must understand the inherent relationships between ideas and their contexts. They must also understand that it is the responsibility of criticism to engage, constantly, in self-critique, and self-critique entails constant attention to the critic's own work, as well as to the work of others concerned with the same problems.

Jean Bethke Elshtain's impressive and vigorously argued critique of feminist discursive practices, a critique aimed at strengthening these practices, is exemplary.[8] Arguing for the development of discursive practices that do not involve domination, Elshtain argues that understanding power involves a consideration of the nature of language and that feminist discourse must itself be analyzed. Examining the limitations of the theories on which feminist discursive patterns are implicitly (or explicitly) based, she then points in directions she feels productive in the construction of "a feminist discourse that rejects domination."[9] She observes, however, that in some cases, the unskeptical commitment of feminists to a particular account of human speech has precluded the possibility that their speech might serve liberatory purposes. Indeed, theoretical and critical work in many areas has proceeded unskeptically from research that has ignored women's experience—research based on the assumption that the male and the masculine are normative—and this continues to skew our ability to produce knowledge about females and males and about the relationship between sex and gender.

In the first words of her book *In a Different Voice*, Carol Gilligan recounted the problems she met when depending on the psychological theories she had been taught and, indeed, had herself been teaching:

> Over the past ten years, I have been listening to people talking about themselves. Halfway through that time, I began to hear a distinction in these voices, two ways of speaking about moral problems, two modes of describing the relationship between other and self. . . . Against the background of the psychological descriptions of identity and moral development which I had read and taught for a number of years, the women's voices sounded distinct. It was then that I began to notice the recurrent problems in interpreting women's development and to connect these problems to the repeated exclusion of women from the critical theory-building studies of psychological research.[10]

The theories were themselves the problem she had to overcome. Similar examples abound in other disciplines, and film theory and criticism have not escaped this tendency to normatize the male and the masculine. We must address the trap described by Robinson, Elshtain, and Gilligan, constantly and consistently remembering that blindness to the nature and origins of the theories with which we work will result in continued oppression.

Feminist film critics of the early 1970s, working in a manner similar to that of literary critics and feminist historians of the period, focused on revealing Hollywood films as oppressive and women as their victims. But by the mid-1970s, as film theory in general became more formalist, feminist film scholars began to turn toward the formal analysis of films and the "spectating subject" the films were said to create (or "center"), a turn away from the "recuperative" approach taken by feminist historians and literary critics, who had begun searching for signs of female resistance in cultural texts and who, by 1980, had identified significant female power in nineteenth-century literary texts and records of daily life. Feminist recuperation, in fact, progressed to the point that the literary critic Judith Lowder Newton felt it necessary to warn against replacing the vision of oppression with "the equally distorted view of Victorian America as an era of female power and sisterly utopia."[11] The term *recuperation* is itself problematic, since it is often used to refer to the co-optation of potentially resistant forces by dominant ideologies, and clearly, feminist recuperation can be naively optimistic. But equally naive is the assumption common in feminist film criticism today: all that is "feminine"—and, therefore, all that is woman—is created and circumscribed by patriarchy, with mainstream texts like Hollywood films serving solely to reinforce patriarchal patterns.[12] Following the recuperative trend toward excavating and recuperating feminine voices established by literary critics and historians, I have focused my attention on very popular cultural artifacts from the past, identifying feminine voices, gazes, and power and examining their struggles with dominant (masculine) voices, gazes, and power. Keeping in mind Judith Lowder Newton's observation that "to examine power in the past is also to clarify the present,"[13] I have analyzed the struggle over gender in films produced and initially consumed more than twenty-five years ago, and I have honed various tools for textual analysis in the process.

Mass-media texts are acknowledged as central sites for the struggle over meaning in industrialized societies, but most cultural studies scholars have concentrated on studies of audiences, technologies, and institutions—neglecting the study of texts, as Tania Modleski points out in her introduction to the anthology *Studies in Entertainment*.[14] Acknowledging the advances in audience studies made by "The Birmingham School of Culture Theory in England" (scholars associated with the Center for Contemporary Cultural Studies at the University of Birmingham), Modleski notes especially their demonstrations of the ways in which particular subcultures negotiate the dominant culture and resist the homogenizing forces of mass culture, but she notes too that, caught up in the effort to account for the active and diverse nature of meaning-making, many scholars have moved to audience studies and away from textual analysis. Additionally, in their articulation of examples of resistance, some of these critics, she argues, have lost critical distance from the culture they seek to analyze, have unwittingly written apologias for mass culture, and have endorsed the pluralism of consumer society—instead of analyzing it. Pointing to critics who place themselves on the Left while attempting to balance between the humanist celebration of mass culture as liberatory and the Frankfurt School condemnation of mass culture as inherently and monolithically oppressive, Modleski warns that ethnographic audience studies—in reproducing the methodologies used by the entertainment industry to measure and construct its audience (surveys, questionnaires, interviews)—may produce collaborations with that industry rather than critical analyses of the industry and the texts it produces.

Modleski calls for a critical view of mass cultural production and mass cultural artifacts, specifically noting the need for additional concentration on the analysis of texts—but not without regard to their social and cultural contexts. The critical view she feels will be most adequate to this task is a feminist one. With this book, I move toward filling the gap Modleski describes, aiming both to chronicle the struggle over gender within the texts that compose a significant Hollywood genre in its heyday and to make an incursion into that struggle by opening up cultural studies for feminist film theory. As Dana Polan points out, however, narratives (and, indeed, theoretical texts as well) are profferings of positions. As critics or historians, we delineate not *the* meaning of a text or period but some *possible* meanings,[15] and I seek with my readings to illuminate the struggle between dominant and resisting ideologies in representational texts and in contemporary feminist film theory and criticism as well. Because I wanted to focus on representations of the American mainstream for the American mainstream (read: predominantly white and middle-class) during a period when gender definition was in a crisis, I chose to focus on Hollywood melodramas released and consumed in the 1950s. I examined films that were widely disseminated, limiting my study to film melodramas that were listed in *Variety*'s annual lists of Top Twenty Moneymakers during the decade and to films given a relatively contemporary American setting. (Because of my focus on consumption, the date given in the text for a film refers to the year the film was included in *Variety*'s list.)[16]

Melodrama and History

Why the 1950s? Why film melodramas? During that decade, the social fabric of America had begun to weaken. The interconnected social institutions composing its warp and woof had never before been called into question as they were in the 1950s. As women of all ages, races, marital and maternal statuses, and socioeconomic classes flooded out of their homes and into the workplaces of America, the family structure began to change, previously sacrosanct gender roles began to alter, and struggles over the meaning of *female* and *male* became particularly evident in the cultural atmosphere. Change was imminent but not yet explicitly acknowledged. Now, with the clarity of hindsight, we can see this upheaval in progress in the cultural documents of the period; mass-media texts of the period provide evidence of a concern with the domestic sphere, participating in what Tom Schatz has characterized as "a radical upheaval in the nature and structure of American ideology."[17] In its final decade as America's central cultural medium, the cinema remained a vital part of American life, and the film melodramas produced in Hollywood during the 1950s were concerned with gender-identity formation and its relationship to family structure: the nuclear family based on the heterosexual married couple. In the 1950s, family values became socially and culturally central to Americans, and Hollywood films interpreted and helped to make sense of this basic social institution, symbolically deploying it across a panoply of permutations. Popular films exhibited and examined the dialectics between class politics and sexual politics, between capitalism and patriarchy. Their material was everyday life, where values and ethics—and conflicts over them—are most forcefully expressed. Taking advantage of the schizophrenic history of the melodramatic mode, itself born in a period of crisis, Hollywood filmmakers combined seemingly prosocial narratives with subtle performances and sophisticated stylization to produce texts that both visually complemented *and* challenged the stories they told.

Hollywood's film melodramas draw on the epistemological assumptions and the rhetorical strategies common to two rather different but ultimately related melodramatic traditions. In his well-known essay "Tales of Sound and Fury: Observations on the Family Melodrama," Thomas Elsaesser points to a popular oral tradition that began with the late medieval morality plays, the popular *gestes*, and other forms of oral narrative and drama, such as folktales and folk songs, and that continued through the cult of the picaresque in "high-brow" literature and in "low-brow" barrel-organ songs, music-hall drama, and the German *Bänkellied* (ballads, or narratives accompanied by music), which Elsaesser finds particularly influential. In performance, the *Bänkellied*'s moralistic plots were overlaid not only with a proliferation of detail but also with a heavily repetitive verse form or with the up-and-down rhythms of the barrel organ, which provided a distancing element of parody. Indeed, theatrical melodrama takes many elements from popular and folk entertainment forms. In "The Melodramatic Field: An Investigation," the long introductory essay to her anthology *Home Is Where the Heart Is*, Christine Gledhill notes that alternative theatrical entrepreneurs—in the effort to oppose the aristocratic theater monopoly held by the few Patent Theatres licensed in eighteenth-century France and England and to attract a broad audience drawn from the middle, lower-middle, and working classes—drew on folk and popular entertainment forms such as the "dumb show, pantomime, harlequinade, ballets, spectacles, acrobatics, clowning, busking, the exhibition of animals and freaks, and, above all, musical accompaniment and song."[18] The texts common to this alternative tradition combined moralistic content and prolific detail with unidimensional, non-psychologically conceived characters who served not as autonomous individuals but who functioned to transmit action and link locales, thereby enhancing melodrama's myth-making function by placing motivation as structural rather than personal. This radical positioning, however, fell by the wayside in the second tradition, one far more important in the historical placing of film melodrama.

This other tradition derives from both the eighteenth-century sentimental novel, which emphasized private feelings and interiorized ethics, and the romantic drama originally used by members of the rising bourgeoisie in the latter part of the eighteenth century to depict their values in conflict with those of the "evil" aristocrats, a depiction most often focused on the interiorized and personalized.[19] By the time of the French Revolution, the term *melodrama* had come to mean what it does still, in its broadest sense: a drama in which the spoken voice is used over a musical background. The bourgeois appropriated classical forms, altering the forms to suit their needs, and one of these needs was for a dramatic form peopled not by the aristocrats, as was tragedy, but by the bourgeois. The tragic hero—indicative, in Greek tragedy, of a social group—became the melodramatic hero, an individual capable of individual error; after all, the myth most basic to the bourgeoisie is the myth of classlessness. The social, in melodrama, came to be expressed as the personal.

In the most influential recent book on literary melodrama, *The Melodramatic Imagination*, Peter Brooks places the birth of melodrama in the context of the French Revolution, arguing that the Revolution

> can be seen as the convulsive last act in a process of desacralization that was set in motion at the Renaissance, passed through the momentary compromise of Christian humanism, and gathered momentum during the Enlightenment—a process in which the explanatory and cohesive force of the sacred myth lost its power, and its political and social representations lost their legitimacy. In the course of this process, tragedy, which depends on the communal partaking of the sacred body—as in the mass—becomes impossible.[20]

The Revolution violently threw truth and ethics into question and sacralized the law itself, instituting the state as moral authority. In this milieu, melodrama functioned to reveal and clarify the "truths" of the new order. Melodrama illustrated and contributed to this epistemological moment, the point at which the myth of an organic and hierarchically cohesive cosmology and society was shattered and the institutions of the Church and the Monarchy, which had supported and been supported by the myth, lost credibility.

In the 1950s, American Ideology faced such a challenge. The acts of almost inconceivable violence with which the United States ended the war with Japan had thrown the stability of human existence into question, and the entrance of large numbers of American women into the work force threw the family, that most basic of social institutions, into question.

American Ideology was in need of melodrama, the modern mode for constructing moral identity. Melodrama, as a mode, pervades many genres and through them presents a way to refuse the recognition of a world drained of transcendence. Since the middle of the nineteenth century, the arts, Brooks explained, have been "constructed on, and over, the void, postulating meanings and symbolic systems which have no certain justification because they are backed by no theology and no universally accepted social code."[21] A complex and dynamic social structure must deal with its internal contradictions in a nonviolent manner, and cultural modes like melodrama provide the locus and strategy for negotiation. Usurping the place of religious education, melodrama has operated since as a site for struggles over deeply disturbing materials and fundamental values. Melodrama became for the Western world the ritual through which social order is purged and sets of ethical imperatives are clarified. Using shared, public symbols, this ritual that is melodrama resolves not crises of order but crises within order, what Stephen Neale has called "an in-house arrangement."[22] Traditionally, melodrama has focused on the problems of the individual within established social structures, and as it attempted to make up for the loss of the categorical but unifying myth of the sacred, melodrama's mythmaking functioned at the level of the individual and the personal, drawing its material from the everyday. The insistence on the importance of the ordinary at least partially accounts for the melodrama's ongoing popularity and flexibility—first in its theatrical forms and later in its various novelistic, filmic, and televisual forms. Melodrama's primary drive is the identification of moral polarities, of good and evil, and as Gledhill argues, it speaks in any discourse "that demarcates the desirable from the taboo."[23]

Indeed, the arts are integral to the production of a cohesive social code. During the nineteenth century, melodrama became the dominant mode for revealing and demonstrating the "moral universe" in Europe and America. As a theatrical form, melodrama became conventionalized, and its epistemological assumptions became manifest in its conventions. The melodramatic mode has frequently been compared to tragedy, a mode characterized by the earlier "tragic vision" dependent on an explicitly hierarchical theology and society and peopled by aristocrats. Melodramatic characters, generally of a lower social status than tragic characters, confront clearly identified antagonists, and the courageous and psychologically unified protagonist expels the external adversaries. The fairly constant constellation of characters (the suffering heroine or hero, the persecuting villain, and the benevolent comic), the extensive mimed action, and the music for dramatic emphasis combine to emphasize clear-cut solutions to conflict—victory, stalemate, or defeat—and equally clear-cut and cathartic emotions for the audience—triumph, despair, and protest. Choices are clear; the major characters are not leaders; rather, they take a side and accept choices made by those who formulate policy. The social order is purged, and its ethics are clarified; they are made legible.

By the end of the nineteenth century, however, middle-class markets were recognized as lucrative and were encouraged to join with more "fashionable" audiences. Lines between the "respectable" and the "popular" became clear, and realism and tragedy became valorized forms for the middle and upper classes, while melodrama was generally denigrated and relegated to working-class entertainments. Middle-class audiences followed the intelligentsia to the "realistic" drama of playwrights like Henrik Ibsen, George Bernard Shaw, and Anton Chekhov. The number of stage melodramas decreased, and by 1900 they had begun to change, in response to their audience's increasing bias toward realism. The film and theater historian Nicholas Vardac noted film's "boundless capacity for both spectacular and realistic pictures" and argued that "audiences had been carefully prepared for the new medium both by century-long support of conventional stage melodrama and by the late century rebirth of theatrical realism."[24] The popularity of realism coincided with "a re-masculinization of cultural values," and the emotionalism associated with moral value in the nineteenth century gave way to restraint. Realism, understated and underplayed, came to be associated with the masculine, and melodrama, associated with "feminine" emotionalism, became a term of derision.[25]

The emergence of the cinema disturbed but did not curb this trend. Melodrama provided the narrative and formal foundation for the cinema—and an audience prepared to understand melodramatic narratives. But despite this heritage, the cinema was to become a remarkably realist medium. Realism, like melodrama, refers both to a set of production techniques and to an epistemology. Realism depends on the assumption that the social world can be adequately explained, through social-scientific methods, and that adequate representation is possible. Melodrama has no such confidence; irrational forces exist in the world, and our representational systems are incapable of adequately and directly representing them. Melodrama, like realism, roots itself in the everyday, but melodrama exploits excessive uses of representational conventions to express that which cannot (yet) be said, that which language alone is incapable of expressing. Melodrama contributed many genres to the cinema, but they were destined to become the terrain for struggle between "realism" and "melodrama." They also, as a result of the gendering of these imaginative modes, came to be delineated and evaluated by their associations with gender. The western, the gangster film, and the "adult" realist drama were constructed as masculine, while only the romantic and family melodramas maintained a nominative association with their melodramatic heritage. And in them the figure of woman became a primary site for the battling voices that expressed themselves in the overlay of genre and epistemology.

Melodrama and Film Studies

A serious consideration of melodrama requires the willingness to look to the personal as political, and the study of film melodrama became acceptable—and in some circles even fashionable—concomitant to the rise of the contemporary feminist movement. This relationship, however, was not as direct as it might seem; other factors seem to have been more significant in encouraging scholarly attention to melodrama. In the 1960s, scholars of theater and literature became increasingly interested in performance and theatricality, and this led them toward considerations of melodrama.[26] Film criticism, not yet secure in academe, was at the time dominated by auteurist criticism, by mise-en-scène criticism, and by genre criticism, but two obstacles blocked a foray into melodrama by genre critics. First and foremost, the genres most often associated with "melodrama"—referred to as "women's films" or "weepies"—lacked cultural valorization because of their association with female audiences, and genre critics kept defensively to the "classic" (or "masculine") genres such as the western or the gangster film. Second and conceptually more difficult (though this was not recognized at the time), considering melodrama a genre opens a Pandora's box of difficult theoretical problems.

Paradoxically, film melodrama came into the mainstream of film studies through a neo-Marxist fascination not with genre but with the possibility of formal contradiction in, and possible subversion from within, film texts. During the early 1970s, the highly stylized film melodramas that Douglas Sirk had directed in the 1950s were "discovered," and the director, his motives, and his films were reappraised. His films were reconstructed as social criticism, and politically oriented critics looked for other such films. A genre was born. The historical genre of "melodrama" had long been understood and accepted (though generally denigrated) by the industry and by audiences; the theoretical genre of "melodrama" was now formed in the mold of a group of Hollywood family melodramas produced by a few talented directors obsessed with stylistic manipulation (which is now valorized by film critics as the "excess" that calls attention to the sociopolitical contradictions inherent to bourgeois stories).[27] Constructing "melodrama" in terms of this small group of films obscured the existence of other melodramatic genres, the melodramatic aspects of genres like the western, the historical variation within individual melodramatic genres, and the relationships between kinds of melodramatic genres.

Writing on film melodrama during the 1970s was influenced more by trends within film studies than by the material itself. Not only is the discovery—or construction—of melodrama attributable to a particular movement within film studies, but the various successive attempts to grapple with the material were colored by other such theoretical movements, and the abilities and inabilities to successfully explain these texts—particularly the shortcomings in the analysis of the representation of gender—are also attributable to these various trends.[28] The primary project of the structuralist neo-Marxists who initially "discovered" Sirk and melodrama was not explaining melodrama; their fascination was with constructing the model that came to be known as the "classic realist text." They explained the novel, the cinema, and television texts in terms of this model, ignoring significant variation across time, space, and media and assuming that practically all mass-produced, mass-consumed texts—among them Hollywood films—were explicable through the use of this model and that generic distinctions were unimportant. Christine Gledhill summarized their model of mainstream texts:

> Classic realist texts, it was argued, reproduce bourgeois ideology because they implicate the spectator in a single point of view onto a

coherent, hierarchically ordered representation of the world, in which social contradictions are concealed and ultimately resolved through mechanisms of displacement and substitution. In this process the spectator is "interpellated" as the "individual subject" of bourgeois ideology.[29]

While acknowledging the existence of contradiction, this model ultimately marginalizes any resistance to dominant ideologies, incorporating Althusser's notion of "interpellation" in a way that gives the reader-spectator no way out, a particularly horrifying thought for women because the female figure was shown to be inevitably and infallibly positioned as an object for masculine desire *and* as the threat of castration.

This latter refinement in the "classic realist text" is indicative of the incorporation of Lacanian psychoanalysis into Althusser's thought and, as a result, into the antirealist film theorizing done by those on and influenced by the editorial board of the British journal *Screen*.[30] Because it showed mainstream texts to be inherently patriarchal, this attack gained feminist support, and because Sirk's highly patriarchal bourgeois melodramas were shown to cleverly subvert themselves, they attracted the attention of *Screen* theorists. The retired director—obviously flattered by the attention—encouraged this reconstruction of his films, films that were produced for a specifically female audience.[31] Christine Gledhill called attention to this "problematic identification of melodrama with bourgeois fantasy" and the "identification of melodrama with women"; the latter logically flowed into an "equivalence between the 'feminine' and bourgeois ideology," an equivalence indicative of the sexist nature of much of the writing about melodrama in the 1970s.[32] The politically oriented *Screen* theorists and critics found films interesting and valuable only if they could be read as ruptured and, thus, as subversive or if they could be shown to be instruments of capitalism.

Finally, in 1977, from within the *Screen* milieu, Geoffrey Nowell-Smith began to articulate the differences between realism and melodrama, and Laura Mulvey examined Sirk's films as embodiments of the intersection of gender and genre.[33] But Mulvey argued that such domestic melodramas served as "safety valves" for capitalism, since they represented larger social conflicts in terms of the personal. However, it is realism, not melodrama, that serves as capitalism's safety valve. Melodrama's history parallels that of capitalist democracy in the modern world, and like the myth of democracy, which obscures the relations of power inherent in the sociopolitical world, melodrama obscures the relations of power inherent in narrative structure. Realism draws from the melodramatic mode not only this tendency to obscure power relations but also a focus on individuals. Additionally, realist texts present the capitalist world both as understandable and as one in which clearly articulated answers exist; they present solutions in terms of individual action, presenting individuals (almost always male individuals) who have control over their destinies if they will just *act*. Hollywood's "social problem" films—which I discuss in chapter 3—are exemplary both of this trend and of the struggle between melodrama and realism during the 1950s as they attempt to organize the same terrain.

Another approach to writing on melodrama in the late 1970s came from a Marxist tradition that differed from that of the structuralist neo-Marxists at *Screen* but that resulted in a similar insistence that melodrama tends to mystify social conflict by relegating it to the realm of the personal; the approach diverged in its insistence that realism can lay bare the contradictions of capitalism.[34] This position depends on the belief that the "real" world is one of socioeconomic relations, with the domestic and personal clearly secondary; it obscures and undervalues the domestic sphere and ignores the differences in the ways that men and women experience the domestic, simultaneously and paradoxically denigrating personal experience and privileging the male one. Further, this approach gives little credit to the audience, which it seems to see as homogenous (and masculine). However, this writing on melodrama preceded significant work on subcultural differences in the use and reading of cultural texts, work dependent on examining (as these critics were, at the very least, doing) previously unconsidered genres—genres popular among populations marginalized by virtue of their gender, class, race, or other similar categories.

Attention to film melodrama eventually led to the examination of the distinctly different ways of seeing and being in the world, ways indicated by the differences between realism and melodrama. In the most important work yet produced on film melodrama, Christine Gledhill points out that both modes attempt to organize the terrain "in which different classes and social groups meet and find an identity."[35] Indeed, the definition of identity—one's place in the world, and the nature of that world—is precisely where realism and melodrama diverge, but it was not until Peter Brooks's *The Melodramatic Imagination* was published in 1976 that melodrama critics began to clearly conceptualize this stickiest of problems in that Pandora's box that *is* melodrama. Brooks's description of the desacralization of Western culture and the resulting epistemological gap in bourgeois ideology led critics to articulate this previously fuzzy question more clearly. Brooks avoids using the conceptual framework of ideological analysis, and this weakens his analysis, but his work has, nonetheless, been fruitful, especially his distinction between melodrama as a mode, characterized by the "melodramatic imagination"—a distinctly modern way of thinking—and the manifestation of the melodramatic imagination in specific forms.[36]

Arguing that Brooks's work allows us to get beyond the troubling duality of classic realist text versus countercinema, Gledhill described three responses to the epistemological gap pointed out by Brooks, three primary modes of modern cultural perception/expression: realism, modernism, and melodrama. Each has a different purpose and deploys different strategies, mode of address, and form of engagement and identification. Realism ignores the implicit gap in bourgeois ideology, confident in "the causal explanations of the human sciences." Modernism obsessively seeks to expose the gap, but melodrama

> takes a different stance; it both insists on the realities of life in bourgeois democracy—the material parameters of lived experience, individual personality, the fundamental psychic relations of family life—and, in an implicit recognition of the limitations of the conventions of representation—of their repressiveness—proceeds to insist on, force into an aesthetic presence, desires for identity, value, and fullness of signification beyond the powers of language to supply.[37]

Recognizing that fullness of signification is beyond the capacities of any mode, melodrama constantly attempts to give material existence to the repressed.

Each mode operates in response to the others, though Gledhill claimed the causal chain begins with realism. Realism, according to Gledhill, "is not static. As the systems of explanation which ground realism change . . . the codes and conventions of realism shift, in pursuit of new 'truth' and greater 'authenticity.'"[38] And as realism shifts, it offers up new material for melodrama. Melodrama, then, is a reactive mode, and it is perhaps this aspect that allows its abiding identification with the feminine. The feminine is stereotypically passive, reactive, and responsive—qualities not necessarily negative. As Tessa Perkins has explained, in the process of stereotyping, traits identified with a group are then valued according to that group's location in the social hierarchy. Females still, in the 1980s, occupy a lower rung in a hierarchy that remains patriarchal. This at least partially accounts for the generally negative scholarly and popular reaction to melodramatic forms—forms compulsively, but guiltily, consumed.

The feminine also continues to be identified with the domestic, the private, and everyday social reality, and this is the terrain and the matter of melodrama, with the family and the community crucial. Traditional (masculine) critics have favored the notion that the individual is separate from society, resting on the assumption that individuals have some meaning apart from and prior to the society in which they exist, and texts that reinforce this view, generally showing a male hero in conflict with a feminine society, came to compose the literary and film canons, those bodies of texts "acceptable" for study.[39] Those texts characterized by this favored myth depict society as a destructive pressure, and although melodrama may focus on problems within society, it shows society as the ultimate answer to those very problems. Those critics who see universalism in the individual condemn melodrama for, in David Thorburn's words, its "habits of moral simplification and its lust for topicality, its hunger to engage or represent behavior and moral attitudes that belong to its particular day and time, especially behavior shocking or threatening to prevailing moral codes."[40]

Such critics fail to understand the central position of melodrama in Western, particularly American, cultures and the complex aesthetic conventions it employs. Melodrama expresses a reality experienced by most of the people most of the time. This means also that melodrama expresses the contradictions that most people live most of the time, as well as the negotiations over the conflicts they cause. Melodrama is, in Brooks's words, a "drama of morality."[41] It takes place within a realm he calls the "moral occult," a realm that sounds remarkably similar to "the ideological," where "truths" and ethics are articulated. Melodrama provides the metaphors for their expression and the ground for struggle over the "real." Melodrama works *from within*; Stephen Neale described melodrama's crises not as crises *of* a legally established social order but as "a crisis within it, an 'in-house' rearrangement."[42] During the 1950s, sophisticated film-makers enriched melodrama, taking advantage of the possibilities of the medium to create complex mise-en-scènes and, as a result, multilayered texts (often with some layers at odds with others) that worked to empha-size and naturalize the complexity of the conflicts they presented. The techniques have by now become commonplace, and some 1980s viewers are amused by the quaintness of even the most complex film melodramas of the 1950s; others are amazed (some are horrified) by the explicitness with which they delineate gender, naturalizing and discouraging attention to struggles over its construction.

Many feminist critics have turned their attention away from the main-stream, assuming that mainstream Hollywood films have already been accounted for by sociological analyses, which identified their content as oppressive to women, and by "semio-psychoanalytic" analyses of filmic enunciative practices, which revealed the oppressiveness of their form and which indicated that possibilities for subversive discourse exist only in formally experimental films. Of those feminist critics who still focus on Hollywood film, most have remained fixated on women's victimization. But there is evidence of resisting voices even within Hollywood films; real struggle goes on within, with, and through mainstream film texts. Some feminists have recognized the existence of contradiction within main-stream films, but few have looked to these films with a recuperative eye. In a 1985 review essay in *Signs*, Judith Mayne pointed in this direction as she described possibilities she saw open for feminist film analysts: "Given classical cinema's obsession with sexual hierarchy, feminist film critics could choose the somewhat obvious task of amassing more and more evidence of women's exclusion and victimization, or they could undertake the more complex and challenging project of examining the contradic-tions in classical films, that is, what is repressed or unresolved."[43] There do exist very different "masculine" and "feminine" views of the world, and—intentionally or unintentionally—they struggle within the institu-tion of the cinema and within feminist film theory and criticism. The impressive evidence that "classic" cinematic enunciation is organized phal-locentrically tells us a very different thing about the nature of the Ameri-can cinema—and about the nature of feminist film theory and criticism—than do my readings, which indicate significant variation even within a film genre that consistently reiterates patriarchy. An approach that constantly returns to female victimization and inflexible patriarchy discourages, whereas my approach enables us to hear the strong, feminine, resisting voices even within mainstream cultural artifacts. As a "recuperative" feminist and a cultural studies scholar, I examine film texts, looking for their internal contradictions and for the (potential) presence of strong feminine voices that resist patriarchal dominance. I examine struggle.

In the chapters that follow, I focus on the problems addressed by feminist film theorists and critics, examining various approaches to textual analysis as they explain or fail to explain the power relations that determine—or attempt to determine—the meanings of gendered categories through ideological struggles within and among a group of highly successful film melodramas produced and consumed in the United States during the 1950s. I employ and examine approaches central to the brief history of feminist film studies, as well as some that have, by and large, been bypassed. I analyze the relation of the film texts to "social reality," focusing on the construction and use of stereotypes; the relation of narrative structure to the representation of gender; the plot patterns used to depict the "family romance"; and the interaction of residual, dominant, and emergent ideologies of race, social class, and gender. I find none of these approaches singularly adequate; each contributes significantly to an understanding of the representation of gender in mainstream cultural texts.

Because I see the audience for this book as a diverse one, certain chapters or portions of chapters will appeal to and address one group of readers more than others. The first section of chapter 1 provides background on the developments and debates within feminist film theory since 1970. Although I begin to lay out the rationale for my approach in this section, much of the information will be unnecessary for feminist film theorists; on the other hand, cultural studies scholars whose work focuses elsewhere will find the section informative. The second section of this chapter chronicles the simultaneous but unparallel developments of cultural studies in the United States and in Great Britain, showing why—until recently—feminist film theory and cultural studies have not overlapped in the States. The chapter's third section outlines the way in which cultural studies scholars have reworked the notion of ideology to overcome the limitations of the classical Marxist interpretation of the base-superstructure model. Here, I resuscitate Raymond Williams's notion of "structures of feeling" as a way to describe preemergent meanings of *female* and *male*—already exerting influence on American society in the 1950s—and I argue that his refinement of "epochal" analysis is one that helps us read the struggles over meaning in cultural artifacts. The final section of chapter 1 addresses the problems for textual analysis raised by recent ethnographic audience research, advocating Williams's version of epochal ideological textual analysis and gesturing toward the analyses of textual elements (such as narrative structure) that are fleshed out in chapters 2 through 5. In each of these following four chapters, I focus on different textual elements and re-read a different approach to analyzing the struggles over the meanings of gender within a group of films, noting the ideological positions privileged both by the films' discourses and by the theoretical discourse on which the analytic approach is based. My analysis and revision of each approach stands as a (not *the*) cultural studies approach to sociological analysis, to narratology, to psychoanalysis, and to ideological analysis. I have grouped together in each chapter similar film melodramas—"social problem" films, female-oriented family melodramas, etc.—and have paired each of the groups with a different critical approach. The rationale for my pairings generally relates to the films' similarities; for instance, the "social problem" films all exhibit an extremely rigid relation between gender and narrative structure, and the critical approach I took to these films focuses on this relationship.

In chapters 2 and 3, I focus on the ways specific textual elements operate conservatively to reinforce dominant ideologies. In chapter 2, I examine the construction of representations of female stereotypes and roles, beginning with a discussion of the limits and advantages of "images of" feminist film criticism of the early 1970s. Then I review Tessa Perkins's analysis of stereotyping as part of the ideological process, proposing her analysis as a more adequate approach to relating the representation of roles and stereotypes to "social reality" than the earlier sociological criticism, which was grounded in a reflectionist theory of representation. In the second section, I synthesize material from histories of women and their "appropriate" roles in the United States, and in the final section, I read seven films exhibited in the early part of the 1950s: *Cheaper by the Dozen*, *Belles on Their Toes*, *Father of the Bride*, *Father's Little Dividend*, *A*

Place in the Sun, *A Streetcar Named Desire*, and *From Here to Eternity*. The readings, focusing on the increasingly negative stereotype of the Woman Alone, analyze representations of women working outside their homes and compare the filmic constructions of gender with accounts of "social reality" provided by American women's historians.

The ideological nature of narrative structure, especially its relation to the representation of gender, is the focus of chapter 3. In this chapter, I trace the influence of the increasing concern with family on the "social problem" film in the period following World War II and argue that by the 1950s, the form had effectively become a subgenre of the family melodrama; whatever the "problem" in these films, its roots and its solution are expressed in terms of family structure, and although some limited resistance is present, the plots are rigidly structured to tie characters to dominant constructions of gender. I explicate the plot pattern common to Hollywood films, a pattern almost inevitably concerned with heterosexual romance, and I review the limited feminist analysis of cinematic narrative structure, showing that—for my purposes—more extensive and helpful work has been done by literary critics, particularly by the feminist literary critic Rachel Blau DuPlessis, who addresses narrative explicitly in terms of its ideological function. The final section consists of readings of five "social problem" films—*Come Back, Little Sheba*; *The Country Girl*; *On the Waterfront*; *The Man with the Golden Arm*; and *Rebel without a Cause*—films in which the struggle between realism and melodrama becomes clear. I re-read them as family melodramas, showing how a rigid narrative structure consistently—regardless of age and class distinctions—positions male characters as active and female characters as simply providers of the grounds for male characters' action.

In chapter 4, I evaluate the usefulness of various theories of psychoanalysis, arguing that the Freudian and Lacanian theories of psychoanalysis, which so persuasively explain the majority of Hollywood films, fail to explain the significant minority of films that focus on the female experience. The theoretical work of Nancy Chodorow and Carol Gilligan—and of their critics—gives us a more adequate basis for understanding the narrative content and plot patterns of female-oriented film melodramas and informs my reading of four films: *Magnificent Obsession*, *Picnic*, *All That Heaven Allows*, and *Peyton Place*. Lacanian theory has also been the basis for the "semio-psychoanalytic" critics of cinematic enunciative patterns, critics who have insisted that the filmic "gaze" is male (or "masculine"), and I challenge this assertion as well, tracing recent arguments among feminists over cinematic spectatorship. My shot-by-shot analyses of scenes from *Picnic* and *All That Heaven Allows* support my argument that even the cinematic gaze and its objects are not gender-bound and that the meanings and uses of cinematic enunciative patterns vary not only from genre to genre but also within genres. Though female characters tend to serve as the object of erotic desire and male characters tend to dominate the agency of the gaze—reinforcing patriarchy—even this tendency is challenged as resisting feminine voices demand to be heard.

In chapter 5, I argue that although Marxist theory—particularly Althusser's theorizing—has influenced feminist film studies, mainstream feminist film critics and theorists have paid insufficient attention to the ways in which race and class inflect the construction and representation of gender; most of the work in the area has been produced by Marxist-socialist feminists, though they have remained a marginalized interpretive community within feminist film studies in the United States. Describing the spectrum of feminisms allows me to place their work, to illustrate the need for additional work in the area, and to lay the groundwork for the readings that follow, in which I trace the interaction of residual, dominant, and emergent ideologies of race, social class, and gender in a group of male-oriented melodramas—*East of Eden, Not as a Stranger*, and *Some Came Running*—and a group of "dynastic melodramas"—*Giant; Written on the Wind; Cat on a Hot Tin Roof; The Long, Hot Summer;* and *God's Little Acre*. I grouped these films together simply because of the similarity of their primary protagonists—either males or male-dominated family groupings. An analysis of competing ideologies of race, class, and gender is informative and valuable in and of itself, whether a film or group of films "cries out" for it or not, but occasionally I supplement these readings with reference to other approaches. In the last section of this chapter, I employ and reflect on all of the approaches addressed in the book in a long reading of an extraordinarily rich, female-oriented film that was produced and exhibited at the end of the decade, *Imitation of Life*.

Finally, in the Epilogue, I reflect on my readings of theoretical and film texts, addressing the questions they have raised for me: To what extent do texts determine the critical approach we use? What is the effect of combining different critical approaches? How does a critic's own ideological position influence her or his readings? What do these readings say about the state of melodrama in the 1950s? Is melodrama inherently conservative or subversive? And what has the "epochal" approach told us about the theories and the films I have considered? In this Epilogue I also discuss the ways we, as critics, discursively construct ourselves and our communities, and I state that addressing the intersection of race, class, and gender is, in my consideration, the most important contemporary feminist project— whatever the approach, whatever the discipline. If we feminists isolate our work on gender, our desire for change and our efforts to intervene in the process of defining genders will be thwarted.

The general goal of feminist intervention is change, and theorizing change is crucial. Elshtain noted women's complicity in the evolution of discourse; we have been and are participants in discursive, social, and political change—not, as many radical feminists would claim, untainted by that responsibility. Even though we may have been shaped by the past, we can consciously act to change our future. Of course, change is neither easy nor simple, and it occurs at a glacial pace, but it does occur. Learning to hear those voices allows us to know our own strength and prohibits us from abdicating responsibility for our own voices. Our theories must open up to explain this variety; we can intervene by skeptically guarding ourselves against unquestioned theory, by altering our own discursive patterns, by making interpretation a conscious and self-conscious process, and by empowering others to do the same, thereby contributing to an emancipatory critical practice. Toward that end, this book.

An

Alternative

for Feminist

Film Studies

1

Cultural Studies

Feminism and Film in the United States

Criticism and theory are processual, characterized by struggle, internal and external. During the late 1960s and early 1970s, as feminists challenged the confines of women's social, political, and economic roles, feminist critics and theorists examined the roles and representations of women in the production, distribution, and consumption of cultural texts; they questioned the process that constructs and reconstructs "woman," aiming to intervene in that process. Feminist film critics in the United States, by revealing the inadequacies of women's roles and images in Hollywood films, challenged the assumption that entertainment texts are either insignificant or neutral; these critics claimed that the films had had detrimental effects on real women and argued for more positive representations of women. Their criticism was characterized by a sociological orientation. The pioneering journal *Women and Film* (published from

25

1972 to 1975) was established to provide an outlet for their work, and special issues on women and film were published by *Velvet Light Trap*, *Take One*, and *Film Library Quarterly*. The high point of this early era of feminist film criticism came in 1973, when both Molly Haskell and Marjorie Rosen published books that surveyed Hollywood's stereotyping and misrepresentation of women and women's experiences.[1]

During this period, American feminist filmmaking closely paralleled American feminist film criticism, with filmmakers' primary concern being the documentation of the "real" lives of "real" women. Feminist documentaries filled women's film festivals in New York, Toronto, Washington, and Chicago. In 1971 alone, *Growing Up Female*, *Janie's Janie*, *Three Lives*, and *The Woman's Film* were released in the United States, products of the first generation of feminist documentarians in the United States.[2] By the mid to late 1970s, however, the arena of American feminist film studies and filmmaking became internally conflicted; documentarians and critics alike faced charges of theoretical naiveté, and sociological feminist film criticism was rapidly displaced from the mainstream of feminist film criticism and theory in the United States by an approach based in semiotics and psychoanalysis, a displacement that had already occurred within French film theory and within the British feminist film theory directly influenced by French theory.

Christian Metz, a French linguist and film theorist, had already produced an important body of work on semiotics and film "language" when his students began asking about fellow Parisian Lacan's new readings of Freud's theories of psychoanalysis.[3] Metz became increasingly interested in psychoanalysis and, attracted to Lacan's ideas, incorporated many of them into his descriptions of narrative form, film language, and reception. Lacan's emphasis on the importance of language in the process of identity development (for Lacan, it was central) appealed to those whose work involved language—particularly those in the areas of literary and film studies. Increasingly—if problematically (see chapter 4)—Lacan's theories became central to much film theory, including—surprisingly—feminist film theory.[4] During the 1970s, film theorists editing and publishing in the influential British film journal *Screen* (among them, feminists such as Laura Mulvey) combined their interest in semiotic analysis and psychoanalysis with a rejection of orthodox Marxist notions of ideology, concluding—unlike their counterparts at the Centre for Contemporary Cultural Studies in Birmingham—that significatory processes are virtually autonomous from other arenas (i.e., the economic) and that it is through the forms of signification that values, ideas, and, therefore, practices are instilled. The overwhelming emphasis on semiotics and psychoanalysis led to the assumption that it is only through significatory processes that human "subjects" are formed and social change occurs, an assumption that continues to plague feminist film theory.

Up to this time, most feminists had been highly skeptical of psychoanalysis, both because it presents the male as the norm and the female as abnormal and because one of its primary practical uses had been to keep women in "their place." Women with "abnormal" behaviors were often sent to psychiatrists—and sometimes to institutions—where psychoanalytic methods were used to modify their behavior so that they could passively fit into the patriarchal scheme of things. But during the mid-1970s, the British feminists Juliet Mitchell, with *Psychoanalysis and Feminism*, and Laura Mulvey, with "Visual Pleasure and Narrative Cinema," argued that psychoanalysis—by allowing for an understanding of women's oppression—had a powerful political potential for feminism. The feminist turn to psychoanalysis was a shocking move, but Mitchell's theorizing quickly spread among English-speaking feminists, and Mulvey's article was published in *Screen* and acknowledged by both British and American feminists as a landmark in the shifting arena of feminist film theory.

The feminist concern for meaning and interpretation remained constant, but the critical and theoretical focus shifted away from the content of films and toward their formal patterns. Drawing on the highly formalist "semio-psychoanalysis" or "cine-psychoanalysis," film critics explicated the way "realist" filmic techniques (particular kinds of camerawork, editing, etc.) give the impression of transparency, the impression that the medium simply records and shows the world "as it is," while the techniques actually function to naturalize dominant ideologies through a manipulation of film language. Semiotics provided the tools for textual analysis that allowed critics to examine the processes by which films encourage certain interpretations; with these tools, feminist critics revealed that the "language" of "dominant cinema" contributes to women's oppression. Because sociologically oriented criticism paid no attention to this aspect of film, it was dismissed as hopelessly naive and it rapidly became passé in film studies—the baby, as it were, thrown out with the bathwater.

By the mid-1970s, American feminists had begun studying film theory in Paris with Metz, with the literary and film analyst Raymond Bellour, and with their colleagues, whose work had already penetrated the male mainstream of film theory in both Great Britain and the United States; by the late 1970s, feminist film theory was an arena no longer clearly divided by the Atlantic.[5] Metz's theoretical work and Bellour's psychoanalytically based textual analyses proved particularly useful for feminists; Bellour's explanation of film form included descriptions of the way Hollywood films positioned female characters for the spectator.[6] In 1976, some of the feminists who had studied in Paris, former members of the editorial board of *Women and Film*, established the American feminist film journal *Camera Obscura*, through which they expressed an explicit concern with structuralism, semiotics, and psychoanalysis.[7] Early issues of *Camera Obscura* included translations of the French theorists and critics with whom these feminists had studied, bringing semio-psychoanalysis—inflected by the editors' own feminism—into the heart of American feminist film studies, where it has remained. The feminist analysis of women's oppression now extended to—but was often limited to—the forms and processes of meaning-making.[8] Hollywood films—characterized as the products of the "dominant" or "classical" realist cinema—were shown to victimize both female characters and female viewers, and many feminist critics and filmmakers turned to the experimental avant-garde for hopes of a liberatory "counter-cinema."

By the late 1970s, this theoretical self-consciousness had become evident in British feminist filmmaking. Laura Mulvey and Peter Wollen made highly abstract experimental films (*Riddles of the Sphinx*, 1976, and *Amy!*, 1980), as did Sally Potter (*Thriller*, 1979). And while the *cinema vérité* documentary form continued to dominate American feminist filmmaking, some filmmakers began experimenting. Michelle Citron's *Daughter-Rite* (1978) seemed to be a documentary but turned out to be a fiction. And the highly theoretical and abstract *Sigmund Freud's Dora* (1979, by Andrew Tyndall, Anthony McCall, Claire Pajaczkowska, and Jane Weinstock) built directly on and from British and French avant-garde filmmaking.[9] In the early 1980s, several books reviewed and consolidated the gains made in feminist film studies; they included Annette Kuhn's *Women's Pictures: Feminism and the Cinema* (1982), E. Ann Kaplan's *Women and Film: Both Sides of the Camera* (1983), and *Re-vision* (1984), the "state-of-the-art" anthology edited by Mary Ann Doane, Patricia Mellencamp, and Linda Williams. Feminist film studies had come a very long way in its brief history, but as in other areas within feminist studies, there remained important unanswered questions.

In the mid to late 1980s, most of the questions central to feminist film theory and even to feminist film criticism concerned textual consumption: the nature of the "spectating subject" and her or his relationship to the filmic text. Most feminist film theorists and critics take a stand on this issue, implicitly or explicitly, and their textual analyses often provide the space for expressing competing positions, the sites for struggle.[10] The roots of the various disagreements surrounding the concept are found in the differences between sociology and psychology and in the distinct notions of spectatorship the two fields have generated. Indeed, the roots of most disagreements in film studies can be found in the seemingly inherent distinctions between the study of social groups (sociology) and the study of the formation and forms of the individual psyche (psychology); moving beyond many theoretical impasses involves moving beyond the notion that these fields—and the theories in which they are based—are incommensurable. The duality of the "social" and the "psychic" may be tired, but its presence lingers, influentially. The constant presence of this duality inhibits the development of what I call a "materialist psychoanalysis" but can also serve as the springboard for its development.

Briefly: "the subject" began its life in film theory as a notoriously ambiguous psychoanalytic concept used to describe the ongoing product-process of discursive practices. The argument follows: the subject and the Unconscious are constructed through the (unconscious) process of acquiring language, which entails a series of repressions. The Unconscious, then, is structured "like" language, although sometimes people forget that the language analogy is just that—an analogy. Cinema too is structured "like" language, and the analogic relationship is even more likely to be forgotten here. Then, a further analogy: because language, cinematic language, the language of the Unconscious, and basically "reality" have now become virtually conflated, the subject is seen to be "appropriately" positioned in ideology through manipulations of "cinematic language."[11] As a result, the subject is considered a discursive phenomenon, and subjects are believed to be formed in and changed through—and only through—discourse. But this discursive subject is distinguished from the "historical" or "social" subject—the "real" human being who lives and acts in the world, the seemingly unified, individual human watching a film. Two of the articles included in *Re-vision* are, in fact, concerned with this issue: the nature of the "spectating subject" and her or his relationship to the filmic text. Teresa de Lauretis's contribution to *Re-vision* (also included in a collection of her essays, *Alice Doesn't*, published the same year) examines the potential of Michel Foucault's "discourse analysis" (referenced in two other articles in the anthology) for explaining a particular reader—in this case, herself. Explaining real readers, she argued, should be the task of feminist critical practice, which she felt no longer needed the demonstration of "the functioning of 'woman' as the support of masculine vision, the restoration of Oedipus' sight, or the odd term in the relations of power."[12] She was, of course, correct, so far as use of the theories and methods for demonstrating such phenomena are concerned. We do not really need yet another explication of the victimization of "woman" by that pernicious male gaze. We do, however, need to question the adequacy of the theoretical framework that insists it has answered certain questions for all texts and all times and places.

De Lauretis attempted, with her writing, to engage in a discursive struggle to "challenge theory on its own terms." In *Alice Doesn't*, she took responsibility for her own voice, confronting the "masters" of semiotics, psychoanalysis, and narrative theory as she struggled to "produce the conditions of visibility for a different social subject"—woman.[13] In the essay included in both books, de Lauretis used Foucaultian concepts and categories to explain her reading of Nicholas Roeg's film *Bad Timing*, finding that the value of Foucault's thinking lies, first, in the insistence on abandoning the notion that a single discursive practice—like the cinema—can be understood in isolation and, then, in the assurance that possibilities for resistance exist everywhere. She saw, however, a danger in the tendency toward totalizing "discourse."

Christine Gledhill expressed even greater reservations about "discourse theory" in her contribution to *Re-vision*. She reworked a previously published exploration of the theoretical underpinnings of feminist film studies, which, she noted, appropriated tools developed within patriarchy for an analysis of patriarchy itself. Reviewing feminist positions in the debates over realism, ideology, psychoanalysis, and cultural practice, Gledhill concluded with an outline of current problems and suggestions for directions in addressing them. Observing that the neo-Marxist, semiotic, and post-structuralist theories of Althusser, Barthes, and Lacan had been assumed rather than explained (and, certainly, never questioned), Gledhill argued that the theoretical framework erected by feminist film critics restricts "the kinds of questions it asks of cinema and the range of film practices it makes available for feminist development."[14] The struggle for social change is, after all, basic to feminism, and we cannot afford to limit our strategies unnecessarily.

Feminists have a greater motivation than many other theorists to link the theoretical with the practical, and as a result, this distinction between discursive subject and social-historical subject has proved especially problematic. The split raises numerous questions, and responses come from such different theoretical bases that they may almost be considered not different varieties of the same species but different species altogether—apples and oranges, so to speak. Primarily, what is the relation between the "social" spectator and the spectator positioned by the text? Additionally, what is the relation between the spectator and film form? How does identification work? How do the unconscious desires of the spectator influence interpretation? How much control can a spectator exert over her or his interpretation? How can we account for the existence of varying defensible feminist readings of a text? And, especially important for feminists, is spectatorship gendered?[15]

The first clear position on the question of gendered spectatorship was constructed in response to the question "Is the gaze [the construction of the characters' and spectators' look or point of view] male?" The earliest, most rigid answer was "Yes, but though the spectator may or may not be male, she or he is constructed by the text as masculine." E. Ann Kaplan presented this position—a bit more sophisticated than the claim that the gaze is "male"—in *Women and Film* (1983). Based on Lacanian psychoanalysis, this response assumes a rather direct parallel between spectating and voyeurism and depends on the assumption that voyeurism is inherently masculine. But even this cinematic voyeurism is not considered truly an *activity*; the spectator passively submits to the text's manipulations. The text controls its own reading.

Laura Mulvey, in "Afterthoughts on 'Visual Pleasure and Narrative Cinema' Inspired by *Duel in the Sun*" (1981), argued for a second position. She argued that spectatorship is indeed gendered but that pleasure in film viewing is inaccessible to the "feminine" portions of the psyche; the female spectator calls up a long-repressed masculinity to engage in the transsexual identification that can allow her pleasure in film viewing. This response is based on Freud's description of female development, a description that initially assumed the masculine as base but eventually came to include bisexuality in that base, still excluding certain experiences (voyeurism among them) from the "feminine." The response—more sophisticated than an essentialist argument in its use of *feminine* and *masculine* as terms not determined by biology—still assumes a passive (male or female) spectator, whose interpretation is controlled by the text itself.

A third position on gendered spectatorship argues that the text presents multiple and contradictory spectating positions and that the female spectator juggles these, identifying with none but rather with contradiction itself. One permutation of this explains the female reader as traumatized by pre-Oedipal separation anxiety (separation from the mother) and as constantly schizophrenic, constantly reading with a knowledge of her involvement in and separation from the text; she sees herself both identifying with the protagonist and knowing more than the protagonist. This response allows the spectator more agency in the construction of her reading and requires that she recognize the text's preferred reading, as well as alternatives to that reading. In "'Something Else Besides a Mother': *Stella Dallas* and the Maternal Melodrama" (1984), Linda Williams took this position, and in *Loving with a Vengeance* (1982), Tania Modleski described readers of Harlequin romances as schizophrenic, simultaneously aware of their identification with the heroine and aware of the superior knowledge provided them by the text and by their knowledge of the rigid formula that governs it. Still, however, according to this response, the alternatives are encompassed by the text; still the text controls its own reading.

A fourth position allows for female spectatorship but assumes that "woman" (an abstract category representative of, but not synonymous with, actual living women) and "feminine sexuality" are so thoroughly colonized by patriarchy that female spectatorship is, therefore, not a viable liberatory subject positioning. In 1985, E. Ann Kaplan—influenced by Julia Kristeva—argued this position in *Cinema Journal*'s "Dialogue" section and later in "Feminist Film Criticism: Current Issues and Problems," a review article for *Studies in the Literary Imagination*. This response assumes that subjects are constructed through language but that "woman is in all cases positioned in a signifying chain based on her representing lack, absence." The response indicates that resistance is possible because the discourses in which language takes form do have gaps that permit "new articulations" through which "new subjects" may be formed.[16] It is unclear, however, just how a lack can fill a gap.

Finally, my own position on gendered spectatorship denies the "radical innocence" of women and points to the ongoing participation and complicity of women in meaning-making processes, indeed in the evolution of languages (including cinematic languages). We are never outside of ideology, and the patriarchal center to a great extent, though not completely, constructs its margins, but the occupants of the margins can resist. We are never able to completely "step outside" patriarchal discourse, as some feminists argue. Patriarchy is not monolithic, but its dominance influences even the feminist discourses that challenge it. But challenge it they do. Ideological struggle is everywhere evident, and patriarchy only partially constructs its opposition. Not even cinematic language is without feminine influences (and female gazes), even though few women have worked in influential positions within cinematic institutions. In her latest book, *The Women Who Knew Too Much* (1988), Tania Modleski's position has shifted to a position closer to mine; her readings of the films of Alfred Hitchcock—an acknowledged master of classic cinematic language—provide evidence of discursive struggle even within films widely held to be highly misogynist. Interpretation, Modleski argues in this recent book, "involves a struggle for survival," and even within Hitchcock's films she identifies for the female spectator "reason to hope that we will be able to survive patriarchy's attacks."[17] Indeed, texts are powerful delimiters of meaning, but they do not fully control their own readings. Research done on actual historical spectators indicates much more agency on the part of the spectator than do the other positions outlined above. Unlike many cultural studies scholars, I remain attentive to the ways texts may manipulate unconscious desires to influence the spectating process and, therefore, interpretation and experience, and my position on the questions of textual analysis and gendered spectatorship, a position that will become even clearer in later chapters, is based in a feminist critique of Freudian and Lacanian psychoanalysis derived from object-relations psychoanalysis (an approach to psychoanalysis considered scandalous by many Freudians and

Lacanians but one I believe may lead us to a materialist theory of psycho-analysis). My intent with this book is to show how textual analysis can be simultaneously responsive to theories concerned with the discursive construction of subjectivity and to research on actual historical readers and their distinctly different responses to the struggle among the elements within a text.

Each of the positions described above implies a stance on the questions central to this book: How do film texts participate in the ideological process? Specifically, how do they contribute to the ongoing construction and reconstruction of gender? Debate within feminist film theory is clearly quite alive; indeed it is lively, but within the arena of feminist film criticism, there exist counterproductive tendencies, as well as highly productive and significant critiques of its direction. One primary difficulty in some of the positions on female spectatorship shows up in a lack of attention to female pleasure, a lack of attention problematic even to feminists within the field. Indeed, pleasure has far too frequently been dismissed as retrogressive; some avant-garde feminist filmmakers have even sought to make films that deny pleasure. And even as feminists have developed the techniques involved in "reading against the grain" of mainstream texts, they have ignored both the systematically resistant discourses within the texts and the pleasures to be found in resistance.

An even greater difficulty is found in the discourse of feminist film theory itself. Although the question of gendered spectatorship is clearly crucial, it, like many questions within feminist theory, obscures other significant questions because of the attention it receives. As they have struggled to carve out and maintain a place for feminism within academe, feminists have often concentrated on questions concerning gender to the exclusion of those concerning race, class, and sexual preference, thus inadvertently reinforcing white, middle-class, heterosexual values by ignoring structures of oppression other than those based on sex and gender difference. Even though this charge has been made against the contemporary women's movement in general, it is certainly worthy in the case of feminist film theory and criticism, a domain that has until very recently been almost exclusively white and middle class. In an article entitled "White Privilege and Looking Relations" (1986), Jane Gaines caricatured the "female intellectual voice" that resonates in feminist film theory and criticism and that acts—intentionally or unintentionally—to police its boundaries. This abstract academic voice also permeates many contemporary avant-garde feminist films, often producing remarkably inaccessible film texts. Two recently published anthologies of feminist media criticism— E. Deidre Pribram's *Female Spectators* and Margaret Marshment and Lorraine Gamman's *The Female Gaze* (both 1988)—included articles that addressed racial differences in the production and consumption of film texts, but the attempt to theorize diversity within feminist film studies remains in its infancy, in part because of the tendency, as Gaines noted, among feminist film theorists and critics to concentrate their attention on the formal aspects of film. Although this has remedied the naiveté of early feminist film criticism, the resulting formalist concentration on cinema as language prohibits "making comparisons between 'actuality' and the text" and banishes "sociological reference points and historical detail from criticism."[18] We must address our own rhetoric, the limitations it places on us, and the possibilities it obscures. Foremost in this process is removing the prohibition against simultaneously thinking the "social subject" and the "discursive subject" so that we can more fully recognize ourselves as both discursive and social-historical subjects, as products of both discursive and extradiscursive phenomena.

My take on the extradiscursive is influenced by the sort of post-structuralist theorizing that insists on human reality/subjectivity as always discursively produced, but although I will agree that we *know* our realities in and through the discursive, I see the extradiscursive differently than do most discourse theorists, who would argue that positing an extradiscursive entails positing an essential, unchanging, and determinant extradiscursive. Such a position is a common response to biological determinism (which post-structuralist feminists see as the ultimately essentialist position) or to the sort of orthodox Marxist reading of Marx's base-superstructure model that sees the model as a description of an extradiscursive economic base that determines the discursive (which is or exists within the superstructure). This is not the way I see the extradiscursive. I see extradiscursive realms (the biological, the economic, etc.) interacting with and changing in relation to the discursive; I see these as, in Althusser's terms, "relatively autonomous spheres" that influence but do not determine each other. I see the social subject and the discursive subject as overlapping but not entirely congruent phenomena; the discursive subject is a product of discursive practices, whereas the social subject is a product of both the discursive and the extradiscursive—and the social subject can act, can intervene. My work is in the discursive realm, and my aim—this should be obvious—is to intervene in the way we collectively and discursively produce realities. Still, I am not prepared to claim that the discursive is the only realm, nor that it is the only realm in which intervention is possible; it is, however, the one in which I work.

Christine Gledhill warned that "conflating the social structure of reality with its signification" will not result in an adequate analysis because the signifying process is *not* the exclusive determinant in the production of the social formation and because this move underestimates diversity. Women experience both the public and the private realms differently than do men not simply because of the differences in their access to and positioning by discourse but also because of the differences in the material conditions of their existence.[19] These conditions are, of course, inflected by race, class, and sexual preference. An approach predicated solely on sexual difference assumes essential gender differences and offers no avenue for change, Gledhill argued, because it assumes that narratives are committed to the compulsive play of difference based on the security of "an already known closure." An analysis of cultural products, such as narrative films, that holds together the discursive and the extradiscursive can aid in the location of spaces in which women can resist patriarchy. Analysis that removes a narrative from the material historical conditions of its consumption is predicated on the assumption of its ideological effectivity and ignores the possibility that it may be consumed differently by different people, by—for instance—women and men or by women of different racial or ethnic backgrounds. Textual analysis must attempt to account for the way cultural texts make available the diversity of interpretations we know to be available, and it must attend to the privileging of certain interpretations over others.

Some recent efforts have been made within feminist film theory to link the discursive and the historical-social subjects. E. Ann Kaplan, for instance, recently argued that "the subjective (psychic) and the social cannot be distinguished." But she then employed an intellectual sleight of hand and dissolved the social subject, stating that "since all subjectivity, wherever experienced, is discursive, it is in this terrain that we must work." The early promise of her position is undercut by her apparent failure to understand the social subject as anything but a discursive product, passively powerless to resist those "new discursive articulations [that] in turn construct new subjects." Kaplan's position turns into semiotic analysis carried to its logical and absurd extreme. As Gaines argued, "Sealed off as it is (in theory), this [feminist film] analysis may not comprehend the category of the real historical subject, but its use will always have implications *for* that subject."[20] We are that subject.

Although feminism has had a greater influence on film studies than on many other areas, film theory has not proven immune to the problems found in other disciplines; it too is dominated by theories that have neglected women's experiences or that have considered them deviant. Too many feminist film theorists and critics have committed themselves to a theoretical base that has obliterated for them the possibility of understanding the participation of film texts in the process of ideological change. In the interest of producing a self-critique that empowers, I will examine the discourse of feminist film theory and criticism by focusing on the advantages and limitations of several methods of textual analysis as they aid or fail to aid in explaining the participation of film texts in the ideological process with, in, and by which we construct our reality. The scope of the book is limited to problems of textual analysis and works toward explaining the circulation of meaning through popular film texts; the book aims to examine how popular film texts provide material for the making of diverse meanings while they guide—or attempt to guide—their own interpretations. The book concentrates on the struggle over gender within and among film texts initially exhibited and consumed during the 1950s, and although their "real"—or original, empirical—audience cannot be fully reconstructed, textual analysis can posit the texts' preferred "subject," as well as resistant readings. An analysis of the sort of readings produced by contemporary feminist film critics illustrates how these films allow empirical, historical subjects distinctly different but defensible readings and how they still actively participate in the struggle over "gender." First, however, it is necessary to consider an alternative to the theoretical framework that so seriously restricts much feminist film theory and criticism.

Feminism, Marxism, and Cultural Studies

The strength of the contemporary women's movement as a social force was obvious by the late 1960s, and by the early 1970s, feminists had begun to evaluate its practice, examining the theories implicitly guiding it. Hoping to find ways of strengthening their practice through more thoroughly understanding women's oppression, many activists turned to Marxist theory, the theoretical tradition that had informed the socialist movement, assuming that it would more or less directly address their concerns, but they found this solution too mechanical and ultimately inadequate. Many subsequently turned away from Marxist theory when they realized that it could not provide the theoretical framework they needed. At the time they were correct; a certain "heart of darkness" lay within Marxist theory. Like the work in many other theoretical arenas, the work in this one lacked substantial attention to women's experiences, and in fact, the entire domestic sphere was undertheorized.[21] Although the labor force must be reproduced ideologically as well as physically, and the reproduction of "properly" gendered individuals is crucial to this endeavor, Marx and the early Marxists paid limited attention to "the woman question" as, for generations, Marxists attempted to account for the production of capital, generally ignoring the all-important "reproduction of the labor force," women's work. In order to be of help for feminism, Marxist theory had to be transformed.

The civil rights movement of the 1960s directed attention to the intersection of race and class among Marxist theorists, but it was only as recently as the mid-1970s that the effects of the contemporary women's movement finally began to be felt in Marxist circles. Only at this point did Marxists begin to seriously consider questions on the relation of modes of production and social class to gender. Questions of concern to feminists in the 1960s, 1970s, and 1980s had not been dreamt of by Marx or Engels, whose concerns—when they wrote on the "Woman Question" in the nineteenth century—were focused on the issue in the context of an evolving socialist movement and entirely in terms of the family, not in the context of a women's movement or in terms preferred by contemporary feminists.[22] Most Marxist analysis, until the last decade, left unchallenged the notions of the unified family and the sexual division of labor, as well as the social and economic consequences of gender differentiation. Neither did it develop the theoretical apparatus for explaining the interaction of discourses of sex and gender with the discourses of class and race (and the nondiscursive experiences that result from their intersection). But relatively recent developments in Marxist theory—particularly developments in the study of ideology within the milieu known loosely as cultural studies—provide a valuable framework for feminist theorists, critics, and researchers, as well as for strategies developed for feminist practice aimed at social change.[23] However, as Elizabeth Long has so cogently commented,

> I am struck by the ways in which summary or presentational statements about British Cultural Studies that have been made in this country have already practiced an exclusion that seems to have marginalized its feminist practitioners, ironically the strand of that tradition that has arguably the best chance of maintaining a critical stance in its appropriation by feminist scholars in America, both because of their connections with a broad social movement, and because of the nature of their practices within the academy.[24]

The movement known as cultural studies, now becoming influential in the United States, is an interdisciplinary approach to the study of the production and circulation of meanings within the contemporary cultures of industrialized societies; to date, analysis has focused primarily on those cultures of the United States, Australia, and Western Europe, notably Great Britain. Like any approach, this one varies from place to place and time to time, according to historical circumstances, but the term *cultural studies* has come to imply the investigation and theorizing of the relations between culture and society that inherently consider issues of power, and in Britain, internal feminist critiques have significantly affected the direction of cultural studies scholarship, complicating considerations of power relations. Until very recently, however, American cultural studies has had a seemingly apolitical bias, and even now Americans writing about cultural studies tend to marginalize the influence of feminism, a theoretical arena in which, as Long correctly argued, ignoring power relations is impossible.[25]

Cultural studies in the United States draws on work from a number of approaches and disciplines; among them are American studies, anthropology, communications research, hermeneutics, history, linguistics, literary criticism and theory, Marxist philosophy, and sociology.[26] Indeed, scholars who now identify themselves with cultural studies emerged from all of these fields; often they found working within institutionalized disciplines frustrating as they approached questions unanswerable without an inter-disciplinary approach, an approach often blocked in the traditional academic disciplines. Distinctly different uses of the term *culture* account for some of the difficulty. The term has a long and complex history, and currently two uses predominate. Matthew Arnold's nineteenth-century description of culture as a society's "best" products still holds sway in many disciplines, especially those—like English literature or art or film—that got their initial purchase on academe as a result of appeals to elitism. Cultural studies scholars, however, proceed from the assumption that a "high culture"–"low culture" distinction is generally nonproductive, and the notion of "best" is itself a social construction. *Culture*, then, takes on an anthropological cast, referring instead to the historically specific meanings and values by which a society defines itself and the practices through which these meanings and values are expressed. Imagining the response of scholars in the traditional disciplines requires little creativity; for them, privileged definitions of *culture*, *art*, and *literature* are commonsensical, and theorizing them only presents a threat.[27]

Even the eclectic approach institutionalized as American studies, which proceeds from a definition of *culture* similar to that used in cultural studies, still lives with the elitist tradition of literary history from which it evolved. It has produced fascinating studies of cultural phenomena, but it has never been noted as theoretically rigorous or consistent; indeed, some American studies scholars avoid theory. However, others—like the communications scholars James Carey and Horace Newcomb, both associated at times with American studies—have not avoided theory and have sought to account for cultural processes, effectively becoming the "first generation" of American cultural studies scholars.[28] As a result, the area of communications research has been, in its relatively short life, one of the more nurturing homes for the developing tradition of American cultural studies. Most histories of communications research have stressed the positivistic media-effects research that came to dominate mass-media studies in the 1950s and 1960s and have ignored the ongoing humanistic analysis of the ritualistic social role of the media.[29] But Carey traces his intellectual lineage to the University of Chicago pragmatists concerned with modernization, specifically to John Dewey, and argues that it is within their work that American cultural studies commenced. It is not, he claims, a new phenomenon at all but the current manifestation of a scholarly tradition as old as effects research.[30]

Carey's work embodies this approach. His distinction between the dominant "transmissional model"—in which communication is seen only as the transportation of a message through space for the purpose of control—and the "ritual model"—which describes the symbolic sphere within and with which we represent our shared beliefs, where we create, maintain, repair, and transform reality—has become basic to many American cultural studies scholars' attempts to explain both the functioning of texts that are mass-produced for mass consumption and their participation in our production, reproduction, maintenance, and alteration of societies and cultures. The transmissional model describes some kinds of communication, and it also explains those mass-media theories that assume a passive audience and overwhelmingly powerful media. In contrast, the ritual model posits social change as a process of collective, mutual persuasion and helps to explain the active role of representational texts and their readers in this process.[31] Influenced by Carey's work as well as by the work of symbolic anthropologists, Newcomb adopted Carey's ritual model to describe television's role as a "cultural forum" for American society. To account for the social role of mass-mediated cultural forms, particularly television, he expanded the notion that culture, meaning, and thought are public and argued that the entertainment forms of our modern and mediated society operate as sites of *"imaginative possibility*, without which we would be unable to try new models, new roles, new theories, new combinations of behavior."[32] Entertainment texts offer an entry into the social rituals that create and give meaning to "reality."

Because of their mutual concern with the creation and re-creation of meaning, American cultural studies and feminist film studies would seem an obvious synthesis, but for at least three reasons, they have not, until recently, begun to merge. The first and most obvious reason has to do with the nature of academic boundaries. Whereas the cultural studies movement has been nurtured in programs oriented to the study of mass media, film is often not studied as such. The study of film has most often been separated from studies of other mass media in the United States and in Great Britain, both by those studying film and by those studying other media. Often included within departments of art or literature—which tend to exclude the study of popular forms—film studies became instantiated in academe as its function as a central cultural medium was ceded to television and as it became possible, then, to argue that film is an art. Indeed, it was film's increasing cultural marginality that allowed it entrance into the university.[33] The formalist tendency in film studies during the 1970s and early 1980s aggravated this tendency, but an increasing attention to film history could bring it toward cultural studies.

However, a second factor has proven problematic. As Elizabeth Long has pointed out, mainstream American feminists have until recently manifested a blind spot toward British cultural studies because of a tendency toward "gender essentialism" and a sympathy with psychoanalytic theories that obscure questions of class and race.[34] And finally, in contrast to the explicitly political British cultural studies scholars, first-generation American cultural studies scholars like Carey and Newcomb have often framed their work in relatively neutral terms, and their work has been labeled apolitical. This apparent failure to overtly consider issues of power and subordination has caused American cultural studies, until very recently, to fail to appeal to many feminists. The most vigorous charges of apoliticism have come from scholars like Larry Grossberg, members of a second generation of American cultural studies scholars (often former students of first-generation scholars) who acknowledge intellectual debts not only to American cultural studies but also to British cultural studies and its Marxist and neo-Marxist heritage.[35] Virtually indistinguishable, theoretically, from other neo-Marxist American communications scholars who identify themselves with the term *critical research*—Eileen Meehan, Jennifer Daryl Slack, Marty Allor, Fred Fejes—second-generation scholars might more accurately be placed within a camp called *critical cultural studies*, since the American situation warrants that distinction. Among this second generation are feminists who call for a feminist cultural studies, which would inherently consider the distribution and manipulation of power.[36]

Carey has denied the charge that cultural studies in the United States fails to consider power, dominance, subordination, and ideology, pointing to theorists like C. Wright Mills and Harold Innis, for whom power was a central issue. Carey contended that the "ferment in the field" of communications research retains overtones of its "cheerful" pragmatist origins while also raising the indisputable fact that social formations are determined by power relations.[37] But the attention to power, dominance, subordination, and struggle within the work of first-generation American cultural studies scholars is so implicit that it is practically invisible. Following the British cultural studies tradition, second-generation scholars find an explicit attention to these issues to be crucial.

Like all critical and theoretical movements, British cultural studies developed within a particular socioeconomic context and in response to the inadequacies of older approaches for answering new, pressing questions. New conditions required new points of departure and new analytic methodologies. An external crisis—the red scares of the late 1940s and early 1950s—purged the American Left, leaving left-leaning intellectuals wary and draining politics and academe of the important and vigorous participation of radical thinkers. But Marxism remained more viable in European politics and academe, particularly within the British "New Left." The atmosphere of the cold war period was daunting in the 1950s and 1960s, but despite the frigidity of the setting and in response to Stalinism—Marxism's internal crisis—humanist Marxists like Raymond Williams, John Berger, and E. P. Thompson (in England), Jean-Paul Sartre and Henri Lefebvre (in France), and the Praxis group (in Yugoslavia) paved the way for what we now know as cultural studies by refusing to reject Marxism, working instead within an atmosphere of critique: the critique of capitalism, the critique of orthodox Marxism, and the critique of methods that proved inadequate for an analysis of post–World War II cultures and societies.

During the late 1950s and early 1960s, Williams and Thompson produced bold, historically based analyses of contemporary British culture, unlike anything being produced by their contemporaries in the States. Their analyses were interventions aimed at addressing the concerns of the New Left: the history and nature of Britain's postwar social, cultural, and economic transformations.[38] Humanist Marxists rejected theories of ideology as "false consciousness," turning to examinations of the ways human beings create their social realities, with an emphasis on the cultural arena as the site for ideological struggle; they considered whole ways of life, symbolic systems, and structures of experience. Culture and interpretation were established as problems central to Western Marxism, the existence of multiple cultures within single social formations was recognized, and the need to understand the mass media and their impact was acknowledged as one of the more pressing problems. As humanist Marxists turned toward analysis of cultural documents, it became clear that cultural theory lacked the necessary sophistication to adequately explain their participation in meaning-making and cultural reproduction. An interchange with anti-humanist structuralism and semiotics marked a revision in Marxist cultural theory, first in France in the early 1960s and then in England and America in the late 1960s and early 1970s, laying the groundwork for contemporary post-structuralist Marxist theory. Human subjectivity was re-theorized, and the concentration on historical, social, and cultural specificity called attention to the ideological practices that determine subjectivity. The social formation itself was reconceptualized, as a structure of relatively autonomous social practices; a concern with ideology was recognized as central, though a fascination with Foucault's antihumanist rejection of individual agency and experience marks the 1980s version of the ongoing reconceptualization of ideology, with terms like *discourse* and *subjectivity* often eliding *ideology*.[39]

The research and theorizing that became known as British cultural studies was finally institutionalized in 1964 at the University of Birmingham as the Centre for Contemporary Cultural Studies (CCCS), a graduate-level research center directed at first by Richard Hoggart (1964–68), then by Stuart Hall (1968–79), and finally by Richard Johnson (1980–88). (Suffering from budget cuts under the Thatcher regime, the Centre's activities have been somewhat curtailed in recent years; it has lost its independent identity, becoming a department within the faculty of commerce and social science.) The CCCS has never considered cultural studies a discipline but rather, in Hall's words, "an 'engaged' set of disciplines" that inhabits the tensions between political and intellectual concerns.[40] Johnson has described cultural studies as a tradition, a movement, a network, a process, and an alchemy; it resists codification and insists on "the importance of critique." By *critique*, Johnson means in its "fullest sense: not criticism merely, nor even polemic, but procedures by which other traditions are approached both for what they may yield and for what they inhibit. Critique involves stealing away the more useful elements and rejecting the rest."[41] Cultural studies manifests a flexibility that feminist film theory and criticism need.

Initially, British cultural studies scholars privileged class, neglecting issues relating to sex and gender difference, but during the 1970s, feminist critiques and the struggles against racism in Britain caused a rethinking of cultural studies' basic assumptions, models, and topics for analysis. Questions of gender and race, displacing the exclusive attention to class contradictions, produced the field's most important recent self-critiques and called attention even to the importance of supportive working relationships.[42] The rhetoric surrounding these changes in direction is indicative of the early lack of attention to the complexity of oppression but is indicative, as well, of a healthy, nurturing, often collective though difficult approach to intellectual labor—an approach from which we in the States need to learn—and of an intellectual flexibility valuable for feminism. Feminist film studies can benefit most from the theorizing about ideology and the related research on audiences—particularly on subcultural and female audiences—that has influenced textual analysis.

Theorizing Ideology

From the beginning, the development of a progressively more sophisticated theory of ideology has been a central activity within British cultural studies, particularly during the 1970s, when the CCCS was under the direction of Stuart Hall.[43] Work on "concrete" case studies has guided and tested that theorizing. Concrete research at the CCCS has proceeded in a variety of disciplines—primarily language studies, literary studies, ethnography, and media studies. Although none of it was restricted by disciplinary boundaries, the work of the CCCS has consistently been influenced by questions and premises traditionally considered Marxist, questions and premises that are (or should be) central to feminist film studies: the notions that cultural processes are bound up with social relations— especially those of class, sex, race, and age—and that culture involves power relationships and is involved in the production and reproduction of asymmetrical individual and social relations. Culture is understood as neither autonomous nor externally determined but as a site for struggle over social differences. Feminism has aided a turn away from earlier forms of ideology critique and toward approaches concerned with the formation of identity, with subjectivity, and with popularity and pleasure.[44]

Both British and American cultural studies are now moving in directions of particular interest to feminists in film theory and criticism. Younger American cultural studies scholars have been attracted by the ongoing

British concern with theorizing ideology—and the varieties and processes of power.[45] Having matured (or begun to mature) during the late 1960s and early 1970s, when active engagement in political issues and movements was a daily experience for many young Americans, these younger American cultural studies scholars—influenced by the often pioneering first generation of American cultural studies scholars but formed by their active confrontations with social and governmental policy—searched for explanations of culture and society that acknowledge those often intangible forces they felt were encompassing and limiting their thinking (and living). The progress made by British cultural studies in developing more adequate ways of talking about ideology appealed to these scholars because it aided in the analysis of cultural phenomena that they had experienced—phenomena often relating to sex and gender—and that were embodying, transforming, and being transformed by those intangible forces so adequately described as "ideology."

By the late 1950s, the inadequacies of the classical Marxist use of the base-superstructure metaphor had become glaringly obvious to the founders of British cultural studies.[46] The insistence on a literal interpretation of Marx's metaphor results in a reductive, simplistic, and inadequate account of the relations between the economic sphere (the base) and the social, cultural, and political spheres of human existence (the superstructure); the classical Marxist model posits a superstructure determined by the economic base and assumes a powerful ruling class that imposes its will on "the masses," forcing them (us?) into a "false consciousness." This deterministic definition of ideology—characterized by Stuart Hall as a "sink hole in history"[47]—posed a major obstacle for Marxist theory, one that British cultural studies theorists slowly overcame through close reading and reworking of various theories of ideology.

Arguing for a position somewhere between camps he characterized as the "culturalists" and the "structuralists," Hall reflected on and distinguished between these two influences in cultural studies, both based on Marxist theory.[48] The earliest influence came from the "culturalists"— among them Raymond Williams—who emphasized human creativity and human experience, placing experience as the source of knowledge, depicting individuals as capable of action, and assuming an identity between experience and social class (homologies like this one abound in culturalist theory). A comparison with the sociological feminist film criticism and documentary filmmaking of the early 1970s is obvious, but there seems to be no evidence of a direct link; both groups emphasized experience, though feminists lacked a serious analysis of social class.

For the sake of comparison, Hall characterized the other camp as "structuralist"; primary among the continental structuralists that influenced British cultural studies was Louis Althusser.[49] Althusser's emphasis on the complex and contradictory relationships between the economic, political, and ideological spheres rang true, as did his lesser emphasis on human agency and his depiction of individuals not as autonomous actors but as (unconsciously) acted upon by social, cultural, political, and economic formations. Both Althusser and Williams rejected the classical Marxist notion of ideology as "false consciousness," which assumed that classes have a "true" and unambiguous consciousness that is obfuscated by "false" ways of living and believing; the notion that ideology is "false consciousness" assumes that a system privileges an elite and manipulates "the masses," the "dupes of history"—always, somehow, other people.[50] Williams stressed that, for Marx, consciousness was "seen from the beginning as a part of the human material social process, and its products in 'ideas' are then as much a part of this process as material products themselves." Althusser described ideology as systems of representation in which people live the (imaginary) relations to the (real) conditions of their existence. It is a lived but not necessarily conscious (perhaps unconscious) relationship of individuals to "reality," and he placed knowledge not as something "found" but as something produced through ideological work.[51]

The obvious comparison between the structuralist camp and that of British and American feminist film theorists of the late 1970s *is* due to a causal link. Feminist film theorists were reading Althusser, Metz, and Lacan, and Althusser, like Metz, incorporated Lacan's ideas into his work, particularly his notions on the creation (or "interpellation") of subjectivity; indeed, Lacan's ideas became central to Althusser's account of the reproduction of ideology. Althusser argued that ideology constitutes individuals as "subjects"—that ideology not only creates individuals but enables a subject's recognition of individual subjectivity. Althusser did not conflate "the subject" with any individual human; rather, he considered "the subject" the position in which individuals are constituted. His work does not help us theorize the relationship between the subject created by the text and the historical spectating subject, and feminist reliance on his theorizing led to a lack of attention to the historical subject. But in his emphasis on the determinate conditions within which individuals and systems of signification operate lies one of the strengths of his theory. He recognized that individuals act in a world not of their making, within a "structure-in-dominance" that reproduces—through "practices and rituals"—the dominant social relations of production (including patriarchal structures, though Althusser neglected this area of analysis). This emphasis led to an analysis of the various structured practices (among them, the cinema) through which social formations determine subjectivity, if not to a further examination of the fact that individuals can—and do—act. However, as Michele Barrett has argued, the Lacanian influence is "so badly integrated into Althusser's theoretical position as to make little more than a dent in the class-based foundation of his theories in general."[52]

Indeed, one of the most profound problems in Althusser's theory is the tendency toward "creeping Marxist functionalism": displacing the subject reduces it to only the pre-given product of ideological positioning, determined by the necessary reproduction of the conditions of production. This leads, in film theory, to the assumption that, for instance, a film's spectator is positioned by the "cinematic apparatus"—the film's discourses and the conditions of production and consumption—and the passivity of the "spectating subject" is assumed. Althusser's theory, then, fails to account for resistance, intervention, and the change that can result. Still, Althusser's recognition of the systematic structuring of ideology and the determinate tendencies of these structures was a major advance.

Althusser also established the importance of social institutions and practices in constructing human subjectivity, insisting that ideas *are* ideology but that ideology appears in practices located within the rituals of social formations. Ideas are registered in language and behavior, in social "apparatuses." As limited as it is, this notion is valuable. Althusser's linking of apparatuses such as education, religion, and media to political structures was a positive contribution, but he linked them far too firmly to the state. It is not difficult to see how such a theory could have arisen in France during the 1960s and 1970s, when many of these institutions were indeed linked directly to the French state; for instance, unlike television networks in the United States, those in France were state-controlled. Still, as Althusser formulated it, the concept of the ideological state apparatus presented an inadequate framework for explaining the situation that has developed, for instance, in the United States, where civil institutions do indeed support and aid in reproducing the state, but only in a complex and indirect way.[53] The base of the problem, it seems, is that—even with his concept of "relative autonomy"—Althusser failed to adequately distinguish between the state and civil society. Although the links between them are important, the distinctions are equally important, especially when considering issues of gender, sex, and sexuality, issues that concern phenomena in the "private" spheres.

Much contemporary "post-structuralist"–"post-modernist" theory is influenced by Althusser's rejection of the idea that a "necessary correspondence," a homologous relation, exists between various levels of a social formation. But many of the theorists who label themselves "post-modernists" have stretched this observation much further, to the position that there is "necessarily no correspondence," that "nothing connects with anything else." In 1977, Raymond Williams outlined the advantages of proceeding from the analysis of structural homologies—notably the often striking "fit" between an abstracted ideology and cultural products—but he also noted the extreme selectivity necessary in establishing such homologies and the "heavy price" paid by such analysis, particularly in the understanding of the contemporary cultural process:

> None of the dualist theories, expressed as reflection or mediation, and none of the formalist and structuralist theories, expressed in variants of correspondence or homology, can be fully carried through to contemporary practice, since in different ways they all depend on a known history, a known structure, known products. Analytical relations can be handled in this way; practical relations hardly at all.[54]

In 1985, Stuart Hall took a position midway between the homologists and the post-structuralists, arguing that neither correspondence nor non-correspondence is necessary, that the ideology of a class is not necessarily determined by its relationship to the economic relations of capitalist production. The British feminist Michele Barrett took a similar position, arguing that although Althusser's reconceptualization of ideology has been useful for feminist theory because it challenged the mechanistic classical Marxist interpretation of the base-superstructure model and included gender as an important factor in the construction of individual subjects, the post-Althusserian rejection of all determinate relations is "not at all useful."[55] Basically, there are no guarantees; the effects of a practice are not given by its origin. Contradiction and ambiguity exist, and action is relatively open-ended. Possibly, for instance, a feminist film might not position its spectator in a way that challenges patriarchy, or a structure that tends to reinforce patriarchy may indeed fail or may fail partially.

Williams found developments in the concept of hegemony—initiated in the 1920s and 1930s by the Italian theorist Antonio Gramsci and extended by British cultural studies scholars—to be a promising alternative to formalist and structuralist theories. A more satisfying and convincing notion of ideology developed and became dominant in British cultural studies during the 1970s and 1980s; this notion combined the useful aspects of Althusser's theory with Gramsci's notion that ideology is a hegemonic process that is multifaceted, constantly challenged, and constantly changing. The concept of hegemony carries much of the richness of Carey's ritual model, but it also carries with it a critical stance and a recognition of the existence of power and dominance simultaneously with inequality and resistance within the ideological process.[56] A brief analysis of the ritual model reveals the distinctions between the two generations of American cultural studies scholars, the influence of British cultural studies on the second generation, and the overlap in the concerns of cultural studies and feminist film theory and criticism.

Although much of the work based on the ritual model is persuasive and the model offers a significant advancement in the understanding that there are various kinds of communication, a central problem exists with the way in which the ritual model is generally used. Describing the transmissional model as inherently focused on power and control leads to the assumption that power is unimportant in ritual communication. This is entirely misleading; significant power exists in and is manipulated within ritual communication. Indeed, the primary distinction between the two kinds of communication described by these models is not that one kind is used for control and the other is not. Rather, these are distinct uses of power, used for distinct kinds of control. Power exerted in the communications accurately described by the transmissional model—telegraph communication, for example—resembles the sort of power often described as repressive, whereas power exerted by communications of the ritual variety—films, for example—involves not coercion but consent, and within the process of attaining and retaining consent (or, in other words, within the ideological process), there is significant struggle between dominant and resistant forces.

Influenced by the theoretical advances of British cultural studies theorists as well as by American literary theorists and philosophers who work in the continental tradition (rather than the Anglo-American tradition), second-generation American cultural studies scholars recognize a theoretical framework that can lead to understanding this power: theories of ideology that constantly call attention to the existence and manipulation of power and to resistance, even with and within mass-produced and ritually mass-consumed texts.[57] But this theoretical arena and its politically loaded vocabulary have generally been ignored or rejected by American analysts who base their work on the ritual model of communication. The ritual model has many virtues, but it fails to account for any of the many kinds and uses of power, particularly the kind of power given and derived through consensual processes. Ultimately, this weakens the model and limits its usefulness.

Theories of ideology are rejected for various reasons: some consider ideology a useless nineteenth-century anachronism; some accuse the term *ideology* of insufficient specificity, since it refers to an amorphous and ill-understood area of human existence; and some dismiss it on the basis of unfortunate and inaccurate theorizing under the rubric, most notably the claim that ideology is "false consciousness." The term *ideology* does have a varied past, but so do other terms we use frequently but rarely question and certainly don't discard. For instance, Raymond Williams tells us that "culture is one of the two or three most complicated words in the English language."[58] But we haven't abandoned the word because it originally referred to the tending of plants and animals. Neither have we dismissed the term *art*—which originally referred to just about any kind of skill—because its initially nonexistent, then secondary, and now dominant reference is to "an abstract, capitalized Art" focusing on creative and imaginative products and their production. The concept referred to by *ideology* too has evolved since it was coined in 1796 by the French philosopher Destutt de Tracy to refer to a science of ideas, a philosophy of mind. Subsequently, it has referred—often pejoratively—to explicitly delineated sets of beliefs and to the notion of "false consciousness," but the most current scholarly use of the word refers to a less evaluative and more descriptive notion based in Marx's distinction between material transformation and the forms in which people become conscious of and participate in conflict and transformation. Used widely among scholars in cultural studies, *ideology* in this latter sense dramatically expands the potential of the ritual model. The close examination of how social and cultural reproduction and change are accomplished is hampered by avoiding this concept, which at the same time links various areas and levels of activity in the production and circulation of meaning while constantly reminding us of power and power relationships, even—perhaps especially—in the rituals we use to shape our reality. Avoiding an explicitly articulated theory of ideology often leads to ignoring the complicity among texts, methodologies for textual analysis, and dominant configurations of ideologies. And by avoiding this theorizing, American cultural studies has alienated feminists. We can remedy that.

Much of the misunderstanding of *ideology* among scholars in American cultural studies may be attributed to descriptions of hegemony like that given by the American communication researcher Todd Gitlin in his widely circulated 1979 article, "Prime-Time Ideology: The Hegemonic Process in Television Entertainment." Gitlin equated hegemony with dominance and described ideology as a rigid but "leaky" system of domination, a system through which a dominant ideology is inevitably reproduced and resistance is defused or drained away.[59] However, the phenomenon at question here is not monolithic but is a shifting configuration of ideologies, and it is not just systemic but is also processual. The process does imply dominance but does not imply the sort of necessarily and inevitably continued dominance Gitlin indicated when he argued, first, that television keeps real alternatives off its (and the nation's) agenda; second, that it is used by established social powers to colonize the consciousness (and the unconscious) of "the masses"; and finally, that alternative and oppositional forms are routinely incorporated and coopted or excluded. Within entertainment texts, Gitlin saw an inevitable move toward homogeneity, with no ongoing and serious resistance to dominance. When he argued that the cultural system functions to frame and form social conflicts into compatibility with dominant systems of meaning, it is obvious that he understood something of the complex relationships between culture and society, but he saw no real potential for change. Although he argued that the hegemonic system must be continually negotiated and that the ideology of capitalist societies is essentially conflicted, Gitlin finally claimed that the core of capitalist ideology remains basically unchanged and unchallenged. He argued that because challenges are waged in the language of liberal capitalist ideology, they are therefore lost from the beginning. He failed to realize that language is not owned by liberal capitalism alone and that intervention—not to mention real change—is possible. We know that change does occur. Simply the existence of feminist scholarship is evidence; its increasing influence on communication studies and the resulting changes in this area provide a case in point. Clearly, the version of hegemony presented in this article resembles more the orthodox Marxist interpretation of the base-superstructure model than it does Gramsci's description of the hegemonic process. Gitlin's version does not open up to theorizing change; it does not account for the existence of resistance, for the process of struggle within the discourse of entertainment texts and the discourse of media criticism, or for the participation of entertainment and critical texts in the process of ideological change.

Ideology is a hegemonic process. Not merely a synonym for *ideology* or *culture*, *hegemony* is best understood in its adjectival form. It refers to a tendency (indeed a very strong tendency) within ideological processes, the tendency and process by which ideologies and configurations of ideologies attain dominance and attempt to retain it. Any particular (large *I*) Ideology is a configuration of many, not always noncontradictory (small *i*) ideologies—positions on and within a variety of arenas of struggle (race, class, gender) that function as strategies through which people negotiate their daily lives.[60] Any national or regional Ideology, for instance, is composed of official and unofficial ideologies, and in them dominant ideologies struggle with residual and emergent ideologies; all exist simultaneously and competitively. But we do not all exist in the same relation to the configuration of ideologies currently dominant. American Ideology, for instance, places us in its matrix by virtue of the particular discourses that intersect in each of us—our particular gender, class, age, sexual preference, race, color, education—and it provides different "road maps" for our economic, political, and social interactions, our actions conditioned by the site at which we find ourselves. We are not, however, entirely predetermined by such placing. American Ideology, for instance, defines *democracy* as a certain political—but not economic—organization, and our participation in this democracy is conditioned by discourses of gender, class, age, race, ethnicity, skin color (and others, no doubt) and by social practices. Although official national discourse prohibits inequity because of racial difference, we know that actual behavior does not reflect this, and ideology is as much practice as discourse. Official national discourse does not reach so far as to prohibit inequity based on gender, sexual preference, or class, and social practice often enforces such inequity, though some state and local governments have attempted rectification and though the resistant practice of subcultural groups actively opposes dominant inequitable practices. "Alternative" families based on lesbian or gay couples co-exist peacefully with traditional nuclear families and single-parent families in many communities, and some local governments have moved to legalize homosexual relationships and to extend benefits to the families of their lesbian and gay employees.

Limitations placed on the meaning of *democracy* have also inhibited moves toward economic democracy in the United States, but limitations have not stifled these moves entirely; producer and consumer cooperatives provide the best example in the United States. The first wave of co-op activity in the States occurred in the 1930s, and institutions established then—agricultural co-ops, credit unions—still thrive. The 1970s saw a second wave of co-op activity, and many of the consumer cooperatives and service collectives established then have survived, and many even pay decent, living wages to their "employees." Of greatest interest to feminists, of course, are ideologies concerning sex and gender and those ideologies (notably those of class, race, ethnicity, national origin, sexuality, age, and education, to mention a few) that overlap and inflect ideologies of sex and gender.

Hegemony does refer to the ongoing manipulation of power in the interests of those people(s) and structures (such as patriarchal social structures) that hold power and exercise it. But this does not imply continued dominance; it refers as well to the tentative nature of dominance and to the processual nature of system, to the possibility for change, and to the fact that ideologies (and even Ideologies) that are dominant are always challenged (sometimes successfully, sometimes not). Ideologies that are dominant may not always be dominant; indeed, resistance is a necessary condition for dominance. Interventions are, indeed, possible (though, of course, they may not always have the effect intended), and this is implicit in a feminist theoretical framework.

Ideology is structured and structuring. But change is not structured in;

the possibility for change is structured in. Struggle is inherent in the ideological process. The possibility for change in the structure-in-dominance is structured in the interplay of discourses (and play is very serious business), but this necessitates neither maintenance of the status quo nor change. Discursive struggle is inherent in the hegemonic ideological process, but the distribution and the deployment of power at various levels of the making and manipulation of meaning make some outcomes (far) more likely than others. But the outcomes are not, as Gitlin would have it, givens. Ethnographic research has shown that people can—consciously or unconsciously—and do make unexpected meaning from the messages they create and consume. And resistant meaning-making reshapes culture.

Williams argued that concentration on an abstracted dominant system (in our case, "bourgeois culture") inhibits understanding historical specificity and internal differentiation. The sort of "epochal" analysis Williams proposed is one expanded to include attention to "residual" and "emergent" elements, which are in themselves significant and which, in comparison, reveal the nature of the dominant. Williams distinguished the residual from the "archaic," which is recognizably of the past. The residual is quite different; formed in the past, the residual is active and effective in the present and may actually have an alternative or oppositional function. One of Williams's primary examples was that of organized religion in contemporary English culture. Although organized religion is predominantly residual, "there is a significant difference between some practically alternative and oppositional meanings and values (absolute brotherhood, service to others without reward) and a larger body of incorporated meanings and values (official morality, or the social order of which the otherworldly is a separated neutralizing or ratifying component)."[61] Within the complex of values that generally serve the dominant configuration of ideologies, there are some that can be—and are—used to challenge the structure itself; for instance, the notion or practice of absolute brotherhood is a distinct threat to a racist social formation. Indeed, some version of the residual must be incorporated into the dominant culture if the culture is to make sense, but to protect itself against the challenge of residual elements, the dominant culture must incorporate the actively residual by reinterpreting, diluting, projecting, and including and excluding in a discriminating fashion. It must respond to the challenge of the residual, but it must do so selectively; risk is there every step of the way.

The residual is more easily recognizable than the emergent, a radically different phenomenon. By *emergent*, Williams meant new meanings, new values, new practices, and new kinds of relationships. Although this sounds relatively straightforward, in fact emergent cultural elements are difficult to distinguish from the elements of a new phase of the dominant culture; Williams here referred to truly alternative or oppositional elements that can be defined only in comparison to the dominant, which will of necessity attempt to defuse the challenge, generally through incorporation. To explain, Williams emphasized that "no mode of production and therefore no dominant social order and therefore no dominant culture ever in reality includes or exhausts all human practice, human energy, and human intention."[62] The most common and obvious source of the emergent is a new class. As it emerges, new ideas and practices will also emerge, and the dominant will attempt incorporation; incorporation, of course, alters dominant ideas and practices. When, for instance, the working class emerged in England, new social values, social institutions, and cultural institutions emerged, though unevenly; the cultural, social, political, and economic develop in relation to each other, but their development is not necessarily "even," or in direct correspondence to each other.[63] Trade unions, working-class political parties, and working-class life-styles emerged with the working class, and the dominant class attempted to incorporate them through popular journalism, advertising, and commercial entertainment forms.

Similarly, in the United States during the 1950s, trade unions, political institutions (the two primary parties and agencies of the government itself), and the popular press explicitly attempted to persuade women—and particularly women who were mothers—that their "proper place" was in the home, and the most popular entertainment forms engaged in the attempt more subtly. But an amorphous, unorganized, and powerful force prevented an easy and expected victory. In retrospect, we can observe a preemergent, unnamed, and unformulated force at work; this force is best described in Raymond Williams's terms—as a "structure of feeling."[64] Williams described kinds of feeling and thinking that are social and material but also embryonic and not fully articulated; they exist in a complex relationship with the already articulated and defined. He referred to a particular—and historically specific—quality of social experience and relationship distinctive to generations or periods that are marked by stylistic changes in language, manners, dress, and buildings. And though Williams associated structures of feeling primarily with emergent classes, feminist scholarship has made it clear that, because of material circumstances, many (most?) experiences and relationships are gender-specific or, at the very least, inflected by gender. Williams also noted another source for emergent ideologies: the realm of the personal, the realm most frequently characterized as feminine.

Williams's description of structures of feeling and the way they interact with established forms presents a way to understand and explain not only the articulated ideologies—residual, dominant, and emergent—evident in cultural artifacts but also those preemergent presences that are embodied and given expression in the implicit tensions often noted as "an unease, a stress, a displacement, a latency: the moment of conscious comparison not yet come." Fixed forms do not speak to these tensions, though the tensions speak in, through, and around them; they do not have to "await definition, classification, or rationalization before they exert palpable pressures and set effective limits on experience and action."[65] Aesthetic forms and conventions often offer the first evidence of a new and widely experienced structure of feeling. The relatively fixed Hollywood genres and their characteristic conventions most often functioned to reinforce dominant ideologies, but Hollywood's most popular film melodramas of the 1950s offer evidence of a structure of feeling that would later find its explicit expression in the contemporary women's movement. What we now know as "women's issues" were everywhere evident but nowhere articulated, and there were certainly no institutionalized efforts to cope with them. Child care for women who worked outside the home was a political issue, but the increasing independence of these women and its impact on family structure, women's control of their own bodies and destinies, even arguments for equal pay were still, for the most part, components of a preemergent structure of feeling. Even today, after many "women's issues" have been articulated, we find in feminist theory and criticism (including feminist film theory and criticism) the ongoing struggle for further articulation, as ways of knowing and feeling that have conventionally been considered "feminine"—and thus have been ignored or dismissed—struggle with established forms for further articulation.

Ethnographic Audience Research and Epochal Analysis: Reading Texts

Half a century ago, Walter Benjamin wrote his now famous essay, "The Work of Art in the Age of Mechanical Reproduction." At its crux is the observation that "much futile thought has been devoted to the question of whether or not photography is art. The primary question—whether the very invention of photography had not transformed the entire nature of art—was not raised."[66] Benjamin pointed out that the transformation of the work of art from its prehistoric function as an instrument of magic to its function as Art (with a capital A) resembles the subsequent qualitative transformation of art brought about by the expansion of availability made possible through mechanical reproduction, the phenomenon that also made it possible for a character in the film *Magnificent Obsession* to joke, "Art's just a guy's name."

Mechanical reproduction changed both the nature of art and the job of the critic. Works of art, dependent on authenticity and uniqueness, are detached from the domain of tradition by mechanical reproduction, and the substitution of a plurality of copies for a unique existence loosens works of art from what Benjamin called their "aura," emancipating them from a parasitical dependence on ceremonial ritual. He also argued that "the instant the criterion of authenticity ceases to be applicable to artistic production, the total function of art is reversed. Instead of being based on ritual, it begins to be based on another practice—politics."[67] Critics had created the need for their expertise in establishing the "aura" of works of art and its subsequent interpretation for the masses, but they have been unable to similarly control the consumption of the mechanically reproduced cultural products—films, photographs, television programs, postcards, advertisements—that are widely available and, as such, are the property of those who consume them. Such cultural artifacts are digested and interpreted in the consumers' terms, not in the specialized terms of the critic. Consumers themselves assume the position of critic, and the political nature of the professional critic's function becomes explicit—in relation to elite as well as popular arts.

The professional critic and the enterprise of textual analysis have been repositioned not just by the increase in the mechanical reproduction of works of art but also by the results of recent ethnographic audience research. Textual analysis shows that texts are definitely organized to encourage certain readings, but ethnographic audience research has shown that mass-media texts are unable to fully control their readings. Theorists and critics must now seek to explain the polysemy that enables multiple readings of the same text, encouraging some over others.

The foundation for the ethnographic audience research of British cultural studies scholars was laid in the early 1970s and was articulated by Stuart Hall in the influential essay "Encoding and Decoding in Television Discourse." Hall related the production and the consumption of television texts, positing that television viewers "decoded" from one of three different positions—dominant, negotiated, and oppositional; his description of these decodings corresponds to various approaches to feminist film criticism and to differing approaches to film melodrama. One sort of decoding suggested by Hall involves an almost direct and uncritical reception of the text's dominant ideological and professional codes; what is encoded by the text's producers is decoded by the viewer, with no attention to or acknowledgment of the text's lack of transparency. This reading is often referred to as the text's "preferred" reading; in this early theorizing, Hall conflated preferred encodings with dominant ideologies. This fails to account for those encodings that actually challenge dominant ideologies—even within the mainstream of the mass media—but Hall's theorizing of this category parallels the theorizing of many feminist film theorists who assume film texts successfully manipulate the passive spectator. Ideology, they say, masks its actions by manipulating film language, and the film text positions the spectator so that she or he, without thinking, accepts the ideology as "common sense." The argument posits that mainstream film texts present woman as an object and that the spectator, unquestioning, accepts this. Film melodramas are seen, then, to use film language to recapitulate the Oedipal romance, manipulating both form and content to firmly position the unsuspecting spectator in patriarchy.

Hall's second category allows for a more skeptical, self-conscious spectator who makes a "negotiated" reading of the text. The spectator understands that the text is organized according to ideological and "professional" (enunciative or, in the broad sense, linguistic-cinematic-televisual) codes, and she or he acknowledges the legitimacy of those codes, as well as the right of the producers to encode as they have. But this sort of reader feels free to negotiate at the individual, personal, situational level. The negotiated reading is "shot through with contradictions," which only oc-casionally become visible; this sort of reading operates through logics "sustained by their differential and unequal relation to the discourses and logics of power."[68] This sort of negotiated reading is identified by another group of feminist film theorists when they point to the reader who can identify the workings of film texts while also considering herself or him-self an individual, or local, exception, sometimes even identifying with the texts' internal contradictions. Taking this approach to melodrama results in a description of the female spectator as aware of her position in patriar-chy while simultaneously (schizophrenically?) considering herself a local-ized exception, limited by patriarchy but with some significant ability to maneuver. Teaching others to consume critically begins with teaching them to see their readings as negotiated readings among many other ne-gotiated readings, and the range of negotiated readings is broad. Some theorists, in fact, argue that all readings are negotiated readings, but this negates the category most significant for feminism—the "oppositional."

The negotiated reading position can, but does not necessarily, lead to oppositional decoding. This step, however, occurs no more inevitably than ideological change results from economic change. Oppositional spec-tators do not simply reject the preferred position taken by the text; they reject it in "globally contrary" ways. Oppositional decoding requires a structural critique of dominant ideologies. The problematics basic to the text become issues for the reader-viewer-spectator, who rejects the domi-nant problematics and replaces them with distinctly different ones. An oppositional reader would identify the sexist nature of representing gen-der common to mainstream cinema—melodramas included—with the structural inequities of patriarchy and would reject them both, attempting to replace patriarchy with a more equitable social formation and to replace film form and content with alternatives compatible with this formation. This is, of course, the project of experimental feminist filmmakers.

Hall's three categories are useful for delineating certain kinds of readers and readings, but ethnographic audience research done in the late 1970s showed both that these categories are not sufficient for describing all readings and that social class is not the sole factor in determining a read-er's decoding (further shifting the British cultural studies focus from class to a more complex intersection of determining factors). Testing Hall's theory, David Morley and Charlotte Brunsdon analyzed the encoding process of the British television program *Nationwide*, paying close attention to a few episodes. Morley subsequently used these episodes in his ethnographic audience research, which revealed a far greater variety of readings than Hall had proposed. Assuming class would be the primary determining factor, Morley had difficulty accounting for the various readings.[69] He found that the readers' class positions did not determine their readings and that some readings ignored the producers' preferred encodings altogether. For instance, a group of young black women from the West Indies missed the preferred reading entirely; they lacked the "cultural capital" to make sense of the show, and the show lacked the "cultural capital" to make sense to them. In an auto-critique of his study, Morley speculated that a number of other factors—such as gender, race, age, education, national origin—must be considered in attempting to account for readings.

Textual analysis can aid in understanding the range of readings a single text can evoke, since such analysis exposes the hierarchies of power at work in and through texts, hierarchies not unlinked to external phenomena such as ownership and control—phenomena themselves linked to race, class, sex, and gender differences. It is within the humanities that impressive tools for the analysis and description of the textual involvement in the realities of power and authority have been developed, but paradoxically, humanities-based scholars have tended to remain buried in the technical and encompassed by the limited questions of single disciplines while the analytical tools they have developed can and should be used for more ambitious projects. Treating romance novels as simply literary, or movies as simply filmic, ignores their existence as social categories; on the other hand, approaching them—and their readings—as temporally and spatially specific leads to an understanding of not just the text but of society as well. Texts are, as Said argued, "worldly"; they exist as "events" when and wherever they are encountered, as parts of our social world and history. They may be, and quite often are, read differently as they travel through time and across space, and their readings are strategies by which individuals and groups constitute and negotiate their identities. Texts participate in the ideological process that constructs real, historical, gendered subjects—human beings. Feminist film scholars are no exception.

Texts are sites for struggle over meaning, and British cultural studies scholars have recently emphasized the importance of textual analysis. Richard Johnson has argued for the value of formal analysis, as well as for studies of textual production and consumption. Most feminists in film and television studies will consider this a "commonsensical" conclusion, coming as they do from text-oriented humanities disciplines, but like many British cultural studies scholars, Johnson comes from the less textually oriented social sciences. Unlike many in the social sciences, however, Johnson insists on crossing boundaries to build on past theorizing of the ideological process, and he calls for "a much more complex model, with rich intermediate categories, more layered than the existing general theories." Speculating that, perhaps, existing theories—and the different modes of research associated with them—"actually express different sides of the same complex process," Johnson suggests that research and analysis that focuses on just one arena in the production and circulation of meanings must take into account others.[70] Studies of cultural production must also include attention to texts and their consumption, just as audience research should pay attention to texts and the process and conditions of production. Text-based studies (such as this one), focused on cultural products, must not ignore production and consumption, assuming that any arena determines another; "effects" are not guaranteed. In a world characterized by difference, struggle is inevitable, and constant emphasis on the dominant values and practices of a given social formation is insufficient for explaining the ideological process through which various groups struggle over meaning; attention to resistance is also necessary. In the hegemonic ideological process, the dominant configuration of ideologies tends to reproduce itself but is never secure. A particularly valuable and flexible approach—and one that allows the incorporation of the most useful aspects of various analytic methodologies—stems from Raymond Williams's recuperative "epochal" approach to analyzing the interaction of cultural elements. Although a reductive epochal approach often results in the sort of limited analysis characteristic of classical Marxism, a more complex reading of competing ideologies allows us to see how alternative and oppositional ideologies (and even those not-yet-articulated structures of feeling) always threaten to alter or displace those dominant ideologies, struggling to determine meaning in cultural practices such as representation. In and among film texts and in and among theoretical and critical texts, differing ideologies struggle for dominance. Multiple voices speak, and multiple readings are possible; some are privileged with more power than others but remain vulnerable to challenge.

Cultural products display and participate in ideological conflict, and though they generally reproduce and reinforce dominant ideologies, they also present alternatives and participate in the evolution of the dominant ideologies themselves. Textual analysis that addresses form, content, and context reveals the interaction of competing ideologies, showing how the formal elements of a text—the narrative structure, for instance—relate to its "content" and how these refer to the material conditions in which the text was produced and consumed. And an examination of various textual analyses reveals the ideological struggle among scholars as they seek to influence the creation and circulation of meanings. For instance, one approach to film melodramas has focused on their "happy endings," arguing that they operate as a safety valve for women unhappy in a capitalist patriarchy. Such an approach depends on the assumption that film texts powerfully control their own readings and that spectators have little choice but to read the texts in the terms dictated by their endings. In fact, the conclusions of popular films do generally support prevailing, dominant assumptions about "reality," and reading the grain of the text—the hierarchy of power that structures it—is important. But the conflicts on which the narratives are based display contradictions within those assumptions, and another approach to film melodrama focuses on explicating their inherent contradictions and depends on an assumption that spectators embody and bring with them to the act of interpretation a matrix of discourses that influence their readings at least as much as the film text itself. Reading "against the grain" of a text reveals challenges to dominant ideologies, as well as the tension between a happy ending and the narrative that (perhaps improbably) leads to it. Although texts are organized to discourage aberrant, unexpected readings, the polysemic nature of textuality allows for these readings, and an analysis of the ideologies that compete within a text is crucial in any examination of the hierarchies of power in entertainment texts and any explanation of the potential for (or actuality of) alternative or oppositional readings. As we will see in subsequent chapters, not all film melodramas are organized in the same hierarchy. Some, in fact, do not end with an unquestioned co-optation of woman for patriarchy; to understand these films, we must of necessity have a conception of ideologies competing not just within a single text but across a genre, as well as among genres. And we must be able to hear silences as readings are not just opened up but closed down by the interaction of

formal elements and the interaction of form and content. For us to understand the variety of feminist readings of film texts, such a conception is
equally necessary.

Though it is important (and relatively easy) to demonstrate the polysemic nature of a film text, of a genre, or of Hollywood cinema during a
given period, it is necessary to go beyond simply demonstrating multiple
views and to examine the contradictions inherent in that configuration of
ideologies called American Ideology, as well as the methods through
which representations of residual and emergent—potentially progressive
—elements enter into this site for struggle. Film texts are not reflections
of American society, in the sense that they present a homologous picture
from which we can unproblematically "read off" the society that produced and consumed them. They are themselves conflicted in many ways.
Texts open up, encourage, or attempt to close down readings through
their story content and the way they represent social reality, as well as
through their formal elements—their narrative structures, their generic
conventions, and the very techniques used to tell them—but because certain theories have exerted a hegemonic force within film studies, critics
and theorists have unnecessarily limited their explanations of the workings of polysemy by confining themselves to currently popular theories
and methodologies. Most notable and perplexing is the dependence of
feminist film scholars on Freudian and Lacanian psychoanalytic theories,
as they inflect Althusserian and post-Althusserian Marxism. This approach has generally eclipsed methodologies based in other psychoanalytic and Marxist theories, and methods based in other areas—such as
narrative theory—have received very limited attention. Critics and theorists have positioned themselves—and have been positioned—in terms of
their stance in relation to the latest fashionable theory, and a skeptical
analysis of the theory and its implications is often neglected. (Some, indeed, have attempted to step outside this debate altogether, usually without complete success.) But although giving in to the faddish flow of a
discipline may be possible for scholars who have no personal and social
stake in their scholarship, for feminists, scholarship has a cause, and such
acquiescence is unforgivable.

Analysis of the narrative and enunciative forms common in our society—and our responses to them—should aim to explain the complex
roles that texts play in the ideological process as they interact with read-

ers and communities of readers; works of art are often, as Raymond Williams noted, especially important as sources of the complex evidence of transformational social processes.[71] And we must not lose sight of the fact that, because of our position in American higher education, scholarly feminist critics make up significant communities of readers. Feminist critics generally constitute identity by resistance to mainstream or "dominant" texts and readings, but few question the authority of the theoretical base from which they work, and many neglect an analysis of their own ideological position. Engulfed in the effort to redefine the discursive clusters relating to genders—"man"-"masculine"-"male" and "woman"-"feminine"-"female"—even feminist critics can lose sight of how they are positioned by other factors such as race, class, or age. With our textual analyses, we do struggle over the meanings associated with these word clusters, but we must not see these clusters as isolated or autonomous, and we must not foreclose attention to the categories that inflect genders and their representations differently. Neither should we pursue textual analysis without acknowledging the importance of analyzing the conditions and processes within which texts are produced and read.

Thomas Elsaesser described melodrama as a cultural form that initially emerged to express the "healthy distrust of intellectualisation and abstract social theory" of a growing bourgeoisie, but he accused its twentieth-century form of encouraging escapism and losing its "subversive" nature. Yet Elsaesser acknowledged that melodrama has also "resolutely refused to understand social change in other than private contexts and emotional terms," insisting that "other structures of experience (those of suffering, for instance) are more in keeping with reality."[72] This once emergent mode, we can see, operated initially as an overtly resistant one, but the focus on the private and the personal has allowed it, even while it became outrageously escapist in some of its forms, to act as a vehicle for expressing the second source for the emergent—the personal. These two sources —emergent classes and the personal—need not be contradictory and may, in fact, be very close. Modes of domination select from the whole range of human practice and, therefore, exclude part of that range. This exclusion is often seen as "the personal," "the private," or "the natural" and, therefore, as beyond intellectualization and abstraction—the most ideologically determined.

If we look to the 1950s in America, we can see a prime example of this "natural" in dominant concepts of gender. Women's problems were as yet not named, not institutionalized, and not fully intellectualized. Williams has noted, however, that in advanced capitalism, "the dominant reaches much further than ever before in capitalist society into hitherto 'reserved' or 'resigned' areas of experience and practice and meaning." In the 1950s, the emergent feminine—and, as a result, the response of the masculine— became most evident in melodrama, where the natural is negotiated. But as Williams also pointed out, "The alternative, especially in areas that impinge on significant areas of the dominant, is often seen as oppositional and, by pressure, often converted into it."[73] Alternative, resisting forms of woman often became so problematic to the dominant that film melodrama translated them into oppositional forms to be excluded or incorporated; we can observe in these films a preemergent force, active and pressing but not yet fully articulated. In them, new expressions of gender struggle for linguistic expression, visions sensed but limited by language and intellect.

Roles,

Stereotypes,

and Popular

Film

Melodramas

of the Early

1950s

2

Re-reading
Sociological
Criticism

Rethinking Roles and Stereotypes

With the resurgence of the women's movement in the late 1960s
and early 1970s, American feminist critics actively began considering both
the positive and negative potential of film. Examining plots and characters
of popular films and concentrating on "images" of women, they focused
particular attention on the stereotypes and social roles of women presented in films, two of the most conservative of the representational practices
that operate to express and support dominant ideologies; at that time,
however, theorizing had not yet developed to the point that analysis could
convincingly tie these representational practices to material conditions.
The two most visible and influential representatives of American sociological feminist film criticism in the early 1970s were Marjorie Rosen,

who wrote *Popcorn Venus*, and Molly Haskell, who wrote *From Reverence to Rape* (both published in 1973). Rosen and Haskell focused primarily on American films, and their books are still in print—an indication that their approach still has a strong popular appeal, even though it was dismissed by semio-psychoanalytic feminist film theorists, who successfully challenged the dominance of the sociological approach in feminist film studies.[1] A primary reason for the dismissal of Rosen's and Haskell's approach is that their critical work proceeded from the "reflectionist" assumptions that films mirror the society in which they are produced and act simply and directly to reproduce dominant ideologies—in this case, patriarchal ideologies. Haskell argued, "Movies are one of the clearest and most accessible of looking glasses into the past, being both cultural artifacts and mirrors." Marjorie Rosen answered the rhetorical question "Does art reflect life?" with the response: "In the movies, yes. Because more than any other art form, films have been a mirror held up to society's porous face."[2] However, Rosen's and Haskell's analyses indicate a more complex theory of the relationship between film and society. While arguing that films directly reflect reality, they implicitly contradicted this position as they compared stereotypes of women in film with the "social reality" of women's lives, finding a distinct disparity. In addition, while emphasizing Hollywood's negative portrayals of women, both Rosen and Haskell implied the contradictory notion that films can, if made properly, act as a force for social change.[3] Still, neither actually theorized beyond this primitive reflectionist stage.

The more rigorously analytical and explicitly theoretical feminist film theory developing during the late 1960s and early 1970s drew consciously on complex theories of signification and subjectivity and on methods of formal analysis evolving in the new field of "film studies"—methods that required looking beyond plots and characters to the realist cinematic enunciative practices that were assumed to be the primary cinematic force in reproducing dominant ideologies. This involved a critique of the reflectionist theory of representation, which assumes a direct relationship between socioeconomic reality and filmic representation (a cause-and-effect precision even Marx warned against). Additionally, reflection theory assumes that films transparently transmit meanings. Critics of the sociological approach pointed out that the medium and the "form" of a text are integral to its "meaning." Indeed, the very term *image* became problematized; while in literary studies, it refers to a metaphorical notion, the *image* is the very matter of film, *imaging* its very process. Indeed, representation is *not* reflection but rather an active process of selecting and presenting, of structuring and shaping, of making things *mean*. Meaning is a social production and practice, and the power to signify, to make meaning, is *not* a neutral social force. As more and more emphasis was placed on the production of meaning in the processes of storytelling and filmmaking, feminist film critics turned away from studies of "images of women" and toward various structuralist—and then post-structuralist—theories and methodologies, primarily those based in semiology and psychoanalysis. "Images of" studies became passé as feminist film scholars and filmmakers became increasingly aware of the role of the medium itself in the process of meaning-making.

One area of agreement between the opposing critical positions concerned the power of the film text to control its own reading; on this issue, semio-psychoanalytic feminist film criticism and theory resembled its predecessor in its assumption that film texts "center the spectator" and "suture" her or him into patriarchal ideology, though the results of ethnographic audience research should make us skeptical of this aspect of both critical approaches. Haskell and Rosen assumed a passive and gullible audience, full of people (women, in particular) who willingly accepted the Hollywood version of life. Rosen answered the question "Does life reflect art?" in the affirmative, arguing that "because of the magnetism of the movies—because the glamor and intensity and 'entertainment' are so distracting and seemingly innocuous—women accept their morality or values." Rosen considered herself a victim of the "Hollywood whitewash" and wondered how many others had also been victimized. Haskell concurred, maintaining that the film industry aided in reinforcing "the big lie . . . the idea of women's inferiority, a lie so deeply ingrained in our social behavior that merely to recognize it is to risk unraveling the entire fabric of civilization."[4] Revealing the victimization of women was their political strategy.

With all their shortcomings, however, both Haskell and Rosen did attempt to analyze the relationship of films to their context; it was Haskell and Rosen's underdeveloped theory that prevented them from seeing the subtleties and complexities of ideological struggle at work in and through film texts. Rosen described the dominant images of women in Hollywood films and examined how they had changed, from turn-of-the-century Victorians to 1920s flappers and vamps all the way to the flower children of the 1960s. Haskell traced female roles and stereotypes across the decades in American film, associating them with various film stars and—contradicting her argument that films mirror society—criticizing them for their inadequacy in representing the "real" conditions of women's lives, a concern shared by American feminist documentarians of the early 1970s.

Rejection—and often ridicule—of "images of" criticism by what became the mainstream of feminist film studies functioned to create, by the late 1970s, the boundaries of a realm accessible only through the recently legitimated film studies programs cropping up in the universities. Many, if not most, film studies programs were formed in or through departments of literature, increasingly dominated by the formalist theoretical reactions (deconstruction, psychoanalytic criticism) to a formalist reaction (New Criticism) to historically oriented studies of literature. Scholarly critics—and students—interested in "social reality" criticism became progressively rarer in film studies. Paradoxically, many American feminists (as feminists, inherently concerned with social issues) became increasingly formalist, following the British in the attempt to conflate form with function and in the assumption that texts govern their reading. Although these feminists came to dominate feminist film studies, they nevertheless composed a marginalized interpretive community, which, like all marginalized communities, found itself defined in great part by its relevant cultural center—in this case, a center dominated (as was most of academe) by white, middle-class men. And although women (many of them feminists) inhabited this realm almost from its inception, the theories that dominated film studies—Lacanian and Freudian psychoanalysis—were theories that posit the male as the norm and place the female as abnormal (see chapter 4 for a more extensive critique). In addition to their inherent sexism, these theories are notoriously complex. Each of these factors further restricted access to what became the mainstream of scholarly feminist film studies.[5] Theoretical expansion is now in order.

Recently, in retrospectives, Haskell's and Rosen's names have reappeared without ridicule in the discourse of scholarly feminist film studies but only to serve as representatives of the "role-image" or "images of" phase in the history of feminist film criticism. However, as the pat answers provided by semio-psychoanalytic analyses of the supposedly homologous relationship between patriarchy and cinematic language became less convincing, even such leaders in the field as Mary Ann Doane, Patricia Mellencamp, and Linda Williams (editors of the 1984 state-of-the-art anthology *Re-vision*) admitted, "Issues which at one time seemed solved—the complicity of a realist aesthetic with a patriarchal way of seeing—have often come back to haunt us."[6] Haskell's and Rosen's theoretical bases do have distinct and well-recognized deficiencies, but their approach holds far too much promise to be discarded entirely. In her contribution to *Revision*, Christine Gledhill called for "cultural analysis [to] hold the extradiscursive and discursive together as a complex and contradictory interrelation."[7] And as the flaws and gaps in semio-psychoanalytic theory and methodology became increasingly evident, Doane, Mellencamp, and Williams acknowledged that "it is of importance to recognize the value of such ['images of'] studies, both as a point of departure for students first encountering the subject and for historians and sociologists who seek more detailed information about the relation of stereotypical images to the epochs that produce them."[8] They left the matter there, ignoring Brandon French's more sophisticated sociological criticism and Tessa Perkins's theoretical work on stereotyping (noted by Gledhill), both produced in the late 1970s. An extension of French's and Perkins's work provides a useful way to examine the interrelation of the discursive and the extradiscursive through the comparison of film content with historical, sociological data.

In *On the Verge of Revolt: Women in American Films of the Fifties*, published in 1978, French replicated some of Haskell's and Rosen's problematic assumptions, but she moved the sociological method further than either Haskell or Rosen had. French focused on thirteen films popular in the 1950s—this close attention marks a break from Haskell and Rosen's sweep through masses of films—and she examined the contradictory positions the films presented on clusters of issues and situations women and men faced in "their transition from the forties to the sixties: romance, courtship, marriage, sex, motherhood, divorce, loneliness, adultery, alcoholism, widowhood, heroism, madness, and ambition." Her analyses of popular films disclosed "a mixture of progressive and reactionary elements" indicative of a "time of conflict and contradiction."[9]

Clearly, French was edging toward a critical approach that acknowledges and examines power and struggle, but her language included those problematic terms *images of* and *reflection*, and at points she seemed to see a rather direct and causal relation among the social, the economic, and the cultural spheres. She argued, for instance, that movies of the 1950s "recorded American women's dissatisfaction and tentative rebellion with a surprising degree of fidelity," doing "it in a way, however, that virtually no one noticed." Moving beyond Haskell and Rosen, French argued that the films' surfaces "promoted women's domesticity and inequality" while simultaneously reflecting, "unconsciously or otherwise, the malaise of domesticity and the untenably narrow boundaries of the female role." The films provided a "double text," with which a film contradicted itself without acknowledging any contradiction. French, herself on the verge of a more sophisticated theory of ideology, pointed to the indirect nature of film documentation of "the practical, sexual, and emotional transition women were undergoing beneath the threshold of the contemporary audience's conscious awareness."[10] She convincingly tied the stereotype of the "woman-as-homemaker" that came to dominate American cultural texts in the 1950s—a stereotype she referred to as "the compulsive whitewash of women's emancipation"—to a schizoid American "defense against terror and catastrophe." In the 1950s, terror came in many forms; French pointed to "the hysteria of McCarthyism, the obsession with nuclear annihilation, and the rabid overreaction to any violation of middle-class decorum, from singer Elvis Presley to 'beatnik' poet Allen Ginsberg." She took the position that, of all the threats to the American way of life, women's emancipation was the most immediate; it presented "a buried threat to the basic tenet of world order, male supremacy."[11] The threat of the Emancipated Woman became, increasingly, a source of terror. (To call attention to specific stereotypes, I follow Rosen's practice of capitalization.)

Stereotypes are powerful discursive forms, and analyzing the stereotypes produced and circulated during a historical period in relation to the material conditions of existence common to that period enriches our understanding of the ideological process that constantly defines and redefines basic notions—like "female" and "male"—and the realities they inflect. Such was Haskell's, Rosen's, and French's project, but they began with the assumption that we all already *know* what stereotypes are. In "Rethinking Stereotypes," Perkins addressed the phenomenon in light of recent theoretical work on ideology, examining the interrelation of the discursive and nondiscursive. Analyzing specific stereotypes gives empirical content to her theorizing (unlike the work of many contemporary theorists, which she feels lacks empirical backing). "Stereotypes," she argued, "seem to be ideological phenomena and should therefore be capable of being accounted for by any theory of ideology; conversely, as ideological phenomena of a peculiarly 'public' kind they may provide a useful means of studying the practice of ideology."[12] Stereotypes are ideology made tangible.

Haskell was satisfied with the assertion, "If we see stereotypes in film, it is because stereotypes exist in society."[13] Perkins only began here. Arguing that stereotypes have their base in material conditions and social practices, Perkins examined the dominant (often misleading) assumptions about the nature of stereotypes, focusing first (and repeatedly) on a central problem in understanding stereotypes: validity. The general assumption is that stereotypes are always erroneous, false in their content, but Perkins pointed out that this assumption avoids acknowledging the "kernel of truth" in stereotypes. They are, she argued, both true and false. They are "selective descriptions of particularly significant or problematic areas and to that extent they are exaggerations."[14] The production of stereotypes involves selecting ideologically significant personality traits common to a group of people and making those attributes seem innate; stereotypes may be held about one's own group, and stereotypes are not necessarily pejorative. The stereotype of the white, heterosexual, upper-class male is held both by members of that group and by others; certainly, for many, this is a positive stereotype and, indeed, is one by which—through comparison—others are defined, often negatively. Stereotypes function to reinforce ideological hierarchies by naturalizing the occupation of certain rungs by specific groups. For instance, because women adopt contradictory (but dominant) value orientations that insist on women as abnormal or inferior, sexual difference becomes the basis for their derogatory self-definition as part of an oppressed group. Stereotypes draw their strength from their ability "to operate as conceptual (cognitive) resolutions of such contradictions";[15] they allow people to think it "natural" that they themselves are "inferior." The political consequences are obvious. The concepts of "responsibility" and "leadership" are generally attached to the stereotype of the white, heterosexual, upper-class male; members of other groups—and stereotypes are a group phenomenon—defer to the implied superiority of this group, often accepting contradictory value orientations that require negative valuations of themselves and others in their group as irresponsible and incapable of leadership. Such evaluation is a central element in stereotyping.

Status refers to a position within society, complete with rights and duties, and *role* refers to the performance of those rights and duties, but stereotypes differ in that this is where what is concealed in the concepts of status and role is made central and explicit.[16] But though stereotypes are primarily evaluative, they are not, as most assume, necessarily simple or rigid and unchanging. Often they may seem simple, but this can be deceptive; it may be that they are operating at a level sufficiently abstract to imply a complex social structure and to necessitate a certain level of cultural competence for their understanding. Perkins gave the example of the "dumb blond." At the most obvious level, of course, this refers to intelligence and hair color. Secondarily—though immediately obvious to those "in the know" (and this entails many "knowers," as stereotypes are by nature widely disseminated)—it "refers immediately to *her* sex, which [then] refers to her status in society, her relationship to men, her inability to behave or think rationally, and so on. In short, it implies knowledge of a complex social structure."[17] And stereotypes—along with the social formation—change. After "women's liberation" had affected all of America —even if only secondhand, through the media, and possibly because of this, more effectively—the "dumb blonde" generally lost her naiveté and took on an increased sophistication; still the stereotype represents women primarily as sexual objects. Marilyn Monroe's wide-eyed innocent had her consciousness raised and was transformed into Loni Anderson's wiser-than-you-know bombshell, most notably as the exaggeratedly "beautiful" Jennifer Marlowe on the late 1970s CBS sitcom *WKRP in Cincinnati*.[18] Stereotypes are also quite flexible; the same stereotype can be simultaneously presented starkly and blatantly (as in cartoons) or "realistically." Anderson's "wise dumb blonde" was manifested "realistically" in her portrayal of Jayne Mansfield in the made-for-television biographical movie and then again as the poor little (gorgeous) girl who held out (withheld) for marriage to the richest man in town in the made-for-television adaptation of *A Letter to Three Wives*. Such flexibility, Perkins argued, allows stereotypes to maintain credibility and communicability.[19]

Perkins described the process by which patriarchal discourse transforms material realities and differences into innate characteristics and then evaluates them in terms of the ideological hierarchy. Illustrating her theorizing about "the sort of determining influences material conditions have on consciousness," she gives the striking example of "the flighty woman":

> Part of the stereotype of women concerns their inability to concentrate on one issue at a time, their mental flightiness, scattiness and so on. In the middle of a conversation about one issue they skip to something completely different. This is all part of the "irrational, illogical, inconsistent" (female logic) stereotype. Now what this seems to me to relate to is a mode of thinking which is essential to the housewife's job. Most other jobs demand concentration on a single issue and the application of one skill at a time; the capacity to keep shifting attention back and forth, and changing skills, is characteristic of a housewife's job. What the stereotype does is to identify this feature of the woman's job situation, place a negative valuation on it, and then establish it as an innate female characteristic, thus inverting its status so that it becomes a cause rather than an effect. . . . the strength of stereotypes lies in this combination of validity and distortion.[20]

Stereotyping results from a remarkably essentialist approach. The particular sort of managerial thinking necessary for running a household is identified and then—because women are hierarchically inferior to men in patriarchy—evaluated negatively; it is made to seem innately and essentially female, and it is conceptually transformed into a cause of female behavior rather than an effect of woman's daily, material existence. The stereotype, as Perkins argued, is both valid and invalid.

Haskell and Rosen were interested in showing trends, and they glanced briefly at many films instead of concentrating on any films in detail; this allowed them to demonstrate the widespread use and acceptance of certain stereotypes. For instance, Rosen called attention to the stereotypical Emancipated Woman, a stereotype that Rosen nominated "The Woman Alone" and that had "long served as subject for on-screen exploration."[21] Her examination of this stereotype showed that Hollywood's representation of spinsters and career women changed with the American sociopolitical and economic conditions. Rosen argued that in the 1930s and 1940s, the Woman Alone had been presented as neither bitter nor neurotic but as a warm, loving, and independent person who maintains an opulent, vital, and productive life-style; Rosen's examples included the roles played by Olivia de Havilland in *To Each His Own* (1946) and Bette Davis in *The Old Maid* (1939), *Now, Voyager* (1942), and *Old Acquaintance* (1943), each of which focused on noble sacrifice—giving up an illegitimate child or giving up marriage to the "wrong" man because the "right" one is already married. The Woman Alone suffers, but she does it with dignity. Think also of Claudette Colbert's working, single mother in the 1934 version of *Imitation of Life*; elegantly clad as well as highly successful (in her pancake business, a business with a domestic orientation), she makes maternal mistakes that are attributed to the demands of her career, not to her unloving nature. In the end, she is willing to sacrifice her own sexual satisfaction for her daughter's happiness.

Haskell saw a "growing ambivalence and coyness" beginning in the films of the 1930s and running into the films of the 1940s. She argued that the limitations imposed by the Production Code (in full force by the mid-1930s) "were catastrophic to the sexually-defined, negligee-wearing glamour goddesses" but "were liberating for active or professional women."[22] In response to code restrictions, flirtation was moved from the bedroom to the office, producing female characters to whom contemporary feminists responded positively.[23] But in the films of the 1940s, Haskell saw "a retrenchment from the feminism of the twenties and thirties" as women in the "real world" got better jobs as a result of the war and began to present the potential for real competition in the workplace. In the "film world," working women were "given a pseudo-toughness, a facade of steel wool that at a man's touch would turn into cotton candy."[24] The man's touch was to become increasingly crucial. In the films of the 1930s and 1940s, if the touch didn't take and matrimony didn't result, the Woman Alone did not resort to hysteria or decline into a "withered, jumpy" old lady but was allowed a dignified martyrdom. Yet in the 1950s, Rosen argued, the Woman Alone as "a natural counterpoint to the decade's exaltation of matrimony" became "a love-starved pariah" and she "figured in fifties' movies as a creature so negative and pitiful that one can interpret the vogue as little other than a reinforcement of the decade's belief in marriage as salvation."[25] Moving toward a more sophisticated theory of stereotyping, Haskell analyzed this development as a reactionary one, but she never made the necessary adjustments to her theoretical statements. Perkins did make these theoretical advances; a stereotype changes,

Perkins explained, because stereotypes "develop about a group because it has, or is presenting, a problem."[26] Her theorizing allows us to see the evolution of this discursive form in relation to material conditions.

As increasing numbers of women entered the paid labor force, changes in the social status of women threatened male supremacy, and the stereotype of the Woman Alone changed. After World War II, it was clear that the workplace was attracting more women than just those from the working classes and that these women were committed to working outside the home—*and* to working for compensation. The 1950 decennial census showed that 46.3 percent of single women in the United States worked outside their homes.[27] By the end of the decade, government researchers revealed that—whether public opinion favored it or not—women *were* a significant presence in the paid labor force, but in the Hollywood genre most directly concerned with the issues of gender construction and family structure—the melodrama—working outside the home became tantamount to prostitution for female characters. The Woman Alone came to embody the threat of female emancipation; the Woman Alone became suspect. The Wife, the Mother, and the Daughter—in their many manifestations—became the only truly viable female alternatives in the film melodramas of the 1950s. To understand the changes in representations of gender construction and the structure of the family during the 1950s, we must place the popular films of the period in the context of interrelated developments in the social, cultural, political, and economic spheres.

Struggling over the Meaning of "Woman"

Although many interpreters now recognize the years following World War II as far from peaceful, popular memory continues to construct this period as idyllic, even bland. In the tumultuous and often frightening years of the 1960s, 1970s, and 1980s, Americans have tended to remember only the positive aspects of the postwar era, only a happy prosperity and a mass move to the suburbs. In their own way, however, the late 1940s and the 1950s were just as tumultuous as the decades that followed.[28] Brandon French noted that, for some, the reemergence of the U.S. women's movement in the 1960s "appeared to combust spontaneously, without any clear origins." She noted, however, that in the conflicts and contradictions of 1950s America there existed a "gathering thunder of revolt that an entire culture chose not to hear, or hearing, failed to comprehend."[29] Indeed, many of the debates that seemed to erupt in the 1960s and 1970s found their most immediate roots in the changing structures of feeling that accompanied the social, cultural, and economic changes of the postwar period. In the mid-1950s, the contemporary historian Eric F. Goldman described the emotional roller coaster experienced by Americans in the decade following the war:

> They were only a handful of years, ten of them, but what other period in American life can quite match them? That taut Thursday when Franklin Roosevelt died and the first sickening fall of an atom bomb, the heartfelt roar when Jackie Robinson trotted out in a Dodgers uniform, the meat you couldn't buy and the apartment you couldn't rent, high prices and boom times and higher prices and boom, boom, boom, a brilliant young man named Alger Hiss, Harry Truman now fumbling, now making the bold decision to go into Korea, Arnold Toynbee and Mickey Spillane, Ezio Pinza singing "Some Enchanted Evening" and the bloody wastes of the Changjun Reservoir, "We like IKE," "WE LIKE IKE," "WE LIKE IKE," pyramid games, the poodle bob, chlorophyll toothpaste, chlorophyll chewing gum, chlorophyll dog food, "Point of order, point of order, Mr. Chairman," a President of the United States, direct and earnest before the Geneva delegates, stirring the world with a simple plea for peace—these and a thousand other memories flood back from the frightening, heartening whirligig years since the end of World War II.[30]

Americans had fought for a dream, but the very defense of the dream had altered it. With the events of World War II, nightmarish elements began to appear in the romantic dream that had been America. The end of the war, though signaling victory, was gained at the price of security; the bomb had been dropped, and now the whole world recognized the possibility of nuclear holocaust. Existence itself—the future of the species—could no longer be taken for granted. By 1959, two of every three Americans considered the possibility of nuclear war the most important national problem.[31] A concern with security—national and personal— became paramount, and anxiety over the increasingly destructive potential of new scientific developments coupled with a growing fear of communism to encourage insecure Americans to return to and justify their institutions. This, Elaine Tyler May has argued, resulted in "an overarching principle that would guide them in their personal and political lives: containment."[32] Cold war ideology and the postwar domestic revival were inextricably linked. A family-centered culture became America's bulwark against fears of another economic depression, against the insecurity caused by the discovery of atomic energy, and against communism.

The experiences of Americans during the depression of the 1930s had paved the way for two different family forms: an emergent form based on two egalitarian breadwinners; and another, more traditional form based on a married heterosexual couple with polarized gender roles—the male breadwinner and the female housewife. But enormous numbers of young adults chose the latter form, determined to make it work for them, even as increasing numbers of women became part of the paid labor force. The potential for developing new ways of structuring families and for radically altered gender roles withered in the face of obstacles to women's employment—poor working conditions, low wages, prevailing social attitudes, and a government policy that encouraged a "family wage" for men and, as a result, female dependence on men.[33]

During the 1930s, 1940s, and 1950s, when the film industry was dominated in the United States by a strongly centralized, vertically integrated studio system, four hundred to seven hundred films were annually produced, distributed, and exhibited by Hollywood's major studios, and these films gained popularity by addressing the concerns of their audiences. By the 1950s, enormous numbers of women were working outside the home, and primary concerns in the United States during the 1950s were gender construction and family structure, concerns linked to changes in employment practices generated by war. During World War II, as men had left workplaces and universities to form the fighting forces, many women had left their homes to staff the offices and factories that supported the war effort.[34] Even white women of the middle and upper classes participated in mainstream economic activities, in the production of goods (exchange values) rather than just in the ideological and biological reproduction of the work force. The war's end put six million out of work, 60 percent of them women, and popular mythology would have us believe that these women returned to work exclusively in their homes, but this was not the case. The implicit challenge to cultural norms became explicit when these women by and large continued to work outside the home after the war ended.

Historians disagree over how to interpret women's employment during and after the war. William Chafe contends that this period was indeed a watershed in American women's history. Karen Anderson argues, on the other hand, that Americans experienced changes in family and employment during the war as temporary and crisis-oriented. Lois Banner also argues that although an illusion of social change existed, reality for women had *not* changed. In fact, Ruth Milkman argues that even during the war when women worked within previously male sectors, they worked in predominantly female departments or in jobs only temporarily reclassified as "female"; sex segregation in the paid labor force persisted during and after the war. Elaine Tyler May argues that Americans adjusted to the increased presence of women in the paid labor force because they perceived it as a temporary response to crisis; after the war, the ideology of domesticity entranced the white middle class, who provided normative values, shaping the dominant political institutions that affected all Americans. May shows that although increasing numbers of wives were working outside the home, most worked less than full time, made less than their husbands, and actually saw their earnings decline. But Heidi Hartmann sees currents of traditionalism *and* change in women's wartime work experiences, and so do I. Andrea Walsh, for instance, gives the following figures: 75 percent of women working in wartime wanted to continue working after the war; of those, 90 percent wanted to keep their wartime jobs rather than give them up; and 50 percent of those who had been homemakers before the war wanted to continue working. This seems convincing evidence that women's wartime employment experiences did indeed heighten their aspirations. And though many women did leave or were forced out of their jobs at the war's end, a majority of them later reentered the work force, and work outside the home gradually became legitimated for women of all ages, classes, races, and marital and maternal statuses.[35]

This radical change came about, however, not as the result of a feminist challenge to the male-dominated, patriarchal society but, initially, as a patriotic and pragmatic response to the threat of war. After the war ended, most women gave financial necessity as their primary motivation for seeking and maintaining employment; although surveys showed that a growing number of women valued employment outside the home for the independence, social companionship, and sense of accomplishment it offered, the aspiration to a higher standard of living motivated most working women. Still, the choice was not an easy one, and working conditions for women were far from favorable. Whereas women's labor had been crucial to the war effort, their labor during the war had not significantly altered the prejudices held by employers and by labor unions that favored white male workers. Women and racial minorities were still the cheap labor force kept in reserve by capital.[36] Some unions ignored security provisions in women's contracts; some unions, seeing women as threats to men's jobs, even prohibited women's membership. Women did, however, provide unions with the excuse to demand more humane benefits.[37] But jobs were scarce, especially for older women and black women, and were no longer available for women in manufacturing or the professions. Sex segregation in the paid labor force reinforced the notion—a rhetorical construction— that women and men inhabit "separate spheres"; only in jobs that had come to be considered a part of women's "sphere" were there many available jobs.[38]

Especially important for women was office work. The service sector was expanding, and the experiences of World War II had removed the conflict between femininity and employment, redefining "women's work," but jobs stereotyped as "female" paid (and still do pay) significantly less than those stereotyped as "man's work." Higher-paying factory jobs were characterized as less respectable, for women.[39] It has become a feminist truism that "if a woman does it, it turns to dirt." As Tessa Perkins argued, stereotypes are constructed by identifying a feature of a situation common to a portion of the population, evaluating it in terms of the hierarchical position inhabited by that group, and establishing it as a characteristic innate to that population, thus "inverting its status so that it becomes a cause rather than an effect."[40] In a hierarchical society, work done by a hierarchically "superior" group will be considered more valuable to society; hence, those in control are rewarded more handsomely, and their work is given a higher status. Americans had fought to end fascist inequities including the repression of women and racial minorities, even as similar inequities were maintained at home during the war, and these inequities continued after the war as well. This contradiction became increasingly evident during the 1950s.[41] Women's wartime work experiences—which had often included "better" jobs, such as welder or pilot, and higher wages than were now available to them—and the obviously contradictory changes in popular imagery from "overalled welders in wartime to those of aproned consumers in peacetime" could not be erased.[42] Still, women were working outside the home, and many families were moving into the middle class because of it.

The acquisition of material goods was a consequence and an expression of this move upward, and—especially in the middle class—the emphasis on the family in the postwar years had to be balanced with the necessity for women's employment. American culture was becoming more and more a consumer culture, and increasingly, materialism became more important, to many Americans, than the desire to keep women at home. "The good life," the historian Karen Anderson has observed, "was expensive, and women had to contribute their share."[43] For a wife to have to hold a position in the paid labor force was considered unfortunate, but worse was the inability to purchase those items that had become requisite for the middle-class home. Americans poured their resources into their homes and into family pursuits, providing an unequaled level of luxury, but family-centered spending was intended to strengthen both traditional values and the notion that the American way of life was superior to any other.[44] Such security was bought with women's participation in the paid labor force. Yet marriage, for many Americans in the 1950s, was about children, and rearing children was consigned to women. However, studies began to show that children of women who worked outside the home were happier and more responsible than those of women who did not.[45]

Some of the women who gave up careers for motherhood raised their children to have expectations different from their own. Referring to the data collected in the Kelly Longitudinal Study—which, over a period of twenty years (1935–55), surveyed six hundred white, middle-class women and men who formed families in the late 1930s—Elaine Tyler May described a woman who had wanted to work in the theater but had given this up to marry and raise children. Her compensation was taking her daughter to plays. A credible interpretation of this report (which May did not make) is that women like this mother displaced their ambitions onto their daughters, encouraging them to pursue avenues closed to the mothers. Such an explanation helps to explain a phenomenon that May did note: baby boomers resemble their grandparents more than their parents.

Like many of the baby boomers, the grandparents challenged sexual norms, increased the rate of divorce, decreased the birthrate, created a unique youth culture, and became political activists. May argued that it was the generation in between—with a strong domestic ideology, consensus politics, and peculiar and pervasive demographic behavior—that was the exception.[46] Overwhelmingly, across race and class boundaries, Americans of this generation married younger and devoted themselves to maintaining their families, even while increasing numbers of wives and mothers worked in the paid labor force.

Working women's self-concepts began to improve, and their role in the family was also altered; because of their financial contribution to their families, working women began to have a more significant voice in decision making within the family.[47] The war had been fought to preserve America's social and political institutions, and the family, the most basic of social institutions, was now faced with a serious challenge. Changes in the construction of gender and generational differences were the basis for changes in the institution; within the family, the status of women and children had shifted.

This shift occasioned debate, and the debate took many forms. The struggle over gender definition and family structure was evident in the popular press. In their 1950 article "What Has Happened to the Feminist Movement?," Arnold W. Green and Eleanor Melnick described the struggle as it occurred in popular magazines and best-selling books.[48] They pointed to the antifeminist Dr. Marynia Farnham as representative of one extreme. A psychiatrist, she coauthored with Ferdinand Lundberg the best-seller *Modern Woman: The Lost Sex* (1947). In this book, Farnham and Lundberg traced a "tidal wave of modern unhappiness," expressed in widespread neurosis, to a home life disrupted by the effects of the Industrial Revolution. This was hardly an original point, but their proposal that the government should support an extensive program to deliver psychoanalysis to the neurotic American masses certainly was. Farnham and Lundberg simultaneously advocated a "reconstruction of the home," which would involve "public recognition of the fact that the psychically balanced woman finds greatest satisfaction for her ego in nurturing activities." The independent woman, they claimed, "is a contradiction in terms," and women who desire to remain childless or single are abnormal. They even advocated barring unmarried women—whom they archaically referred to as "spinsters"—from teaching children, arguing that "a great many children have unquestionably been damaged psychologically by the spinster teacher, who cannot be an adequate model of a complete woman for boys and girls." Although they would not prohibit women from working—and indeed they acknowledged that, except for a tiny minority, women had always worked outside the home—they circumscribed permissible areas, for those women "intellectually equipped for more technical achievement than their sisters," to biology, psychology, sociology, medicine, pedagogy, philosophy, and anthropology. And though they would not entirely prohibit women from entering "the male area of exploit or authority"—including the areas of law, mathematics, physics, business, industry, and technology—they argued that "government and socially-minded organizations should . . . make it clear that such pursuits are not generally desirable for women," so as to combat the fantasies of "masculine-complex women" and to emphatically shift prestige, honor, subsidy, and public respect to "those women recognized as serving society most fully as women."[49]

In another best-seller, *The Common Sense Book of Baby and Child Care* (first published in 1945 but reprinted regularly throughout the 1950s, indeed until this day), Benjamin Spock encouraged mothers to remain at home with their children. And like Farnham and Lundberg, Spock advocated government allowances for "all mothers of young children who might otherwise be compelled to work," arguing that "useful, well-adjusted citizens are the most valuable possessions a country has, and good mother care during early childhood is the surest way to produce them." Spock, however, made no wide-ranging proposal for social change. He did acknowledge that some women, out of economic necessity, would have to work and that others, "particularly those with professional training," would be unhappy not working. But Spock urged those mothers "who don't absolutely have to work but would prefer to—either to supplement the family income, or because they think they will be more satisfied themselves and therefore get along better at home"—*not* to work outside the home. For Spock, a woman's preference was negated by childbearing. Mothers, he felt, should realize that steady, loving care is vital to a small child; this "might make it easier to decide that the extra money she might earn, or the satisfaction she might receive from an outside job, is not so important after all." Spock did limit this advice to mothers of infants, noting the need for children to associate with other children and the adequacy of many nursery schools.[50]

Spock's pragmatic approach to the problems of childrearing is indicative of the "middle ground" that Green and Melnick considered the prevailing opinion, especially in contrast with extremists like Edith M. Stern, who—in an article entitled "Women Are Household Slaves"—called housewifery a "brain-dribbling, spirit-stifling vocation."[51] Green and Melnick pointed to Margaret Mead as an exemplar of the middle ground. Mead had examined several other cultures and argued that the patriarchal family structure was not universal. In her books, Mead gave evidence that the roles considered "male" or "female" were not biologically determined. The influence of her work can be seen in what Green and Melnick described as the "prevailing social reality":

> The opinion appears to be growing that both sexes are headed toward a common appreciation of *both* traditional and new women's roles, the latter representing real, but secondary, contributions to the world's work outside the home. This would seem to be indicated for as society is presently organized the majority of women will not, or cannot, follow either pattern to ideal extremity. They thus are being advised to get both society and home life in a balanced perspective.

Green and Melnick contended that the structural changes in the family that had occurred by that time (1950) would prevent a return to an earlier balance of sexual differentiation and that impassioned rhetoric from either extreme would have little effect, "for by now there are more men who benefit from women's work than who suffer competition from the sex." The feminist movement, they said, was not dead, but it had changed. Most modern feminists and women leaders tended "to be married women, with one or two children, who are more and more insisting on the combination of modified career and modified traditional role, at the same or different periods of the woman's life cycle."[52]

Most men and women were not yet actively questioning their own traditional attitudes about their "place," but they were being bombarded from all sides by contradictory positions, not only in these popular nonfiction treatises but also in advertisements, popular novels, songs, television shows, and films. The *New York Times* published an interchange between Sloan Wilson, who had attacked career women in an article entitled "The

Woman in the Gray Flannel Suit," and Reka Hoff, a lawyer who responded in a letter insisting that she was neither the "neurotic" nor the "compulsive half-woman" Sloan wrote about. Hoff summarized, "If unmarried
their career is designated a 'substitute' for marriage; if married, their career is designated a 'substitute' for motherhood; if a mother, their career
brands them as selfish and neglectful."[53]

Still, many Americans reacted to the drama and the trauma of the postwar years by attempting to return to traditional institutions, and working
women presented a direct challenge to traditional constructions of gender
and family. With the postwar baby boom, the attention of the nation
turned to the family and to its youth, and educational institutions took on
increased importance. Religion too offered hope, and many Americans
turned to their churches. Church membership rose from 64.5 million (50
percent of the population) in 1940 to 114.5 million (63 percent) in 1960,
and religious affiliation became a component of the American way.[54] Billy
Graham swept through the nation, saving thousands—on television.
Mass-media institutions took on more importance than ever before. Each
year, television entered increasing numbers of homes, challenging the centrality of both radio and film but not entirely supplanting them. The radio
networks poured their resources into television and left their radio hold-
ings to founder. Many local affiliates abandoned the networks and developed programming strategies that complemented rather than competed
with television. With the transistor, radio became portable, and "drive
time" replaced evening "prime time" in importance to radio broadcasters
and advertisers. Radio accompanied people as they drove to work, cleaned
house, and lounged at pools. Innovative local broadcasters pioneered new
programming formats, focusing on sports, cash giveaways, local news,
and—previously taboo—recorded music. Adapting for survival, radio
turned to specialized audiences: ethnic groups, farmers, religious denomi-
nations, and young people. Although opposed by racist conservatives,
recorded rock 'n' roll—adapted from black rhythm 'n' blues (called "race
music" in the record industry)—swept the airwaves and was adopted by
America's newly rebellious youth, who began to define themselves in
terms of generational difference, as "teenagers."[55] Films like *Rebel without
a Cause* and *The Wild Ones* highlighted the challenge that teen differentiation posed to the family, and even on television, teens' presence was felt.
The television program *American Bandstand*, initiated in Philadelphia in

1952, was designed specifically for teenagers. The most famous rock 'n' rollers appeared on the show, and teens showed up regularly to do the latest dances. ABC picked up the series in 1957—the year after Dick Clark became its host—and *Bandstand* became the first network television series devoted to rock 'n' roll, an acknowledgment of the new importance (and buying power) of young people.[56]

Television also brought to the people the activities of the House Un-American Activities Committee; in their zealous attempt to purify the nation, the members of the committee committed such unforgivable excesses as their numerous attacks on prominent filmmakers. In the 1950s, the film industry not only had to respond to these right-wing political challenges but also had to restructure itself and to compete with television for its audiences. The studio system was in decline. The Supreme Court's 1948 *Paramount* decision forced restructuring by demanding that the vertically integrated Hollywood studios divest themselves of their exhibition outlets, those theater chains that had, until that time, controlled 70 percent of first-run exhibition. The studios also moved away from production and concentrated on distribution; independent production decreased costs on some films as much as 50 percent. Even so, production was down and so were profits. Before World War II, four out of five films broke even on their U.S. bookings alone. By 1950, the number had declined to one in ten. Risks were high, and the number of films produced yearly fell from an average of 360 in the early 1950s to fewer than 200 by the end of the decade.[57]

Reactions within the industry varied, but all of the major studios except MGM (RKO, Warner Brothers, Paramount, and Twentieth Century-Fox) drastically reduced their production activities, eliminating the stock-company system and concentrating on aiding independent productions, which they would later distribute. The studios also used other strategies in their effort to attract moviegoers. Americans had attended the movies in record numbers just after the war, but as the population made its massive move to the suburbs and focused its attention on family life, attendance began to decline rapidly. The industry began to experiment with drive-in theaters, with wide screens, with lusher-than-ever color, and even with 3-D and smell-a-vision. Industry-wide, the move to exploit film's differences from television changed the visual nature of the cinema. Although 3-D foundered, wide-screen and lush color became common. With the loss of an integrated production-distribution-exhibition system, the emphasis shifted to producing big money-makers (the initial move toward the "blockbuster").[58]

The subject matter of Hollywood films also changed. Television's general co-optation of the mass audience altered the notion that films were family fare and should be acceptable for all viewers. Venturing into previously taboo areas, the film industry aimed its products at an adult audience and provided controversial stories, often based on popular novels and plays that had already proven lucrative. Films were no longer considered an inevitably good investment, and bankers demanded every possible assurance that their investment would be returned. The previous success of a story encouraged investment, and some adaptations worked; others didn't. An important part of the imported prestige was the nature of the content and its influence on original screenplays. Whereas novelists and playwrights had long traded on the existence of an implicit classification system that allowed for adult entertainment, filmmakers were only now being allowed this privilege. Challenges to the Production Code resulted in a relaxation of censorship, and male-oriented melodramas began to include increasingly "sophisticated" (read "sexual") subject matter, often resulting in films concerned with human sexuality and "realistic" topics such as drug addiction (*Come Back, Little Sheba*; *The Country Girl*; *The Man with the Golden Arm*), labor union corruption (*On the Waterfront*), and juvenile delinquency (*Rebel without a Cause*).[59]

Some studios specialized. MGM, for example, concentrated on the musical, a genre with which television could not yet compete.[60] Others recognized the potential for catering to portions of the audience, rather than to the ostensibly ageless, sexless (read "male"), mass audience. Some studios were occasionally rewarded by massive success as they produced films that, though seemingly aimed at a specialized audience, addressed the concerns of many Americans. Universal, for instance, focused much of its talent and money on providing products for a predominantly female audience, producing female-oriented melodramas whose central problems were precisely those of gender construction, sex roles, and family structure (*Magnificent Obsession, All That Heaven Allows, Imitation of Life*).[61]

Some people within the film industry—conscious of their personal images and the associated stereotypes—took their part in the ongoing debate over gender and sex quite seriously. In one anecdote, the free-lance photographer Eve Arnold, in the text that accompanies a collection of photo-graphs she took in the 1950s, characterized the decade as a "corseted" time, commenting in an aside that "surely there is a correlation between how people dress and how they think." In *Flashback!*, Arnold included two photographs that exhibit a coy, happy, and voluptuous Marilyn Monroe. They are followed by two pictures of Joan Crawford. In one, Crawford is seriously considering business at a meeting of the Pepsi Cola Board of Directors. In the other, she is being fitted for a dress; she wears only its bodice, over one of those constricting girdles that reach from the waist most of the way down the thighs. She appears pinched and uncomfort-able. Arnold tells of the meeting: "The first time I met Joan, she stormed into Tina Leser's (the dress designer), where I was to photograph her. She was so angry that her hands shook and the tiny poodles that she wore like twin muffs yapped, cowered, and danced around on her wrists. She had come from Actor's Studio, where she had seen Marilyn Monroe. Joan kept sputtering over and over: 'She doesn't even wear a girdle. Her ass was hanging out. She's a disgrace to the industry!'"[62] The meeting of the stereotypical Corseted Woman, embodied in Joan Crawford, and the ste-reotypical Loose Woman, incarnate in Marilyn Monroe, pitted the sexual-ly uptight against the sexually titillating—abstract polarities, extremes in the struggle to define "woman." In Crawford and Monroe, visions of femininity clashed; in the 1950s, the old America—that "corseted" so-ciety—met the new.

Working Women in Film Melodramas of the Early 1950s

The disintegration of status for the Woman Alone was neither immediate nor direct, but it is clearly evident in the presences and ab-sences expressed through the stereotype. As women became an increasing-ly large portion of the work force—competing with men for jobs—the increasingly frightening specter of the Working Woman, conflated with the Woman Alone, began to haunt the melodramas early in the 1950s. The motives of female characters who worked outside the home became associated less with necessity than with moral inadequacy. Variants of the Woman Alone can be found in seven popular films of this period, with the most threatening manifestations appearing in films oriented around young, working-class men. *A Place in the Sun* (1951), *A Streetcar Named Desire* (1951), and *From Here to Eternity* (1953) define their female characters in terms of the male characters and in terms of moral polarities. Haskell noted the preponderance of male-oriented films in the 1950s and the dearth of good female parts, and popular melodramas evidence this trend. Even the lighthearted *Father of the Bride* (1950) and *Father's Little Dividend* (1951)—which tell the story of a young upper-middle-class woman, Kay (Elizabeth Taylor), as she moves to establish her own family unit—focus primarily on her father (Spencer Tracy) as he struggles to accept her, first as a Wife and then as a Mother, and himself, as the Bride's Father and then as a Grandfather. In the *Father* films, the Working Woman's presence is felt in her distinct absence. Her explicit presence is made palatable in two other films because the Working Woman is based on a real-life superwoman whose wifely and maternal activities are placed in the foreground. *Cheaper by the Dozen* (1950) and *Belles on Their Toes* (1952) were based on the story of the enormous, but remarkably still middle-class, Gilbreth family first popularized in the book *Cheaper by the Dozen*. The films tell "the story of our family and, first and foremost, the story of my father and my mother," Jeanne Crain's voice-over informs the audience.

Adapted from the best-selling family biography by the same name, *Cheaper by the Dozen* reached *Variety*'s year-end list of top twenty money-makers in 1950.[63] The book—by Frank B. Gilbreth, Jr., and Ernestine Gilbreth Carey—had reached number five on *Publisher's Weekly* nonfiction best-seller list for 1949, selling 241,093 copies in stores and an additional 247,000 copies through the Book-of-the-Month Club.[64] That the film adaptation was made at all and that it was immensely popular indicate both the conservative fiscal policies of the Hollywood studios and the American population's increasing fascination with the family. The story begins sometime in the 1920s and chronicles the lives of Frank and Lillian Gilbreth and their *twelve* children; the Gilbreths, in their quantitative excess, exemplify the ideal American family. An industrial efficiency specialist who was credited with making an important contribution to advanced capitalism in streamlining, mechanizing, and dehumanizing human labor, Frank Gilbreth looked forward (if his work can, indeed, be considered progressive) in the public sphere and backward in the private sphere, with very traditional notions of how things should work in the family. Indeed, the film tells us that even the idea of having an enormous family was his, not his wife's. Much of the book's charm lies in the humorous descriptions of efficiency measures he introduced to the family and insisted on as the logistics he felt necessary for managing a fourteen-person household. Benignly patriarchal, Frank Gilbreth got his way; he was, after all, the Father, the source of wisdom and leadership.

Jeanne Crain—as Ann, the eldest daughter—narrates the film in voice-overs, and much of the film's story line involves her maturation, but still, Father (Clifton Webb) dominates the film, as well as the family. Lillian Gilbreth, the Good Wife and Mother (Myrna Loy), bears and raises a dozen children while assisting her husband with his experimentation and consulting work, all with never a hair out of place. Conveniently, Frank Gilbreth does much of his work in his home, since Mother's place is clearly there and he can't get along without her assistance and support. He imposes old-fashioned mores on his children, and the film delivers a conservative and well-articulated line on gender construction. Mr. Gilbreth, with his wife's support, refuses his daughters' requests—indicative of a preemergent female independence—to cut their hair short, wear makeup, or don bathing suits that would bare their knees. Eventually, of course, the eldest daughter rebels, but she quickly learns the *real* value of her father and his ideology when, at a dance, Tom—her dance partner and the best "catch" around—admires her father for insisting on chaperoning:

> Believe me, if I ever have a daughter, I'm sure gonna watch after her. You aren't gonna find me letting her run around with alot of guys, you know, trying to act funny. . . . You wouldn't catch me marrying anybody whose folks let her act like that either. . . . A fella likes to run around with them, you know, just for a good time before he gets married, but when it comes to settling down, none of those flappers for me. I want a girl I can respect.

Just as the rhetoric of the 1950s is now being reinvoked by members of the religious Right as part of their attempt to effect a general sociopolitical move to the Right, the rhetoric attributed to the 1920s is here forcefully reinvoked in the 1950s. The film offers a paean to those who retain the values of times past, when boys were All-American Boys—allowed, according to the double standard of the day, to sow wild oats—and when Good Girls were traditionally feminine, carefully protected, and ultimately married—not like "them," the Flappers, the Bad Girls who grow into Dark or Evil Women Alone. The key word here is, of course, *married*. In 1950, the decennial census report indicated that, for the first time, women outnumbered men in the United States, and the pressure was on. Women were told—in films like this and, often, in the popular press—that if they didn't marry young, they might not marry at all. Women began marrying younger than they had at any other point during the twentieth century. Spinsterhood, they were told, was the dreaded option; new ideas and new social practices were practically guaranteed to insure a life alone. Dividing women into exclusive categories, the film represents the Flapper, lively and independent, as destined to be the Woman Alone and—ultimately—doomed.[65] The implicit evaluative aspect of this stereotype served an additional, nondiscursive function: as women married, they generally left the work force (at least temporarily); had this held true after the war, the marriages of women at a younger age would have eased the postwar job squeeze for men.

Ann finally learns the lesson her father worked so hard to teach—that independent women aren't "Ladies," aren't to be respected, and most important, aren't to be married. They may be fun, but their market value is nil. Secure in his ideology and in the knowledge that his wife would, as always, implement his decisions, this narrative agent, Father, is free to die. Closure becomes imminent. With his wife's support, he has successfully integrated his eldest child into his value system and has indicated the centrality of the male to this "female," domestic genre. Even the primarily feminine task of ideological reproduction is usurped by the male: Father is the actor, Mother his support.

After his death, Mother calls the family together, asks for their cooperation and sacrifice, and vows to carry on. She enters the economic mainstream as her husband's proxy, insisting that she is just that and not an independent agent. In fact, she is independent; in rhetoric, she is not. In the film's final scene, Mrs. Gilbreth ascends the house's large central staircase and walks past the family portrait as Ann's voice-over addresses the now absent but still very present patriarch: "She'll go right on, following in your footsteps, to become the foremost woman industrial engineer and, by 1948, America's woman of the year, but wherever you are, Dad, somehow I'm sure you never doubted it for a moment." While he was alive, however, Mr. Gilbreth was content to take full credit for their joint work.

And even though the story is primarily concerned with the feminine arena of ideological reproduction and even though its narrator is female, its telling is nevertheless structured around a dominant male, and he is the primary agent in the process of ideological integration depicted in the film.

Lillian Gilbreth did, indeed, go on to win fame on her own, as a psychologist and consulting engineer. She was, in fact, one of the most prominent businesswomen and certainly the most famous female engineer of the 1950s. She wrote four books on scientific management before receiving an award in 1951, and in 1954 she published *Management in the Home*, a scientific response to *Cheaper by the Dozen*. She was an active consultant into her seventies and continued to lecture into her eighties. According to Eugenia Kaledin, most of the few successful businesswomen of the 1950s "survived by entering fields of little interest to men," fields like poetry recording and doll making. Lillian Gilbreth was one of the few clear exceptions.[66] However, the fact that this working woman became a success in a "man's world" is overshadowed, in both *Cheaper by the Dozen* and *Belles on Their Toes*, by the invocation of the cultural "ideal." Men are central even to the female-oriented melodrama, evidence of the conservative nature of the genre and its role in ideological reproduction; even "feminine" domestic concerns are negotiated in terms of the "masculine." The fact does remain, however, that this woman, Mrs. Gilbreth, did go on to work outside the home, sacrificing to keep her family together in the wake of her husband's demise. Lillian Gilbreth was an early version of the intimidating stereotypical Superwoman, the woman who has it all— family and career—and who manages it all with grace, composure, dignity, and beauty. Molly Haskell argued that a character like this could appear in a 1950s film only if she was based on an exceptional real-life woman: "Generally—and typically—the only films that allowed dignity to working women were those based on historical figures, real-life women, the singularity (and therefore non-applicability) of whose achievement would not make them a threat to men. Or to other women."[67] The story of the real— but exceptional—Lillian Gilbreth is easier to dismiss than a stereotype, its specificity less frightening than a generalized abstraction.

The success of *Cheaper by the Dozen* led to the production of a sequel, *Belles on Their Toes*, which—unlike its predecessor—did not make it to *Variety*'s top twenty list. The center of *Belles on Their Toes*, however, was not male; more of a "women's film" than its predecessor, the film focused both on Mrs. Gilbreth's professional and personal tribulations as she fought to establish herself in the business world while holding together her family and on daughter Ann's courtship and marriage. It begins as Lillian—called by the diminutive "Lilly" throughout the film—and Ann (played again by Myrna Loy and Jeanne Crain) meet the rest of the family at the "baby's" graduation ceremony; the remainder of the story is a flashback that chronicles Lillian and her family's activities from the death of her husband to the award she received in 1951. The theme of sacrifice, common to the "women's films" of the 1930s and 1940s,[68] pervades this film. Ann, in love with an attractive young doctor, turns down his marriage proposal when her mother is offered a teaching position at Purdue. Why? The family, of course. Ann feels that it is her responsibility to help her mother, who has herself sacrificed for the family, and she wants to wait to marry. But Mrs. Gilbreth, when she finds out, insists that Ann live her own life: "Is that why you think I've kept this family together? So I can have spinster daughters around the house? . . . What I've been sacrificing for is to have someone like Bob love you and marry you." The specter of the Woman Alone is too ugly even for a woman alone. Lilly Gilbreth has little room in her life for anything but her work and her children, and her sacrifice is cheerful. Sam Harper, the industrialist who—after delivering the memorable line "No man that's worth anything would take instruction from a woman"—was the first to hire her, tries desperately and sporadically to propose to Lilly during a chaotic evening at the Gilbreth household, but he is forced to resign himself to the fact that Lilly does not have room in her life for anything or anybody else. She concurs, but not unhappily, "No, Sam, I guess I don't." Why? The Family. The mother can sacrifice; she, after all, has had a husband and family, but the daughter's sacrifice would make her a "spinster." Horrors! Being a widow was still acceptable, but being a spinster was not. This changes as the genre evolves. By the late 1950s, this sort of sacrifice is depicted in film melodramas as *counter* to the interests of the family, and the Widowed Woman Alone becomes increasingly neurotic (*Picnic* [1956] and *Peyton Place* [1958]) or selfish (*Imitation of Life* [1959]). In the melodramas of the late 1950s, widows, instead of devoting themselves solely to their children, begin to take mates, reforming "complete" family units. Thus the centrality of the male and the equation of love and romance with marriage in this "women's" genre becomes increasingly evident. The Woman Alone becomes an incomplete woman.

Early indications of this trend are evident in the particularly stable family units represented in *Father of the Bride* (1950) and *Father's Little Dividend* (1951), based on loving, heterosexual relationships. As was to become typical of the genre, a contemporary setting allowed the films to comment on both contemporary and traditional notions of sexual difference, family structure, and individual behavior. The films' narrative conflicts arise naturally from family life and are a result of "natural" changes within its realm. Focused on major social-familial rituals—courtship, marriage, birth, christening—the primary changes involve the status and role of a young woman, but the films are narrated by her father, Stanley (Spencer Tracy), privileging his point of view and explicitly attempting to naturalize certain approaches to and attitudes about the rituals the two films depict. Both open with Stanley directly addressing the camera—and thus the audience. He opens the first film with "I'd like to say a few words about weddings" and the subsequent film with "I'd like to say a few words about what's happened to me over the past year." Stanley is the center of both films, even though the stories are ostensibly about his daughter, Kay (Elizabeth Taylor). It is Stanley's reactions that are important: the reactions of the father as he loses his "little girl"—becoming the Father of the Bride—and finally has to admit that he's growing old, that he is a Grandfather. Kay's transition into adulthood occasions the articulation of the "natural," and Stanley is its agent, the voice of ideology.

Both films are structured as flashbacks. In *Father of the Bride*, Stanley tells of his surprise when Kay decides to marry and of the trauma involved in his adjustment to the idea. At the engagement party, one of his male buddies ribs him: "Enjoy your moment in the limelight. From now on the gals take over. Your only function is to pay the bills." The ritual moves immediately to the material, and the two are intertwined throughout the rest of the film. The stereotypes of men as Providers and women as Consumers take over, although the increasing number of working women was only beginning to have any real power over large purchases. Stanley, wanting to avoid not just the pomp but also the expense of a large church ceremony and the ensuing reception, discusses the upcoming wedding with his wife, Ellie (Joan Bennett), who understands the proper role of the wedding in her upper-middle-class society. The ritual display of wealth is requisite, and she ties it to her daughter's emotional state, making Stanley feel guilty for not wanting to spend money on the wedding and gesturing toward another stereotypically "feminine" trait, manipulativeness:

ELLIE

There's only one time in a girl's life that she can be married in a bride's dress, just one, and I don't want Kay to miss it the way I did.

STANLEY

Miss it? Why didn't you have it?

ELLIE

Because you didn't want it. So I pretended I didn't either. A wedding, a church wedding—it's what every girl dreams of—a bridal dress, orange blossoms, the music. It's something lovely for her to remember all her life, and something for us to remember, too.

Ellie's implicit reference to virginity—the only time a girl (not a woman) is allowed to be married in a white bridal gown is the first wedding, the wedding of a Virgin—is glossed over by her sentimentality and the assumption that their daughter has abided by the prohibition against premarital sex. And though she may have acquiesced in her husband's wishes for their own wedding, Ellie is not about to allow Stanley's aversion to ceremony and expense to prevent Kay from fully participating in this central social ritual. Any real financial reason for Stanley's aversion is negated by the film's ideal, 1950s suburban setting. Little reference is made to the past, to times when, during the depression and World War II, many people, even those of the middle class, did without the bridal gown, the music, and the flowers. In the 1950s, with a new prosperity, America's love for the material flourished, and ritual events were once again a prime arena for the material display of values and social class. This scene is only one of many that stress sexual differences in attitudes toward money. Women are depicted as the spenders, men as the breadwinners. None of the female characters in either film work outside the home; the Woman Alone is conspicuous in her absence. Women's knowledge of money and money matters is represented as implicit. Just after meeting his future son-in-law, Buckley (Don Taylor), Stanley tells the camera-audience, "In half an hour, I had told him more about my affairs than I'd told Ellie in a lifetime." Men talk to each other—but not to women—about finances. Women must intuit the amount of disposable income their husbands bring in, and of course, they are accurate (indicative of the power of the stereotypical female intuition). Ellie knows Stanley can afford a big wedding, no matter how much he squirms at the thought.

Both films posit this sexual difference. Men pay for material possessions; women revel in them. Men pay for weddings and the costs of having a baby; women collect the plunder, the loot. Men worry; women are self-assured. This dichotomy is exhibited most vividly in relation to the major rituals. Kay, unable to sleep the night before her wedding, retreats to the kitchen, where Stanley, wakened from a Kafkaesque nightmare sequence (about the impending wedding, of course), finds her. She's worried, and he reassures her, not realizing that the next day during the wedding, she will wait, he narrates, "for the proper moment with the calmness of a general watching his forces deploy into battle" while Buckley will have "the haggard look of a man who'd just completed a dangerous bombing mission." The military metaphors make explicit the iron underpinnings that *all women* possess (at least according to stereotype) and vividly contrast these with the masculine weakness Stanley makes clear during his opening monologue in *Father's Little Dividend*: "You women may not sympathize; you may think men have it easy, but that's where you're wrong. Man is a very delicate and sensitive mechanism. If you treat him right, flatter him and butter him up a bit, he's good for years, but if somebody rocks the boat, well, you know how it is."

However charming Stanley's plea for pampering, his monologue puts into words the often unspoken assumption that it is a woman's place not so much to be submissive but to tactfully—and charmingly—manipulate her man. Diplomacy is the woman's craft, and man is her target. And she has the strength in the family, even the strength to overcome parental and in-law pressures to abandon her ideas about natural childbirth and breast-feeding. Kay, traditional in most ways, bucks her parents and Buckley's to practice more contemporary methods—and to naturalize them for her audience. Kay foreshadows some of Elizabeth Taylor's later characters; the actress often played the doting young wife, with no context outside that of her relationships with men. Haskell argued that Taylor "bridged the gap" between sexy stars, like Marilyn Monroe, and their opposites, the serious actresses of the theater. But, as Rosen pointed out, Taylor was not "perfect": "Alone among the young wives, she served as a positive screen model for a loving woman able to vocalize her needs and desires. Fans never felt that she could ignore herself for very long, and it was this ego and impatience and self-involvement which sparkled in contrast to all the perfect, selfless martyrs . . . who sobbed and suffered for their men rather than themselves."[69]

In *Father's Little Dividend*, Kay insists on natural childbirth, and she receives the expert support of her doctor—who, in the manner of Dr. Benjamin Spock, advocates doing what comes "naturally" in child rearing and who reassures her husband and both sets of parents that these methods are quite safe and quite traditional. Even though the children—Kay and Buckley—have their own home, the residual ideal of interlocking extended families is encouraged by the parents' constant attention to the affairs of their children. In this case, visits to the doctor are in order. An initially shaken Stanley yields to the authority of the medical doctor, who presents an argument for natural childbirth. Eventually Stanley himself adopts the persona of the expert and reassures Kay, "When the time comes, you mothers seem to have a courage and strength you never knew you had." Mothers, the film preaches, are not social but natural constructions, and women's strength and diplomacy ultimately have one aim: the creation and maintenance of a nuclear family.

Family is the ultimate issue in these films. Other issues, like aging, materialism, and the appropriate methods for childbirth and child rearing, are subsumed in the narrative drive toward the happy ending that overcomes all odds, all conflicts. Even a seeming infidelity turns out to be extreme fidelity. A pregnant Kay, thinking Buckley is being unfaithful, leaves him, running home to daddy. Father is horrified; divorce would make Kay a Woman Alone—and one with a baby! Although American divorce rates were soaring, this film worked hard to present divorce as almost unthinkable. The crisis is resolved by the revelation that it never existed. To make their little nuclear family secure, the Good Young Husband, Buckley, has stayed late at the office to earn extra money for his family, not to be with another woman. The family is the central problematic and its preservation the goal; the genre concerns itself with a multitude of topics surrounding the familial institution, the gender differentiation, and the division of labor that supports and defines the family. Various approaches to family matters are offered, and the society's concerns are worked into the fabric of this commercial product through the topics avoided and those explicitly discussed, the issues that must be resolved, the narrative structures devised to express and to answer the questions raised, and the rhetorical uses of the cinematic technique. The sumptuous black and white of these two films encourages a romantic vision, and the Kafkaesque dream sequence, the flashbacks, and the extreme close-ups on objects seem to pull the viewer away from a realistic perspective. But the emotional accuracy exploited in Stanley's voice-over and the filmic work establishing his point of view posit a powerful sense of reality and of the righteousness of the films' ideological stance: that although the creation and maintenance of family structures may be difficult, it is the only correct goal, and the only path to this earthly nirvana is found through the acceptance of prevailing notions of proper sex roles. The Woman Alone doesn't figure into the game plan at all. The historian Carl N. Degler described the 1950s as "the decade of the baby boom" and of the "new emphasis in the media upon home and traditional roles for women." The nature of courtship, marriage, and family life was changing, but according to Degler, "the attack on women as workers outside the home mounted even as the number of married women in the work force rose."[70] These four films challenge the legitimacy of the working woman and privilege the return to tradition, but the existence of the two sequels exhibits the temporary nature of narrative resolution and the tentative nature of even dominant ideologies.

In the film melodramas of the 1950s, idealized images of the family and family members were presented and tested. The stable family unit, which had been used as the background for earlier comedies like the Andy Hardy and Henry Aldrich films of the depression and war years, takes on central significance in both the family comedies and the melodramas of the early 1950s, and in both, a happy ending is assumed. However, in the melodramas, the tone is far more emotional and psychological, and the stakes actually *seem* to be in question. As the melodrama developed in the 1950s, the family itself became less stable, presenting in many instances the source of difficulty. The characters interact as the structure of inequality generates tension, conflict, and change. Heidi Hartman asserted that "the underlying concept of the family as an active agent with unified interests is erroneous" and offered "an alternative concept of the family as locus for struggle."[71] This concept opens the possibility of studying the

representation of the conflicts that result from unequal divisions of labor—both by class and by gender, both within the family and outside of
it, in the larger socioeconomic sphere. Film melodramas exhibit and examine these conflicts, and although it is this very topicality for which
melodramas have often been denigrated, here also lie their strength and
importance. Within these films, the family may be the source of the conflict, but it is also the solution. The narrative resolution almost inevitably
functions to preserve and perpetuate the institution of the family and the
society built upon it, but the existence of the genre points to the necessity
for a discussion of the contradictions inherent in this basic social institution, and although the resolutions common to the genre tend to reinforce
dominant notions of family and gender, the genre also enables a presentation of alternatives. The genre's structures and demands for the negotiation of societal differences provide a forum for a discussion of problems
that seem to be contemporary or topical, for a discussion of questions
simultaneously personal, social, and economic. The forum, however, is
limited. In it, in the 1950s, the Woman Alone, antithetical to family,
becomes flat—and unhappy. This is *not* the forum for *her* story.

In *A Place in the Sun* (1951, an adaptation of Theodore Dreiser's
American Tragedy), the young and handsome George Eastman (Montgomery Clift), having fled his evangelistic family in search of a better life,
has been given a job by a distant relative in a clothing factory. He falls in
love with the beautiful and wealthy Angela Vickers, the Ideal Bride (Elizabeth Taylor, again)—but finds that this ideal is available to only a few.
Highly valued by all—men who want her and women who want to be
her—the Ideal Bride is evidence of a stereotype held by many groups,
even by those to whom it refers. Some, however, want to embody this
ideal but can't; a young factory worker, Alice Tripp (Shelley Winters),
doomed never to be the Ideal Bride, throws herself at George. George,
however, is obsessed with Angela, who, at the center of an aristocratic
social scene, reciprocates, even though it is painfully obvious to all concerned—especially to her family—that George's breeding and upbringing
are not equal to hers. George dallies with Alice, and his indiscretion
catches up with him; Alice becomes pregnant (then the standard Hollywood end to premarital sexual activity). Pregnancy, of course, demands
marriage. But marriage to Alice would prohibit George's romance with
Angela and would, he thinks, also inhibit his upward socioeconomic mo-

bility, his "American dream." He contemplates murdering Alice, and even sets it up, but at the last moment he can't go through with it. Fate steps in, and Alice drowns accidentally, just as George had planned.

Even Shelley Winters's considerable acting talent could not flesh out the character of Alice. As in most films of the period—even the melodramas—the male protagonist is at the film's center. Winters's Alice merely provides the foil for the protagonist's angst, and the simplicity of her character powerfully indicates the "naturalness" of the stereotype of the Woman Alone—a desperate, single, working woman. Living alone, she is assumed to be "loose." Her independence, her separation from a family, is identified—and is identified with promiscuity. She is not bound to a protective man. The trait—promiscuity—is made to seem innate to the working woman and is negatively evaluated. Even though over 52 percent of the female labor force (29 percent of the total female population) was composed of married women (46.5 percent of them with "husband present") and only about 32 percent were single women,[72] the single working woman represents them all in the stereotype of the Working Woman. The independent working woman, the Woman Alone, was a reality that challenged the notion that the family is both "natural" and sacred, a notion still dominant, even in the face of newly changed circumstances. Women now outnumbered men. A holdover from the lengthy period in which men outnumbered women in the United States, the bachelor could be presented as a positive figure (often even as a romantic figure), but the spinster—a Woman Alone—could not. In this particularly profamily period, she was shown to desire the security of family, and family was represented without working women; the necessity of female employment was obscured by the prevailing rhetoric that marriage provided salvation.

The Nice Girl, a far more prevalent stereotype in family melodramas, is found in the character of Angela Vickers, who securely lives at home with her family and who is defined by, and under the protection of, her father. She provides the contrast to Alice, the Woman Alone. Working and living alone, which makes her an inherently sinful woman, Alice frantically looks for the mate that she knows is statistically not assured; ultimately—and as a result of the sort of double standard depicted in *Cheaper by the Dozen*—she relinquishes the fantasy as she surrenders her virginity. Her fate indicates the increasing severity with which the Woman Alone came to be treated. She sinned and was punished, not with a lonely life but with death. Angela, on the other hand, is the virginal side of the "age-old dualism between body and soul, virgin and whore."[73] However, the tragic character in *A Place in the Sun* is George, who "should have known better." Wanting too much, he fell into another negative American stereotype—the Gigolo.

That configuration of ideologies known as American Ideology includes within it the notion that although it is marginally acceptable for a woman to marry up, it is entirely unacceptable for a man to rise in status and wealth through marriage. Even "true love" will not suffice as an excuse. The American work ethic is itself gendered. Women are born into a class and are awarded as prizes to the men who "deserve" them, generally men of their own class; if they are very, very lucky, that man will be of a higher class than theirs. Men must do their own climbing; they must earn their socioeconomic rise through hard work. George "deserved" Alice, not Angela, and after Alice's death, he is tried and convicted for her murder, a murder he had contemplated and prepared but had not actually committed. His felonious plan to circumvent his destiny was bound to fail. Melodrama performs here that function formerly enacted in religious ritual: it makes clear the set of ethics basic to the dominant configuration of ideologies. In post–World War II America, upward mobility was becoming increasingly common (due in large part to the two incomes possible when women worked outside the home), and the desire for upward mobility provided material for a number of Hollywood melodramas. But even though that American dream was sanctioned by and in these texts, they also preached that success is accomplished through hard work and that attempting a more direct route to wealth will result in punishment. The attitude of the melodrama was remarkably feudal: characters achieve happiness not just by working hard but also by accepting the roles to which they were born.

A Streetcar Named Desire (1951), another early male-oriented melodrama, also focuses on the interaction of people from different socioeconomic strata, and it was also indicative of the conservative fiscal policies influencing the film industry in the 1950s. The film was adapted from the play of the same title by Tennessee Williams. The play premiered in New York on December 2, 1947, and toured the country, returning to New York on May 23, 1950, for two weeks at the City Center; it won a Pulitzer Prize and a Critics Circle Award. Staged by Elia Kazan, the play starred Marlon

Brando as Stanley Kowalski, Kim Hunter as Stella Kowalski, and Jessica Tandy (and later Uta Hagen) as Blanche DuBois. It was also a hit in Paris and in London, where Vivien Leigh starred.[74] In the film, the Good Wife, Stella (Kim Hunter), quietly accepts the life-style that her husband, Stanley (Marlon Brando), provides. Their shabby apartment in a seedy section of New Orleans is, however plain, their home, and she willingly suffers the implicit abuse of a macho, working-class husband. Then her sister, Blanche (Vivien Leigh), the Woman Alone, arrives. Blanche has never been able to accept either the fact that their family lost social and economic status after the Civil War or the fact that she, unmarried, needs to work to survive. She continues to pretend that she's a "Lady," deserving of both attention and material luxury. In Blanche, the Woman Alone–Working Woman is crossed with the stereotype of the Southern Lady, genteel and fully aware that she deserves attention and support. Her facade of gentility and her insistence on special treatment enrage the earthy Stanley, and class warfare begins, within the family.

The director Elia Kazan's strength lay in his ability to work with actors, and in this film, the performances draw heavily on regional, ethnic, and class stereotypes—notably those of the fallen southern quasi-aristocracy and the first-generation immigrant. The inarticulate anger of Brando's Stanley and the quiet stoicism of Karl Malden's Mitch as they confront the shallow pretension of Leigh's Blanche offer a representation of the working class that is simultaneously attractive and heart wrenching. Passionately honest working-class men, Stanley and Mitch are repulsed by Blanche as she refuses to acknowledge the economic reality of her position and the obsolescence of her fantasy. Stella, in contrast to Blanche, represents many of the characteristics traditionally considered appropriate for women. Even torn between strong-willed characters, Stella remains passive. She never resorts to bitterness, and she is willing to allow her class position to be determined by her husband; she stands by her man. She is the Good Woman, the Wife.

The unmarried and desperate Woman Alone, Blanche attempts to maintain a facade of respectability, at least in front of her sister. But eventually Stanley discovers that, with all the family money long gone, Blanche— who has implicitly taunted him with her own repressed sexuality—has supplemented her meager income by exchanging her sexual favors for expensive gifts, an activity sanctioned only within the institution of mar-

riage and an activity here directly associated with a working woman unwilling to accept the demeaning poverty her economic status demands.
Stanley and, especially, Mitch are unable to accept, unable to acknowledge, the central contradiction that refuses the alliance of gentility and
sexuality and that produces neuroses—neuroses that can never be acknowledged. The Woman Alone becomes the Whore.

Stereotypes depend on the implicit and shared knowledge of explicit
values, values concealed by "roles." Women may be Daughters; they
should be Wives; they may be Mothers. Indeed, in the 1950s, Wives
should be Mothers. The film version of *From Here to Eternity* (1953) expresses this clearly. Set in Hawaii in the weeks before the bombing of Pearl
Harbor, the film chronicles the formation and disintegration of two very
different couples. Army Sergeant Milt Warden (Burt Lancaster) falls in
love with Karen Holmes (Deborah Kerr), his commanding officer's wife.
Their romance proceeds surreptitiously but surely, and its progress would
seem to condone adultery. But Karen's marriage isn't a True Marriage.
Her husband is a drunken philanderer whose deviance has caused her to
lose a child and become barren. The film encourages its audience to believe that she wants—like *all women*—to have a "normal" happy family.

Brandon French pointed out a major disparity between the story told in
the film and that told in James Jones's novel, on which the film was based.
In the novel, Karen has a son. Independence is what she longs for, but she
is confined by her sexual role, by economic limitations, and by emotional
traps. Still, she feels there must be a life more fulfilling than hers, but this
preemergent longing for independence threatened dominant notions of
"woman." In contrast to the novel, the film presents marriage and motherhood as women's primary necessities. In the film, Karen hopes that this
virile sergeant will provide them, but her ambitions prevent her from
being satisfied with marrying a man of his rank, and ambition proves her
downfall. She asks him to enter officer's candidacy school. The army is
Milt's life, but his long-standing aversion to officers cannot be overcome
even by his love for Karen. He knows his place in the army's hierarchy and
has no desire to leave it, to move among the Organization Men who put
on airs as they conform to the expectations of peers more concerned with
socioeconomic status than with individualism. Milt's masculinity is tied to
what he perceives as freedom within a system, freedom he must forfeit to
become an officer. He won't compromise his pride for their love and her
ambition. She takes his refusal of upward mobility as a personal rejection,

commenting perceptively, "You're already married—to the army." She returns to her husband, the stereotypical 1950s Empty-but-ambitious Executive, Company Commander Dana Holmes (Philip Ober), who, satisfied with the facade of a marriage, doesn't want a divorce. Karen queries Milt, "I wonder why men feel differently about it than women?" Why, for men, is the institution more explicitly an economic one? Milt, naturalizing the difference, responds simply, "It's just not the same."

It's not the same for Robert E. Lee Prewitt (Montgomery Clift) and his love, Alma "Lorene" Burke (Donna Reed), either. This parallel romance is doomed by the same incompatible, gender-based, stereotypical notions of marriage: is it a trap or is it security? An orphan, Prewitt joined the army at seventeen, and the army has also fulfilled his need for family. In it, he quite successfully learned to bugle and box, gaining an identity. As the film begins, he has been transferred from the Bugle Corps to an infantry unit because of his boxing prowess, but—having once injured someone when boxing—he refuses to return to the sport. On the instructions of Company Commander Holmes, he is severely punished for his principled but stubborn stance. From Holmes's perspective, Prewitt is letting down the company. Another young soldier, Maggio (Frank Sinatra), takes up for Prewitt and is also punished. They become buddies and head into town together on payday. Maggio takes him to the New Congress Club, where Prewitt meets "Lorene" (whose real name is Alma), one of the "girls" at the club. He convinces her that he's not like all the other guys, and she tells him her life story. After three years of dating a rich boy, she was ditched for a more suitable woman of his own class, and she ended up at the New Congress Club, "two steps up from the pavement." Prewitt falls in love and wants to marry her, regardless of her past, but she resists, not wanting to be a soldier's wife:

> Nobody's going to stop me from my plan, because I want to be proper. In another year, I'll have enough money saved. Then I'm going back to Oregon, and I'm going to build a house for my mother and myself and join the country club and take up golf, and I'll meet the proper man with the proper position. I'll make a proper wife who can run a proper house and raise proper children. And I'll be happy because when you're proper, you're safe.

In this case, it is the woman who desires upward mobility and is willing to work for it. Although she is naive about the route to the "proper," Alma understands perfectly the social importance of economic success, and she understands too that love, possibly fleeting, is an unsatisfactory basis for marriage. But the film proves her ambition to be misplaced.[75]

Prewitt and Alma continue in their relationship, and it is to her that he runs, going AWOL after killing the man responsible for Maggio's death, the cruel Sergeant Judson (Ernest Borgnine). As the Japanese begin to bomb the harbor, Prewitt—still weak from the wounds he received in the fight with Judson—wants to return to his company. She begs him not to, even promising: "Oh, Prew, don't go. I'll do anything you want. We can go back to the States together. We can even get married." But his ties to the army are stronger than his ties to Alma, and he leaves.

Both Prewitt and Milt experience the army as home and family, and both have strong ideas about how it should be run. Neither can stomach personal compromise or corruption within the army. They have developed a mutual admiration for each other, and it is their friendship that structurally pulls the film together. When Prewitt, running frantically back to his company, fails to respond to an order to halt, he is shot down. Milt delivers an on-the-spot eulogy: "He was always a hardhead, Sir, but he was a good soldier. He loved the army more than any soldier I ever knew." Milt looks down at Prewitt's body and picks up his bugle mouthpiece, poignantly punning, "You just couldn't play it smart, could you?" But then, neither could Milt.

In an epilogue, Karen and Alma, strangers, meet on a departing ship and briefly talk of their men. Alma prepares herself for a better future by describing her "fiancé" as a bomber pilot, but Karen silently realizes the truth when she hears his name and sees the mouthpiece in Alma's hand. They bid the island and their pasts farewell by tossing their leis onto the water. Neither passion could be fulfilled by family. Both characters were Women Alone before—Karen implicitly, Alma explicitly—and both are ambitious. Their ambition is shown to be destructive to the men—Milt and Prewitt—who were tied gallantly and irrevocably to constructions of masculinity and individuality incompatible with "female ambition." Clearly, the film's end indicates that the failures of these Women Alone are personal, not institutional—indeed, that the thwarting of female ambition is not structurally determined. Just as clearly, the contradictory concepts governing these gendered roles have their base in the shifting social and economic tides of the 1950s.

3

Re-reading Narrative Structure and Gender

Narrative Structure and the Representation of Gender

Realist and melodramatic texts share many of the same strategies, among them the narrative structure characteristic of what has come to be known as the "classical Hollywood film" (a remarkably homogenizing and reductive notion). Based in the (also homogenizing and reductive) model referred to as the "classic realist text"—which focuses on storytelling strategies the cinema shares with other media—the classical Hollywood film is remarkably realist. It presents a coherent reality in which individual identity is unified and clear and in which characters' actions are goal-oriented, motivating a formulaic plot pattern. The exposition lays out the situation and the primary conflict, showing psychologically defined individuals striving to solve problems or attain goals; the middle drives inexorably toward an absolute truth as the protagonist struggles with other individuals or with a hostile (often social) environment; and that absolute truth (the "truth" of dominant ideologies) is revealed in the plot's logical conclusion, the happy ending achieved through individual action. In some films, however, the motivation for the happy ending fails to convince, revealing contradictions in the ideological problematic the ending seeks to reinforce. On occasion, for instance, an epilogue may be used in an attempt to gloss over the dangling difficulty. Sometimes it works; sometimes it doesn't. One thing it certainly does is make clear the need to examine the relationship between story content and story form even, perhaps especially, in films with convincing endings; aesthetics are irrevocably linked to ideology.

When we consider that the classical Hollywood film generally has two plot lines and that the goal of one of them is the formation of a heterosexual couple (which depends, of course, on concepts of "female" and "male"), the ideological nature of plot structure becomes abundantly clear.[1] But most recent film criticism has concentrated less on narrative strategies common across media than on cinematically specific narrative strategies, and feminists have been particularly fascinated with the "gaze" or the "look." Reacting to this obsession, Christine Gledhill argued, "A mainstream feature film is not constituted simply by a series of looks; it is above all *fiction*, deploying a range of strategies."[2] One of the most powerful—and generally conservative—of those strategies is plot structure. Gledhill lauded the recent expansion of the study of film melodrama and included in her anthology, *Home Is Where the Heart Is*, articles addressing a variety of issues and texts. The essays are within what she admits is a limited field—white, Anglo-Saxon, generally Hollywood cinema—but among them she includes only one that addresses, as a primary concern, plot structure; indeed, analysis of this particular fictional strategy has been underrepresented within film studies and, significantly, within feminist film studies.

In *Women's Pictures*, Annette Kuhn described a feminist and "structural" approach to film narratives, suggesting that "we may consider how 'woman' as a structure or narrative function operates within the textual organization of certain types of film." It may be possible, she suggested, "to isolate recurrent or typical narrative functions or interactions of character and narrative action in dominant cinema" and relate them specifically to "woman." Analyzing the "woman structure" involves seeing "woman" not as a "concrete gendered human being who happens to exist on the cinema screen" but as a "structure governing the organization of story and plot in a narrative or group of narratives"; it also involves comparing representations with the condition of women in society but definitely without the assumption that texts directly reflect society. The point, Kuhn argued, is to ask "whether there are any recurrent structures of enigma-resolution, of movement of plot from disrupted beginning equilibrium to resolution, associated with woman as a narrative function." At the time, Kuhn could present few examples of feminist narrative analysis. She cited an unpublished paper in which Mary Beth Haralovich analyzed ten randomly sampled Warner Brothers films from the 1930s and 1940s; Haralovich concluded that "narrative closure is always dependent on the resolution of enigmas centering on the heterosexual courtship" and that female characters who, in the beginnings of these films, played an unusual role in the production process ceded their control to a male character by the end of each film. Kuhn also cited a 1972 study by Elizabeth Dalton, who showed that female characters are recuperated into a heterosexual bond by the ends of films. Kuhn herself did an analysis of *Mildred Pierce*, showing that although there seems to be "a tendency on the part of the classic Hollywood narrative to recuperate women," "woman"—as character or structure—can be the motivator of the narrator, setting the plot in motion. However, for the film to end "happily," the female character still must be returned to her "rightful place." Fortunately, Kuhn concluded, "things are not always so clear cut in dominant cinema"; attempts to recuperate women are not always successful or convincing.[3] A few other examples of feminist analysis of cinematic plot structure have surfaced, but the trend has not been strong. Lucy Fischer showed, in an analysis of the female doppelgänger in "women's films" of the 1940s, how plots participate in the evaluation of female characters in terms of established patriarchal assumptions about femininity, masculinity, and mothering. Diane Waldman connected textual variations within the Gothic romances of the 1940s with the historical situation of American women. And in her controversial reading of *Stella Dallas*, Linda Williams focused on the film's ending.[4]

Endings fascinate most analysts of narrative structure. For instance, in his masterful review of formalist narrative theory and its limits, *Reading for the Plot*, Peter Brooks moved toward an explanation of the diachronic, processual aspects of plot, but even as he described the beginning, he defined it in terms of the end: "The sense of a beginning, then, must in some important way be determined by the sense of an ending." The end calls, across the bulk of the middle, "to the beginning and transforms it."[5] And the middle, in Brooks's psychoanalysis of narrative structure, is shown to "create a delay, a postponement in the discharge of energy," but it too is determined by the end and functions to make that "ultimate pleasurable discharge . . . more complete."[6] Plot, Brooks argued, is about boundaries; narrative "has something to do with time-boundedness," and the plot "is the internal logic of the discourse of mortality."[7] Brooks's analysis, as usual, was brilliant, but he stopped short, failing to consider the other sorts of boundaries created and enforced by plot—especially gender boundaries. "And they got married and lived happily ever after" means "they got married, and he lived happily ever after; she worked and waited." Endings always call attention to the overlay of narrative and social coding.

In *Reading for the Plot*, Brooks reconstructed "Freud's masterplot," reading narrative fiction as a psychoanalyst reads an analysand. Not unlike Freud's analysis, however, his normatized the masculine. Narratives have a "right end," but reaching a "wrong end" frightens less than the "fear of endlessness." Meaning and recognition come only in reflection, and endlessness, for him, apparently challenges the possibility of signification. Brooks associated serialization—often considered "feminine"—with prostitution (complexly, still reductively, associates).[8] Freud's association of the sense of justice and finality with the masculine resonates in Nancy Chodorow's and Carol Gilligan's association of the sense of separation with the masculine. The sort of narrative dominated by its ending indicates a valorization of the discrete, the individual, the masculine. Females, Gilligan and Chodorow have argued, are more flexible; they are less concerned with judgment and more concerned with relationships and connection than males; their (ego) boundaries are more fluid.[9] Associating serialization with the feminine makes sense, in light of these arguments; the negative valuation does not. In fact, Brooks acknowledged the existence of what he called "the female plot," and in a discussion of ambition, which "may in fact be a defining characteristic of the modern novel," he credited "the female plot" with taking "a more complex stance toward ambition" in "a counter-dynamic which . . . is only superficially passive, and in fact a reinterpretation of the vectors of plot." But though it would seem that this "female plot" should figure prominently in his analysis, Brooks, in a footnote, acknowledged one feminist literary critic (Nancy K. Miller) and discussed a single folk tale that "in some measure represents the female plot, a resistance and an 'endurance': a waiting (and suffering) until the woman's desire can be a permitted response to the expression of male desire."[10] And he dropped the matter there, precisely where feminist critics begin.

In *Writing beyond the Ending*, Rachel Blau DuPlessis analyzed narrative structure in terms of its ideological function, concentrating most of the book on the narrative strategies used by twentieth-century women writers. She described a consistent, coherent project uniting these writers, a project that examines and critiques the psychosexual and sociocultural construction of women, delegitimating "cultural conventions about male and female, romance and quest, hero and heroine, public and private, individual and collective, but especially conventions of romance as a trope for the sex-gender system." Explaining her analysis in terms of the hegemonic struggle for the construction of new kinds of consciousness, DuPlessis explained narrative as a special expression of ideology "by which we construct and accept values and institutions."[11] As social institutions are called into question, so are the narrative forms that legitimate and support them:

> Once upon a time, the end, the rightful end, of women in novels was social—successful courtship, marriage—or judgmental of her sexual and social failure—death. . . . the reproduction of these relations in consciousness, in social practice, and in ideology turns especially on the organization of the family, kinship, and marriage, of sexuality, and of the division of all sorts of labor by gender. The point at which these basic formations cross, where family meets gender, where the division of labor meets sexuality, is the heterosexual couple.[12]

Narrative "scripts" help to organize experiences, priorities, and patterns of behavior; as Ideology functions on a grand scale, narrative functions on a smaller scale. Transindividual assumptions and values are most clear in narrative resolution. In resolutions, narratives can attempt ideological solutions to the contradictions that fuel them. But the traces of conflict and contradiction may remain, and DuPlessis argued, "Subtexts and repressed discourses can throw up one last flare of meaning."[13]

DuPlessis described the dominant model of the nineteenth-century novel (to which twentieth-century women writers reacted) and showed how the narrative form and its strategies muffle the female protagonist, repressing her quest for selfhood and valorizing sexual asymmetry in the form of the heterosexual couple as it opposes homosexual ties. The five "social problem" films that reached *Variety*'s Top Twenty Moneymaker lists during the 1950s operate, like the nineteenth-century novel, to re-press female independence and to reinforce male dominance. In them, patriarchal dominance does meet resistance, but plot structure is its powerful ally. Each of the films examines an important social problem, and although the films offer a range of representations of both males and females, all depict the primary victims of the problem as male. They are similar in their basic narrative structure, indicating a relatively uniform approach to the family even across a spectrum of characters from various socioeconomic strata. Central to these films is a structuring absence, most frequently the result of a traumatic loss, and the conventions of this basically conservative narrative structure dictate the representation of gender.

The Social Problem Film after World War II: Evolution of a (Sub)Genre

As the United States redefined its role in global affairs during the postwar period, archetypes dependent on its self-image—archetypes such as the hero—underwent basic changes. Film genres also began to shift, hybridizing and taking on previously taboo subject matter. Some Hollywood filmmakers—influenced by Italian neorealism, the American documentary tradition, and their own wartime documentary-making experience—explored the seamier side of life. Representing the frustrations as well as the aspirations of their American audience, they confronted the inequities within American institutions and examined their influence on the lives of individual Americans. Their films, known as social consciousness or social problem pictures, were a site for the struggle over gender and also for the related struggle over ways of knowing—realistic and melodramatic. And they featured many of Hollywood's most talented performers. In 1945, Ray Milland and Jane Wyman starred in Billy Wilder's *The Lost Weekend*, Hollywood's first realistic depiction of alcoholism. In 1946, William Wyler directed Fredric March, Myrna Loy, Dana Andrews, and Teresa Wright in *Best Years of Our Lives*, which focused attention on the concerns of returning soldiers and their families: unemployment, physical handicaps, and the psychological problems of readjusting to family life after living in a predominantly male environment and after experiencing war. In 1947, social problem films composed 28 percent of Hollywood's total film production.[14] Elia Kazan directed Gregory Peck, Dorothy McGuire, John Garfield, and Celeste Holm in *Gentleman's Agreement*, an exposé of anti-Semitism in high-society circles, and Edward Dmytryk's *Crossfire*, with Robert Ryan, Robert Mitchum, Robert Young, and Gloria Grahame, dealt even more candidly with the problem of anti-Semitism, substituting it for the touchier issue of homosexuality at the core of Richard Brooks's novel on which the film was based. In another adaptation, from Robert Penn Warren's *All the King's Men* (1949), Robert Rossen directed Broderick Crawford in an elaborate exposé of political corruption. And Kazan addressed racial prejudice once again with Jeanne Crain, Ethel Barrymore, and Ethel Waters in *Pinky* (1949), one of the few social problem films to be organized around a female character. In this film, community pressure forces a black woman passing for white to admit her blackness and give up her white lover.

But as politicians and the public turned their attention toward Hollywood during the McCarthy-HUAC witch-hunt in the late 1940s and early 1950s, the number of social problem films dwindled, and by 1954 they made up only 9.2 percent of the films produced by Hollywood.[15] Nonetheless, the bolder producers and directors continued to turn them out and were rewarded by the critics, the Academy of Motion Picture Arts and Sciences, and the moviegoing public. These were films Hollywood was proud to call its own, but even though they examined various social problems and focused on issues of concern to their audience, they presented no real challenge to the status quo. On the surface, the films addressed social problems, but the form's ultimate function in the 1950s came to be a celebration of the family. Readings of these films have traditionally concentrated on the "problems" presented and the political positions taken, but here I offer a re-reading.

In the wake of World War II, women's roles were changing, and so were family structures and standards of living. Industry retooled to produce the housing and appliances demanded by young Americans newly married and beginning their families in the increasingly popular suburbs. The media exploited this trend and was, in turn, exploited by the industries that benefited from it. Films of the immediate postwar years, like *It's a Wonderful Life* and *The Best Years of Our Lives* (both 1946), celebrated the middle-class family and depicted the construction industry as crucial to the resolution of interpersonal conflicts in the narratives. Homeownership and housing starts were on the rise, and television surpassed 85 percent saturation in the United States, with programming running thirty-eight hours a week (presenting a significant new challenge to the cinema). Advertisers took advantage of and encouraged the increasing materialism, and television commercials and magazine ads sold consumer goods by focusing on home and family. Advertisers encouraged commodity fetishism with commercials that championed a traditional view of the nuclear family and its members. Extensive national advertising campaigns focused on the family, depicting in mini-melodramas a dramatic lack that could be filled with the appropriate products. By 1953, the Columbia Broadcasting System was the most powerful advertiser in the United States, and its top ten advertised commodities were all related to the household.[16] Family had become an issue in a way that it had never been before. Always present in the fictive media, it was now in the limelight, and as concern for the structure of the familial institution and sex role differentiation increased, the socially conscious, realistic social problem film evolved into a version of the family melodrama and provided some of the most notable and successful films of the 1950s: *Come Back, Little Sheba* (1953), *The Country Girl* (1955), *On the Waterfront* (1954), *The Man with the Golden Arm* (1956), and *Rebel without a Cause* (1956). All were financially successful, listed in *Variety's* Top Twenty Moneymaker lists, and some are still considered important—some are even still popular. Several received major awards or nominations, particularly pleasing such critics as Bosley Crowther of the *New York Times*, who favored "serious" (male) films that dealt with "significant" social issues and espoused liberal causes. But, as my readings show, the problems presented by these films—alcoholism, labor union corruption, drug addiction, and juvenile delinquency—are basically family problems, and they can be solved only by a return to traditional family values and structure.

The Social Problem Films of the 1950s

Michael Wood charged that Hollywood's most significant contribution to the myth of the Social Problem "is that there is only one problem." All social problems are treated in the same way in these films. *Crossfire*'s substitution of anti-Semitism for homosexuality provides a prime example of the problems' interchangeability in film. The problem can be named, and social institutions are created to cope with it. Alcoholism, juvenile delinquency, drug addiction, labor union corruption—in Wood's terms, all are reduced to the simple but overwhelmingly frightening "Other," the deviance from normalcy.[17] What Wood does not indicate, however, is that in these films, normalcy, the "Self," is male—white male. The orientation of these social problem films is distinctly male—white male; although female characters may play crucial roles in solving the problem, the problem is rarely theirs. The problem gives these films a rationale for doing the same thing that "women's films" had already been doing—defining and celebrating the family. And the rigid narrative structure of these realistic social problem melodramas—considered "serious" films by the same critics that denigrated and dismissed the more explicitly melodramatic "women's films"—operates primarily to squelch any deviation from dominant constructions of "female" and "male," dictating the characters' actions so that characters of all ages and social classes behave according to gender-determined patterns.

Of these five films, three focus on chemical addiction: the problem in *The Man with the Golden Arm* seems to be heroin addiction, focusing on losses of freedom. The problem manifests itself as alcoholism in *Come Back, Little Sheba* and *The Country Girl*, stemming from the loss of a child. The sensual excess provided by drugs responds to deprivation. The two other films center on the loss of familial trust and respect: the problem manifests itself as labor union corruption in *On the Waterfront*, political excess leading to corruption; in *Rebel without a Cause*, the problem appears to be juvenile delinquency, and this is the only one of the films to share the visual excess common to the explicit family melodramas of the 1950s. But the disturbing and disruptive problem in each film is within the family, and the structuring absence in each film relates to the structure of this institution. The fact that the problem is named would seem to root it in the public sphere, making its orientation implicitly masculine, since, until the advent of the contemporary women's movement in the 1960s, women's problems were not considered social problems. While men were considered to exist in two spheres—the public, or social, and the private, or domestic—women were conceived of only in terms of the domestic, and their problems had no sociological tags. But problems are expressed as those of the male characters. The function of the female characters in these social problem films of the 1950s is to maintain the integrity of the family; they provide the possibility for the solution.

Michael Wood was correct in defining a single problem, but he overlooked the fact that there is also only one solution in these films. Although the male must remain separate and capable of individual action, he and his problem exist within a social grouping; he and his problem are domesticated. The solution—the riddance of deviancy—inevitably results from his individual action and includes reintegration into the domestic-civilized order. The political becomes domestic, political action personal. The same is true of the female-oriented film melodramas, or "female weepies," of the period, but in the female weepies, conflict emanates from the environment itself; it is a given, inherent in the family and in the attempt to integrate the family into a larger social order. The social problem films are motivated by a structuring absence, expressed through a loss of family, a loss involving one of the things most valued by Americans of the period. In each of the films, the primary male character's reactions to, or attempts to cope with, his loss are deviant, and they extend beyond the immediate individuals to affect their families and communities. Though the films gesture toward realism in their attempts to describe an unpleasant but scientifically explicable society, ultimately the force of a disintegrating family pushes toward emotional excess better categorized as melodrama, and the films are plotted to leave the viewer (and the protagonists) exhausted as well as triumphant. In each, as the deviant male character is finally reintegrated into the domestic and communal order, the order is redefined. In depicting deviance, then, these films forcefully portray the range of the permissible, the norm, the ideal.

Because *The Man with the Golden Arm* (1956) dealt with drug addiction, a topic prohibited by the Production Code, Otto Preminger released the film without the previously requisite "Seal of Approval," and it met with great success. The country was changing, and it became clear that the Legion of Decency could no longer dominate Hollywood. People flocked to the theaters to see what they had been missing. The topic was sensational, and a furor surrounded the film's release. But what they saw was essentially a permutation of an already established formula. On the surface, this film appears radical, a challenge to prevailing authority, but at the film's base is a very conservative championing of the family, of aspirations to upward mobility, and of traditional gender definitions.

Frankie Machine (Frank Sinatra), a recovering junkie and a former card dealer in an illegal gambling operation, returns from a stint in the penitentiary to find his clinging and crippled wife, Zasha (Eleanor Parker), unchanged. She torments him with reminders that it was his drunken driving that put her in the wheelchair that we (but not he) soon find out she doesn't need. She fakes paraplegia and begs him to go back to his illegal work rather than risk financial security by trying to make a go of a career in his chosen profession, as a jazz drummer. She is pathetically afraid that he will leave her if he knows the truth, that she can indeed walk. And her fears are not unfounded. As she refuses to be the Good Wife, Frankie—who married her out of guilt—is obviously attracted to their neighbor Molly (Kim Novak), who takes on the wifely role that Zasha refuses to fill. She encourages Frankie's musical ambitions. Eventually, after Frankie yields to the pressures to return to his former milieu, job and all, and becomes readdicted to heroin, Molly supports his efforts to quit cold turkey. Following a fight, the pusher Louie (Darren McGavin) searches for Frankie, inadvertently discovering Zasha's secret. Desperate, she struggles with him, finally pushing him to his death through the top-floor banister of the tenement building in which they live. Frankie is the prime suspect until, dried out—"the monkey" off his back—he returns to tell Zasha he plans to leave her, to try to straighten out his life. Desperate again, she runs across the room to him just when the police and a substantial portion of the rest of the cast arrive to discover, with Frankie, her secret. They also realize her guilt, and she runs through the tenement to the fire escape, where she jumps or falls to her death. Frankie, freed to pursue an upwardly mobile life with the "good" and wifely Molly, walks off with Molly at his side.

The film follows a narrative pattern already established by other social problem family melodramas: a previous disaster, having something to do with the institution of the family, results in a fall from socioeconomic grace and an involvement by the male protagonist in deviant behavior (alcoholism, juvenile delinquency, etc.). As the film begins, some progress has been made in combating the deviance, but a crisis arises and leads to reinvolvement. The female lead, long-suffering but supportive, is tempted to leave her man but ultimately overcomes temptation, resisting because the solution for her as well as her man is in the re-creation of a domestic order, a family. The male acts independently to overcome his deviance and, with his woman's support, faces domestic bliss. This pattern structures both *Come Back, Little Sheba* and *The Country Girl*. In them, the value of the family is revealed by the severity of the fall that results from its loss. The fall from socioeconomic security or the frustration of socioeconomic upward mobility is represented as disastrous, and the loss of a child is represented as the most devastating loss an individual can suffer. That loss removes part of oneself, one's hope, the possibility of genetic immortality, and in a society centered on families, the loss of an only child or of the possibility of childbearing transforms a person into an outsider, an Other.

In the opening scene of *Come Back, Little Sheba* (1953), Lola Delaney (Shirley Booth) comments, "We haven't any children, you know," informing us that this absence is the problem. Its manifestation is in Doc Delaney's (Burt Lancaster) alcoholism. Doc, a chiropractor, turned to drink after he was forced to quit medical school to marry and support his pregnant sweetheart, Lola. A subsequent miscarriage left her unable to bear children. Even their surrogate child—the small dog, Sheba—is missing and presumed dead. The combined losses of child and potential social status led Doc to drink and Lola to sloppy listlessness. Resisting the role of wife, she sleeps late, doesn't make breakfast for her husband, puts minimal energy into her home, drifts around in a robe, and daydreams while listening to the radio. The crisis arrives after they take in a lodger, an attractive coed named Marie Buckholder (Terry Moore), and the Delaneys struggle with their repressed desire for parenthood. Doc, jealous of Marie's young and virile suitors and protective of her virginity, mistakenly assumes that she has given in to the lustful suggestions of the track star "Turk," and after a year of AA-inspired sobriety, he sets out on a binge the very day that Lola cleans the house and prepares an impressive dinner for her surrogate daughter's real fiancé. After being gone all night, Doc returns home and lashes into Lola, revealing his repressed rage and resentment. His AA compatriots take him to the city hospital, where, strapped down and enclosed in a wire cage so that "he can't hurt himself," he once again dries out. At this point, Lola doubts. Tempted to leave her husband, she calls her mother, long-distance, and asks if she can return home. Her father won't have her. With her untimely pregnancy, Lola lost more than a child; she lost a parent. Ultimately, her choice is life with Doc or life alone. Her mother offers to come to visit her, but Lola refuses. Conflating husband and father, she admits to Doc, when he finally returns home: "I'd never leave you, Daddy. You're all I got, Doc. You're all I ever had." She and their house have undergone a remarkable transformation. With her realization that she would never leave Doc—a reinforcement of the then still dominant notion that marriage is forever—Lola has given up her dream that Little Sheba and her own youth will return; she has accepted her "fate." She has changed visibly, now wearing a crisp, pastel shirtwaist dress. She has replaced kitchen curtains, has painted the icebox, and is now prepared to make Doc a "nice, hot breakfast." Marjorie Rosen suggested that in the 1950s, "women's films" became "'how to's' on catching and keeping a man"; she considered this film in that category, an indication of the struggle between realism and melodrama within the text and an acknowledgment that the film's primary lesson teaches women how to keep their men and teaches men what women *should* be. The film ends with Doc signaling his reintegration into the domestic order by saying, "It's good to be *home*." Lola smiles as she scrambles his eggs, and the music rises, melodramatically punctuating the message of the narrative.

The Country Girl (1955) follows the same basic narrative pattern; its inflections on the theme are based in class distinctions. Georgie (Grace Kelly), the female lead, has always had money. Noble, beautiful, and impeccably bred, she has stood by her man even into poverty and is able to make a dingy hotel suite seem homey and comfortable. Her husband, Frank Elgin (Bing Crosby), has fallen from the heights of stage success and of his marriage to this attractive, upper-middle-class young woman. His career is on the rocks; they have lost their only child, a beautiful and cheerful son, in a traffic accident, and Frank holds himself responsible. Maintaining the sort of masculine prerogative represented in *Cheaper by the Dozen*, Frank makes the decision to have no more children, rendering Georgie childless and, therefore, marginal. The problem lies in the shattering of the family structure; Frank's response is alcoholism. The dramatic situation that incites the crisis involves a bright young director, Bernie

Dodd (William Holden), who wants to give Frank a chance to return to the stage in a starring role. Bernie, misogynist, believes Frank's egotistical lies and considers Georgie responsible for Frank's continued failures when, in fact, she is responsible for holding his life and career together. Bernie's confrontations with Georgie allow explicit commentary on the nature of woman, marriage, and the family. During a pre-Broadway run of the show in Boston, Frank reads an unflattering review and goes on a bender. As Bernie and Georgie arrive at a police station to pick up Frank, we see a picture of what Frank and Georgie could become. An older, obviously poor woman is bailing her husband, unshaven and stooped, out of jail; she is so familiar with the procedure that it is obvious this has happened many times before. At this point, Bernie informs Georgie that he wants her to return to New York immediately, that he will take care of Frank. During this confrontation, Bernie discovers that Frank has been lying to him. He is so surprised that Georgie really is a "loyal, steadfast wife" that he begins to fall in love with her, providing her with a potential and romantic escape from her unnamed, unpleasant problem. Later, after the show opens on Broadway, Bernie pleads: "A job is home to a homeless man. Now the job is finished. Where do I go?" After all, in the family melodrama, male characters desire integration into the social order symbolized by the nuclear family. Georgie is touched by his plea, but when Frank gives her the opportunity to leave him, admitting that he's not absolutely sure that he will stay on the wagon, her eyes show her love and devotion, and she follows him out of the opening-night party. Bernie watches them from a second-story window as together they walk toward home.

Through their deviant actions, the male leads in these films push themselves outside the social order, giving themselves an undesirable freedom. The melodramatic deployment of the symbolic family—still, in these films, a stable symbolic construct—illustrates the aberrance of their behavior. The male characters have lost family, and there's little else left to lose, except, of course, their strong, stoic, long-suffering wives. All three male protagonists become dependent on an external, false support, and by doing so, they reject the very real support of their wives. The solution is reintegration into the family, and although the wives provide the material and grounds for this domestic order, this solution can be achieved only through individual action on the part of the male, reinforcing an ideology that valorizes the individual and that places action as masculine. Each of the three female leads—tempted to leave her husband—rejects independence, realizing that the solution, for her too, lies in the re-creation of the familial institution. But even though their situations, actions, and reactions are similar, the characters are distinctly different in socioeconomic status. This difference is revealed not only in the films' settings and costuming but also, and more vividly, in the performances of the actors and in the dialogue.

Frank and Georgie, in *The Country Girl*, speak perfect Standard English, pronouncing each word completely and using correct grammatical structures. They both look respectably middle class, he in suits and ties and she in the conservative skirts, blouses, sweaters, and horn-rimmed glasses that provoke Bernie to say: "You try to look like an old lady, and you're not. . . . There are two kinds of women—those who pay too much attention to themselves and those who don't pay enough." Georgie, generally tidy but matronly, can look gorgeous—and almost virginal—in a low-cut black evening dress. In *Come Back, Little Sheba*, Lola and Doc, older than the characters in the other two films, are firmly established in the middle of the middle class. Lola wears sloppy robes and undistinguished dark dresses, but Doc always dresses in conservative and well-fitted suits. Her speech reflects a working-class background, but his is the overly correct language of the upwardly mobile, until he drinks. Then his physical appearance and normally proper language deteriorate, and he seems the stereotypical drunk and violent working-class man, releasing his repressed rage by lashing out at his wife:

DOC

What are you good for? You can't even get up in the morning and cook my breakfast.

LOLA

I will, Doc, I will.

DOC

You won't even, won't even sweep the floors 'til some Bozo comes along and makes love to Marie. And then you fix things up like Buckingham Palace—or a Chinese joint with perfume on the lamp bulb and flowers. And china, gold-rimmed china, china my mother gave us. My mother didn't buy these dishes for sluts to eat on.

(Pulls the tablecloth off the table, breaking dishes.) I'm gonna get me a drink.

Doc Delaney's violence sharply contrasts with the pathos of Frank Elgin, who can only whimper and lie when Georgie and Bernie find him drunk. This indicates a distinct difference in the representation of social class. Frank, formerly a successful singer and actor whose manners indicate "good breeding," turns inward on himself when he drinks. Doc Delaney, whose ambitions were thwarted by his early defiance of social conventions and "the laws of God" and who subsequently drank up what he describes as a sizable inheritance, betrays a lesser socioeconomic status and his ambitions toward wealth when he drinks. He has become mired in the middle-middle class and turns his anger and frustration outward toward the world and the people around him.

Molly, Frankie, and Zasha, in *The Man with the Golden Arm*, represent the working class. Relatively uneducated, they punctuate their language with grammatical errors and mispronunciations. Zasha's marginal literacy produces such gems as the banner "Wellcome Home Frankie" and the title to her morbid scrapbook, "My Scrapbooit of Fatal Accidence." The characters' class status is most vividly pictured when contrasted with another. When the artificiality of the working-class neighborhood setting (which looks almost like the set of a musical) begins to look almost natural, a more "realistic" setting reinvokes not only the artificiality but also the life it represents. In a sequence shot on location, Frankie and Molly meet on a downtown street, in front of a department store. Contrasted with the photographic realism of the on-location shooting is the artificial display in a department store show window—a mannequin couple posed in a middle-class kitchen. The "wife" stands at the sink, dressed in a crisp cotton dress and an apron (the picture, as we saw at the end of *Come Back, Little Sheba*, of normalcy); the "husband" wears a suit as he sits at the kitchen table reading a newspaper (literate, well-dressed, "normal"). Even this clearly artificial setting appears more realistic than the interiors of the dingy one-room apartments in which Frankie and Molly live. In them, the kitchens share space with everything else. Frankie's and Molly's comments on the window display reveal not only their class status but their attitudes and aspirations as well:

FRANKIE

Will you look at this production? And only for cookin'? Now, who would want a thing like that? Boy, it's goofy, huh?

MOLLY

It's pretty, huh? I wonder what he does for a livin'?

FRANKIE

(shrugs) Him?

MOLLY

Oh, must make a nice dollar. Look at the way he dresses her, kitchen like that.

FRANKIE

I notice he don't help her none, though. I bet he never even married the girl. Look at that—she ain't even wearin' a ring on her finger.

MOLLY

She takes it off when she cooks, maybe. And he's tired, after a hard day's work.

FRANKIE

All right, let him sit there, but at least he could talk to her once in a while. Doesn't have to sit there with his nose buried in a magazine. I would talk to her.

And they begin to playact, calling attention to Kim Novak's incredible ability to become, like a mannequin, the perfect woman of the 1950s. With her exterior coolness and perfect body, she becomes an object, an object who—with her distanced, troubled gaze—clearly sees a problem in this process but who is unable to articulate just what is wrong. Molly initiates the play:

MOLLY

What would you say?

FRANKIE

Well, I'd say, how ya been? How did it go today? What's for supper?

MOLLY

Steaks. Steaks for supper, and everything went fine today.

FRANKIE

Steaks? Good. Now how about you and me steppin' out tonight after we eat?

MOLLY

Why don't we just stay home? Turn on some music?

FRANKIE

Yeah. I like that better (he comes closer, kisses her on the cheek). Just stay home and turn on some music.

Whereas Frankie wants *out* of his current life, Molly knows what it is she wants out of hers *for*. She wants the crisp cotton shirtwaist, the apron, the steaks, the kitchen with modern appliances, a whole room just for cooking—and a man who supports her. She is ambitious, but not just for herself. Indeed, she knows that she can never rise on her own. She knows too that although "steppin' out" is not only a pleasure but a necessity for those who can afford nothing but run-down, one-room apartments, staying in and enjoying one's home is a possibility and a pleasure for the middle class. Interestingly, the scene from *Come Back, Little Sheba* in which Doc and Lola are happiest takes place in their living room when they turn on the radio and dance together to its music, remembering their youth and courtship.

Though distinctly different in socioeconomic status, all of these characters, male and female, aspire to complete their lives through integration into a domestic order. Most of them aspire to a higher socioeconomic order; certainly all of the men do, and the women are supportive of their men's aspirations. None of these characters question the nature or value of the domestic or social class to which they aspire. But the characters in *On the Waterfront* and *Rebel without a Cause* do question these things, and more. The major characters in these two films are young, and youth is presented here as the time for questioning and the time for establishing the ethical imperatives by which to live an entire life.

For Terry Malloy (Marlon Brando), in *On the Waterfront* (1954), the search for ethical imperatives extends beyond the dockside wisdom that "You don't ask no questions and you don't answer no questions." This stance promotes survival but doesn't satisfy Terry. A ruined boxer who works on the waterfront docks controlled by his brother Charley's (Rod Steiger) boss, the corrupt labor union leader Johnny Friendly (Lee J.

Cobb), Terry becomes involved in the union's suspect activities. But when he realizes that his actions have contributed to the death of Joey Doyle, "the best kid in the neighborhood," Terry faces a moral crisis, which is only intensified when he falls in love with the kid's sister, the pale, pure, and virginal Edie (Eva Marie Saint). In need of guidance, Terry begins to look to the local priest, Father Barry (Karl Malden), for advice and support. Terry's "natural" support should have come from his older brother, Charley, but Charley violated familial trust by failing to act as Terry's protector and by involving him in fixed fights in which Terry took dives, dives that eventually ruined his chance for success as a boxer.

Chastened by Edie after her brother's death—"You're in the church if I need you? Did you ever hear of a saint hiding in a church?"—the priest initiates an investigation into the inequities and criminal activities perpetrated by the local dockworkers' union hierarchy. The battle between good and evil—the stuff of melodrama—clarifies in the film's emotional climax as Charley attempts to persuade Terry to accept a lucrative and corrupt position on the docks in return for his silence. Terry finally confronts his brother, who lamely responds by blaming Terry's manager for his ruined boxing career. An unbelieving Terry responds:

> It wasn't him, Charley. It was *you*. You 'member that night in the Garden, ya came down my dressin' room. Ya said, kid, this ain't your night. We're goin' for the prize on Wilson. You 'member that? This ain't your night! My night! I coulda taken Wilson apart! Then what's happens? He gets the title shot outdoors in a ballpark and what do I get? A one-way ticket to Palookaville. You was my *brother*, Charley. You shoulda looked after me a little bit, so I wouldn't have to take those dives for short-end money. . . . I coulda had class. I coulda been a contender! Instead of a bum. Which is what I am. Let's face it. (pause) It was *you*, Charley.

Finally seeming to comprehend how absolutely he has failed as Terry's protector, how completely he has violated their familial bond, Charley at last moves to protect his younger brother, sacrificing himself. Terry turns to Edie, to whom he had confessed and who no longer wants to see him. He forces himself on her, kissing her until she calms down. The scene is classic in its assumption that the woman doesn't know what she wants, that a man—through brute strength—can show her that lust and "love" are the true way. And she acquiesces. Romance overcomes her antipathy to the man who called her brother to his death. Rape becomes romance.

Edie, having overcome her temporary doubt, now stands firmly beside her man as they discover Charley's bullet-riddled body and as Terry vows to avenge their brothers' deaths. By testifying in court and courageously overcoming the physical pain inflicted by Johnny Friendly and his goons, Terry destroys Friendly's power base and restores order to the union, clarifying the ethical imperatives of the social order into which he may now be reintegrated. With the priest, Edie watches as Terry leads the other workers away from Johnny Friendly and reclaims the union for its proper owners. Terry and Edie overcome their loss of family and face a life together.

Terry and Edie survive the shattering of their families by combating an external adversary, by confronting a "social problem." In *Rebel without a Cause* (1956), a "social problem" appears to exist—juvenile delinquency. But this problem is clearly artificial and on the surface. More like the female weepies than any of the other four films discussed here, *Rebel without a Cause* depicts the institution of the family as inherently flawed. Though the social problem has a name, "juvenile delinquency," and an institutionalized method of dealing with it, the problem at the core of the film was as yet unnamed, and the rules for coping with it were still uninstitutionalized.

Jim (James Dean) and his parents have moved from town to town, trying to escape the necessity of dealing with their personal differences and their familial inadequacy. His parents simply cannot give Jim the guidance he needs, and the family is shattered not through the physical loss of a child or parent but through the loss of the family bond dependent on trust and respect. Jim's "henpecked" father (Jim Backus) will not stand up to his overbearing wife (Ann Doran) and mother-in-law (Virginia Brissac), two of the least sympathetic creatures imaginable; their characters act to reinforce the notion that, given power in the family, a woman will abuse it. After being challenged and called "chicken" by the peers at his new high school, Jim searches for the ethical imperatives that will enable him to cope with the dangerous car game proposed by the other students. Testing his father and still hoping for some semblance of idealism in him, Jim demands, "What do you do when you have to be a *man*?" His parents' moral ambiguity—expressed most vividly when, after the game turned deadly and Jim's challenger died, they encourage him *not* to tell the police about the incident—drives him to look for answers outside the family, initially in a bottle and later from his peers.

Judy (Natalie Wood) turns to Jim after her boyfriend is killed in the game of chicken. Judy has, by this time, lost not only her boyfriend but also (symbolically) her parents; she left home after an emotionally charged family "scene," when her father (William Hopper), embarrassed by her sexual maturity, would no longer allow Judy to kiss him on the cheek and her mother (Rochelle Hudson), weak in contrast to Jim's mother, would or could not challenge her husband. Jim and Judy are joined by the emotionally troubled and physically immature Plato (Sal Mineo), and the three of them temporarily form a self-contained surrogate family unit, complete and separate from the world, the model provided by the isolated, suburban nuclear family. The three, children of the upper-middle class, fittingly play out their fantasy in an abandoned mansion, even playacting the upward mobility foremost in the fantasies of most middle-class Americans of the period. Eventually, Jim and Judy, having assumed the roles of Plato's surrogate parents, leave him asleep and go off to explore the mansion. Plato awakens and goes berserk in response to the abandonment that is all too like the pain he suffers in real life, where he lives parentless, with a maid, most of the time. Violent characters intrude from the outside, and Plato, in his frenzy, threatens wholesale slaughter. Jim, in the most mature move of his life, manages to restore Plato's trust, but this game also has gone too far. The fantasy family is destroyed by Plato's death, and Jim's father comforts him, "You did everything a man could." Father and son embrace, as the mother looks on, tears in her eyes. The father vows, "I'll try to be as strong as you want me to be." Jim introduces Judy to his parents; Jim and Judy have each other, and they present themselves to the world as the nucleus of a newly born family. His parents, finally united, come together and look on approvingly.

Both of these films critique American values and aspirations. Terry is leery of ambition in *On the Waterfront*, explaining, "I always figured I'd live longer without it." He questions the lucrative corruption in the labor union that terrorizes and silences him and his fellow dockworkers. And Edie questions too. Asserting the very characteristics her father nurtured by insulating her in a convent, she defies him by refusing to return to "the Sisters" and vowing instead to get to the bottom of her brother's death and the union corruption responsible for it. Though their problems seem to be of a different magnitude than Terry's and Edie's, Jim and Judy, in *Rebel without a Cause*, question their elders, also seeking transcendent truths on which to base a set of ethics. Judy wants to know *why*. Why has her father rejected her? Jim, demanding guidance, asks most succinctly, "How can a guy grow up in a circus like this?"

But *Rebel without a Cause* goes even further. Most social problem films bore a remarkable resemblance in both style and content to documentaries of the period. Almost invariably shot in black and white, they rarely employed extreme angles that would call attention to filmmaking techniques, encouraging the illusion that the camera functions simply as a utilitarian tool for recording reality. Some were shot on location; some were even shot with largely nonprofessional casts. The emphasis was documentary realism. Nicholas Ray's use of cinematic techniques in *Rebel without a Cause* confronted traditional notions of realism. Ray's use of wide-screen and its deep-focus capacities developed what André Bazin would later argue is a more authentic mode of representation than that based on a montage of cause and effect shots, a more conventionally realist style. Particularly in his shot compositions, Ray took advantage of wide-screen's potential for placing characters and objects in a complex and multilayered environment, linking foreground, middle ground, and background in the same shot. His almost Brechtian use of color—for instance, his jarring use of red for Natalie Wood's first costume and for the jacket James Dean wears throughout the film—drew on melodramatic style to emphasize a different sort of realism, a psychological realism that encourages the viewer's awareness of the process of representation. Ray's work simultaneously provided complexity of detail and the abrupt violence of subjectivity. His subjective camerawork encouraged an awareness of point of view and individual experience. A particularly notable example is the dizzy, circular-moving shot when Jim lies on the living room couch and watches his mother enter the room. Portraying the modernist split on a psychic level, Jim longs for unity—with his parents and with his peers—and is repeatedly and frustratingly blocked from it. A shot like this one enforces our awareness of the physical and psychic distance between Jim and his mother, the perversity of their relationship. We feel it in our guts; we cannot help but be aware of it. But though Ray's revolutionary use of technique offered a new awareness of the institutional structures it represented, its challenge was to the notion of "realistic" representation, not to the institution Ray so viscerally and evaluatively represented.

Neither of these two classes of social problem family melodramas—that which deals with rejection from and reintegration into the social and domestic order and that which questions this order—challenges the validity or value of the family structure and the gendered meanings it implies. The second class, although questioning, questions perversions of the structure. It proposes not a radical restructuring but a return to a more righteous order. *On the Waterfront* does not challenge the institutions of the family or the labor union but seeks to restore those that have strayed. Similarly, *Rebel without a Cause* portrays a weakened family structure in order to present its salvation. In both classes of social problem films, the characters "freed" by loss of family desperately seek its reformation, desperately desire a place for themselves in a domestic and social order. And although this order depends on the female for support, in this sort of narrative structure the order is impossible without the commitment of the male. Here, the female provides the materials and grounds for the order, but it is the individual and independent action of the male that constructs or reconstructs the order. The external nature of what is frequently read as the problem not only obfuscates its real nature but also allows for an external and artificial solution. The male solves the problem in his public persona, in the sphere of the "social," and in this narrative pattern, that external solution automatically translates into a solution for the real problem, the healing of the shattered family structure.

The demands of this narrative structure emphasize the effects of external phenomena on the family but simplify the effects by their heroic and individual solution. In a time when the family structure was meeting the challenge of the increasing independence of women and children, the social problem films pictured a range of characters, from all socioeconomic (but not racial) strata, whose distinct differences were obscured by their overwhelming behavioral similarity. These films pictured a family dependent on masculine strength overcoming despair and on feminine fortitude in the face of change. They showed a desperate and basic need for children and parenthood, a need for strong family ties and durable family structure. But although their discourse of deviance defined the norm and although their resolutions expressed the dominant ideology of the period, the conflicts around which the films revolved and the tenuousness of their resolutions indicated significant struggle and challenged the notion that this social unit was actually unified. Robert Ray, writing about the experience of the ambiguous happy endings, observed that

> the more realistically the problem pictures portrayed postwar America's sociological crises, the more they enabled the audience to recognize the transparently mythological status of their reconciliations. Having sat through sustained and graphic depictions of anti-Semitism, class divisiveness, and drug abuse, a viewer could hardly accede to the abrupt resolution of these matters offered by the problem pictures' traditionally optimistic conclusions.[18]

Triumphant but exhausted, heroes and spectators cannot but see the tenuousness of resolution. Melodrama has shaken the sphere of realism and the security of Truth. These social problem films are clearly male-centered and clearly offer one version of gender and family as the Truth, but the more explicitly melodramatic "women's films" present another vision, and they present it in a different manner. For instance, they present a different relation between gender and narrative structure; whereas heterosexual coupling provides the happy ending for the female-oriented film melodramas I examine in chapter 4, the route to that resolution is different. The organizing character, with whom the spectator can identify, is female, and she is generally the character whose action enables narrative resolution.

Hollywood's genre films did, of course, reproduce and reinforce dominant ideologies, but they also actively participated in the ideologies' evolution, and an analysis of narrative structure alone is insufficient. Genre theorists like Stephen Neale and Tom Schatz have recently concentrated on the active social role played by genres and genre films, and their work opens the way to the analysis of genres in their contexts. Neale and Schatz see genres not as simple commercial constructs or as direct reflections of society but as actively functioning components in the construction of sociohistorical reality. As Neale put it, "They are determining factors, not simply determined ones." The interaction of genres and film audiences took the form of an active but indirect dialogue; Schatz has argued that during the period when vertically integrated studio systems dominated the film industry, studios repeated and handed down, "with slight variation, those stories that the audience has isolated through its collective response."[19] Because genres condense real-world experience into narrative patterns, it is only in relation to the social process that narrative structures and phenomenological components have meaning.

An examination of specific narrative patterns uncovers the contradictions inherent in American Ideology and displays the methods through which representation operates to mystify existing domination, inequality, and injustice. It can also show how narratives allow residual and emergent—potentially progressive—elements into the ideological process. It is the nature of genre films to foreground basic social conflicts; they exist as much to challenge as to reinforce our values. Indeed, their often improbable happy endings call attention to the unsatisfactory nature of the dominant ideology's social "solutions." They highlight ideological contradictions, exhibiting and participating in constant renegotiation. The rhetoric of narrative resolution expresses both the dominant ideology and the contradictions that produce narrative conflicts. Endings also gesture back to the variety of possible solutions presented and rejected in the process of the narrative, solutions that provide entry into the text for expression of residual and emergent ideologies. For an accurate description of the workings of the ideological process within narratives, we must balance analysis of foregrounded and backgrounded elements, privileging neither.

*The "Family
Romance" and
"the Gaze" in
Female-Oriented
Film Melodramas
of the 1950s*

4

Re-reading
Psychoanalysis
for Feminist
Film Studies

Style and Substance in the Family Melodrama

In the aftermath of World War II, upwardly and physically mobile families were uprooted, and American commitment to the extended family (always more of a utopian fantasy than an actuality) waned. Indeed, even the nuclear family seemed threatened as increasing numbers of women left their homes to enter the work force. Sociohistorical and economic conditions began to allow questioning of the very institution on which American society was based, asking whether the family is a "natural" or a social collective, and Hollywood too moved in this direction as film-makers working in a variety of genres turned to the family. In the postwar

1940s and in the 1950s, John Ford's westerns came to rely heavily on the family milieu; the plot of *The Searchers* (1956), for instance, is organized around the reunification of the family. Alfred Hitchcock's suspense thrillers, always concerned with romantic heterosexual couples, often focused on the endangered nuclear family during this period. Both *The Wrong Man* (1956) and *The Man Who Knew Too Much* (1956) depict external forces pressuring a family unit and chronicle the resulting interpersonal conflicts. But the genre that most effectively and directly addressed this institution was the family melodrama. In *Genre*, Stephen Neale pointed out:

> Generic specificity is a question not of particular and exclusive elements, however defined, but of exclusive and particular combinations and articulations of elements, of the exclusive and particular weight given in any one genre to elements which in fact it shares with other genres. Heterosexual desire . . . is of course by no means exclusive to the musical or to the melodrama. But the role it plays in these genres is specific and distinctive.[1]

Many of the most talented directors of the period worked partially if not exclusively in the family melodrama during the 1950s. Among others, Douglas Sirk, Vincente Minnelli, Nicholas Ray, and Elia Kazan saw in the family—and the heterosexual couple on which it is based—a charged constellation of characters whose interactions they combined with subtle performances and innovative uses of production techniques and technologies to produce a rich and ambiguous group of film melodramas that simultaneously championed and criticized the institution of the family and the gender roles it entails.

For these directors, melodrama became a "particular kind of mise-en-scène, characterized by a dynamic use of spatial and musical categories, as opposed to intellectual or literary ones."[2] With lush color, wide-angle and deep-focus lenses, crane and dolly, these directors refined a generic style far more sensual and emotionally evocative than any seen before. Cinemascope, for example, enables the sweeping panoramas used in westerns to encourage a powerful sense of the American landscape, but directors like Nicholas Ray (in *Rebel without a Cause*) and Elia Kazan (in *East of Eden*) used it to increase the actual physical distance between characters on the screen, representing the emotional distance between characters.

Likewise, they used deep-focus lenses—with the ability to clearly depict objects and characters composed on several planes of action—to visually represent emotional complexity, developing in the family melodrama increasingly complex aesthetic patterns. Tom Schatz commented:

> Perhaps the most interesting aspect in the evolution of the genre is that its classical and mannerist periods are essentially indistinguishable from each other. Because of a variety of industry-based factors, as well as external cultural phenomena, the melodrama reached its equilibrium at the same time that certain filmmakers were beginning to subvert and counter the superficial prosocial thematics and clichéd romantic narratives that had previously identified the genre. No other genre films, not even the "anti-Westerns" of the same period, projected so complex and paradoxical a view of America, at once celebrating and severely questioning the basic values and attitudes of the mass audience.[3]

Gender construction had been central to melodramatic film genres, but increasingly during the 1950s, gender was defined in terms of the family. Elements of the "women's films" and family comedies were combined to produce a discernibly different sort of film, focused on the family. The family provided the background for conflict in genres such as westerns, war movies, *film noir* thrillers, and of course, family comedies, in which familial conflicts enhanced plots centered on external complications. During the 1950s, a distinctly family-oriented melodramatic form developed, a form focused on conflict indigenous to the family.

Hollywood's family melodramas of the 1950s have often been described as texts that lay bare contradictions within American Ideology.[4] Indeed, the central problematic of the family melodrama concerns the construction of gender and family relations, and since a major function of popular narrative *is* ideological reproduction, the existence of *radical* challenge would be shocking. But instead of tracing the struggles waged in and with these texts and noting the challenges posed by resisting "voices," film theorists like Laura Mulvey have mistakenly argued that family melodramas operate as an ideological safety valve, when in actuality their ideological function is far more complex. Mulvey observed:

The workings of patriarchy, the mould of feminine unconscious it produces, have left women largely without a voice, gagged and deprived of outlets (of a kind supplied, for instance, by male art), in spite of the crucial social and ideological functions women are called on to perform. In the absence of any coherent culture of oppression, the simple fact of recognition has aesthetic importance; there is a dizzy satisfaction in witnessing the way that [in family melodramas] sexual difference under patriarchy is fraught, explosive and erupts dramatically into violence within its own private stamping ground, the family.[5]

Describing the potential for spectators' recognition of sexual inequity in family melodramas, Mulvey distinguished family melodramas told from a man's point of view and those told from a woman's, arguing that although "irreconcilable social and sexual dilemmas" can be resolved in the male version, the female version "offers a fantasy escape," producing "an excess which precludes satisfaction." These films "evoke contradictions rather than reconciliation, with the alternative to mute surrender to society's overt pressures lying in defeat by its unconscious laws."[6] Her argument posits, then, that the female-oriented form functions solely to reinforce dominant ideologies. However, it would seem that this focus on the contradictory nature of the female-oriented family melodrama should lead in the direction of a richer notion of the text, a notion closer to Bakhtin's description of the text as a heteroglottic "weave of voices."[7] It should also call attention to the distinctions between "masculine" texts, which, Mulvey claimed, aim to unify, and "feminine" texts, which resist closure as they disperse meaning. But even in these female-oriented family melodramas, woman, for Mulvey, remains gagged and, therefore, mute. Woman, for her, has no "voice." In fact, the dominant narrative practices of Hollywood films in the 1950s did follow a pattern that reinforced patriarchy and repressed the feminine; however, even though this pattern was the dominant pattern, it was by no means the *only* one. Even in male-oriented texts, and especially in female-oriented texts, there are exceptions and challenges to this dominant pattern, exceptions that "speak" in different "voices," and the inability to "hear" these voices is rooted in the very psychoanalytic theories that have informed recent feminist film theory and criticism.

Feminism and Psychoanalysis

Because psychoanalysis attempts to theorize the construction of the individual identity within the patriarchal family and, at the same time, to account for patriarchy itself, feminists have argued that it offers some potential for the demystification of the status quo and, therefore, for an analysis of gender representation. However, the move to psychoanalysis was not made until the mid-1970s. The practical use of psychoanalytic theory had frequently resulted in attempts to brainwash (condition) women who did not "fit in" to their proper "place" in patriarchy and, sometimes, had resulted in the imprisonment of many women in mental institutions. In addition, scholarly critics like Kate Millett, offended by Freud's misogyny, rejected psychoanalysis out of hand. Toril Moi recounted the "unremittingly negative account of psychoanalysis [that] remained mostly unchallenged among feminists in England and America" until the 1974 publication of Juliet Mitchell's *Psychoanalysis and Feminism* pointed toward positive feminist uses of psychoanalysis.[8]

In her pioneering 1975 *Screen* article "Visual Pleasure and Narrative Cinema," Laura Mulvey laid the groundwork for a political use of psychoanalysis in feminist film studies, charging that previous work in the area had not sufficiently addressed representation of "the female form in a symbolic order in which in the last resort, it speaks castration and nothing else." Claiming that psychoanalysis gives an "exact rendering of the women's frustration experienced under the phallocentric order" (a claim I dispute), she launched her examination of filmic representation of women on the basis that "psychoanalytic theory as it stands can at least advance our understanding of the status quo, of the patriarchal order in which we are caught" (a claim I do not dispute).[9] Many on the Left have considered progressive political analysis (generally Marxist) incommensurable with psychoanalysis,[10] but many feminists, even Marxist feminists (with the inherent feminist focus on the private sphere), have, since the mid-1970s, turned to psychoanalysis for an explanatory theory. The American literary theorist Jane Gallop, for example, has supported the political use of psychoanalysis. In *The Daughter's Seduction*, she argued:

> One of psychoanalysis' consistent errors is to reduce everything to a family paradigm. Sociopolitical questions are always brought back to

the model father-mother-child. Class conflict and revolution are understood as a repetition of parent-child relations. This has always been the pernicious apoliticism of psychoanalysis. . . . [And] what is necessary to get beyond this dilemma is a recognition that the enclosed, cellular model of the family used in such psychoanalytic thinking is an idealization, a secondary revision of the family. The family never was, in any of Freud's texts, completely closed off from questions of economic class.[11]

Freudian and Lacanian psychoanalysis became a primary tool for feminist film analysis, initially among the members of the editorial board of the British film journal *Screen*, among French film theorists, and later among their students and readers, many of them American. However, although these theorists and critics were generally critical of the power imbalance inherent in society and in the modern nuclear family, they based their work in Freudian and Lacanian theories of psychoanalysis, which describe the masculine as normative and the feminine as aberrant. These theories, unless modified significantly, cannot account for resistance and ideological struggle; they represent, instead, the psychic mechanisms for reinforcing dominant ideologies. The resulting film theory does explain a remarkable number of Hollywood films, but it fails to explain and, in fact, misrepresents a significant minority of these texts. This theoretical approach—which incorporated the totalizing notion of classic realist cinema with the universalizing of a male-oriented theory of psychoanalysis—underestimates both the complexity and variety of mainstream narratives and the potential for consuming them in ways that challenge patriarchy.

The earliest influence of psychoanalysis on film theory and criticism produced an approach focused on the Oedipal "family romance," which, it was claimed, generates plot patterns. Popular in the late 1960s and early 1970s, this Freudian mode of interpretation, which concentrated on narrative content, began to lose favor in the mid to late 1970s, when film theorists turned to a second strain that had a more linguistic orientation, focusing on filmic texts as signifying processes and analyzing their enunciative patterns.[12] But even in the late 1970s, Stephen Heath and Geoffrey Nowell-Smith, writing for *Screen*, argued, "To understand melodrama in the cinema is necessarily to attempt to focus the investment in a constant repetition of family romance fantasizing both in its themes and its process of relations and positions of the subject-spectator."[13] While many film theorists were moving away from this (chronologically) first strain, these *Screen* theorist-critics believed, correctly, that the first is as important as the second strain, especially in relation to the family melodrama, but interpretation in terms of Freud's description of the Oedipal scenario is, alone, insufficient.

Freud's description of the family romance depends on a notion of psychic development beginning with a masculine origin that he dissimulated as unisex. He described male development as normal, juxtaposing female development in terms of its deviance from this norm. According to Freud, the relationship of the male child with his mother eventually takes on sexual overtones, and the child begins to see his father as a rival for his mother's affections. He fantasizes about murdering or castrating his father but then fears retaliation (his own castration) and so denies himself the love for his mother, instead identifying with his father, and is reassured of his sexual superiority to all that is feminine. For the male, the entry into the adult social order is the road to normalcy, and he "naturally" transfers his early, primary, narcissistic self-love to "normal" object love, first to his mother and later to some other woman.

For the female, Freud believed, this was impossible. Focusing on anatomical difference, with the male as norm, Freud posited a "genital trauma" in the female child as she realizes that she is anatomically "inferior"—she does not possess a penis. She comes to despise herself and all those like her, especially her mother, and the feelings of castration and inadequacy manifest themselves in "penis envy." She turns angrily from her mother, who is not only penis-less but also a rival for the affections of her father, now the object of her love. Eventually, she regains self-esteem through a narcissistic vanity. But, according to Freud, women never develop "normal" object-love, which he privileged as ethically superior; they experience, he argued, an artificial object-love through their children. Women may appear to "win," but there is no normalcy for women. Woman is the unknown, the unknowable, the Other—not male. Fundamentally narcissistic and penis-less (castrated), woman only artificially displaces her narcissism with object-love.

Laura Mulvey has used Freudian theory in attempting to explain how the female viewer derives pleasure from a Hollywood genre film that is "structured around masculine pleasure, offering an identification with the *active* point of view."[14] She argued that this identification allows a woman spectator "to rediscover that lost [masculine] aspect of her sexual identity," the never fully repressed bedrock of feminine repression. Mulvey insisted that such an accomplishment is derived through a transsexual identification in which the female spectator temporarily remembers her masculine, active stage. Within a theory based on Freudian psychoanalysis, as Mulvey's is, the male or masculine is inherently, essentially both active and normative, and the female or feminine is explicable only through reference to this norm.[15] Within this realm of film theory, then, there is no way to explain resisting, different "voices" that function at both the narrative and the enunciative levels, and there is no way to explain the pleasure of the female spectator without reference to a masculine "norm."

Indeed, a primary obstacle for feminist film studies is this dependence on Freudian and Lacanian psychoanalytic theories, which tie gender to biology rather than to social structures. Both Freudian and Lacanian theories of psychoanalysis operate conservatively to extend and naturalize the repression of women, defining "woman" in terms of aberrance and deviance and effectively obscuring any variant "voice." According to Lacanian psychoanalysis, in fact, sexuality is produced only in and through language, and language constructs woman as *not* man. The male—or masculine—voice that dominates our society and structures sexuality and gender also structures the very theories we use to explain them. Male-dominant theorizing consigns women to an inevitable secondary status and obscures nondominant voices.[16] Recent developments in psychoanalytic theory and in the social sciences challenge Freud's attitude toward narcissism and his interpretation of psychosexual development; however, most psychoanalytic film theory and analysis remains based on either an orthodox Freudianism or on Lacan's re-reading of Freud, which is also skewed in favor of the masculine.[17]

Lacan argued powerfully that the individual *is* constructed socially; he saw the individual as constituted through language, through a process of initiation into "the" symbolic order that establishes for the individual a sense of separateness from the rest of the world and awareness of the nature of signification. Sexuality, he argued, is only ever in language, and language defines woman as *not* man. This symbol system privileges, not surprisingly, the masculine authority it supports and is supported by; it expresses prohibition and the law in terms of the phallus, which Lacan claimed is an abstraction with no necessary reference to anatomy. Even within the Lacanian tradition, challenges have been made to this theory. Some of his followers assign femininity a prelinguistic, presymbolic point of origin. For Lacan, however, there is no prediscursive reality, and these challenges attack the very crux of his theory, the determinant nature of the Symbolic.[18] But his arguments are persuasive, and even if the terms he uses and his privileging of the masculine are offensive, his emphasis on the social construction of individuals is useful. And his argument that authority is vested in the masculine is, at least in our society, difficult to dispute; a Lacanian approach does account for the bulk of Hollywood films, which are, in fact, male-oriented. As Jacqueline Rose argued: "Lacan gives an account of how the status of the phallus in human sexuality enjoins on the woman a definition in which she is simultaneously symptom and myth. As long as we continue to feel the effects of that definition, we cannot afford to ignore this description of the fundamental imposture which sustains it."[19]

But significant problems within Lacanian theory limit its usefulness for cultural studies. Lacan's emphasis on the linguistic obscures, even ignores, the very real nonlinguistic determinants in the constitution of an individual. And there is a distinct tendency on the part of Lacan and his followers to universalize his theory, to assume that all individuals ("subjects") in all societies at all times are constituted in the same way. This transcendentalism is basically incompatible with any notion of historical materialism. In a critique of what he and his compatriots at the Centre for Contemporary Cultural Studies at the University of Birmingham called "screen theory," Stuart Hall addressed this problem in Lacan's theory, arguing that subject formation is neither transhistorical nor transsocial. He noted that it is "difficult, if not impossible to square this universal form of argument with the premises of historical materialism . . . which historicizes the different forms of subjectivity and which needs a reference to specific modes of production, to definite societies at historically specific moments and conjunctures. The two kinds of theory are conceptually incompatible in the form of their argument."[20]

Because of the tendency to universalize, the Lacanian approach fails to account for differences among various patriarchal ideologies, for any nondominant ideologies, and for any concept of struggle and change in ideology. In addition, Lacan's highly phallocentric theory appears to consign women necessarily and irreversibly to patriarchy, and although it is the case that our society is patriarchal, this approach fails to account for the challenges to and changes in our social structure, challenges and changes that mitigate against patriarchy. Although the Lacanian description of identity development has value as a description of the status quo, it is incomplete and cannot be used to explain ideological change. Neither can it explain all cultural texts, even mass-produced texts, even in a patriarchal society.

Mainstream film texts cannot be removed from the material conditions in which they are produced and consumed nor separated from the ideological struggles of which they are a part. They are not simple texts; they not only are not necessarily ideologically coherent but also are not monolithically repressive.[21] They are participants in an ongoing ideological process; real ideological struggle goes on in and with mainstream entertainment texts, and ideological struggle goes on in theory as well. To understand and explain this struggle and the existence and role of "different voices" in Hollywood's films, we must read Freudian and Lacanian theories of psychoanalysis with the eyes of contemporary feminism—if we keep these theories at all, which some theorists feel we shouldn't. I find them helpful but feel that we must rework these powerful theoretical constructs in ways that both acknowledge the validity of female experience and help to explain the active role of women in ideological change. The work of Nancy Chodorow and of Carol Gilligan—and that of their critics—offers fertile ground for feminist film theory.

Chodorow's pioneering *The Reproduction of Mothering* has been hailed as "the most comprehensive and articulate explanation of gender difference as a social fact to date."[22] Because of social, economic, political, and cultural inequities, women's experiences of the world are distinct from those of men, and they develop in qualitatively different (not inferior or superior) ways. Chodorow presented a basic re-reading of Freudian theory, a theoretical account for the asymmetrical organization of gender, which she contended is generated by and reproduces women's mothering. Chodorow works in the tradition of "object relations" theory, which posits, like Lacan, that the individual is a social construction but which claims, against Lacan, that the child's social relations determine psychological growth and identity formation. Object-relations psychoanalysts focus their attention on the infant-mother relationship, seeing the mother as the infant's most important object, and Chodorow described the process by which women reproduce themselves by producing female children who want to mother.

Chodorow drew on clinical evidence and a consideration of the social setting in which it was obtained, and she presented a positive reassessment of female development. Rejecting Freud's emphasis on the child's discovery of anatomical difference, she focused much more extensively on the pre-Oedipal phase. Her evidence showed that the first identification for both male and female infants is with the primary parent, the mother, contradicting Freud by asserting that the boy's development involves a negation of the primary identity but that the girl's does not. Chodorow also countered Freud in her insistence that the girl child does not give up her attachment to her mother during the Oedipal stage but develops instead a triadic model for relationships. The male, on the other hand, represses his identification with the mother and develops a sense of difference and separateness. Because girls are parented by a person of the same gender, they experience themselves as more continuous with the external world than do boys. Girls develop more flexible ego boundaries and more fluid senses of identity; they define themselves in terms of relationships rather than in terms of separateness and individuality. Also, because they don't develop the masculine sense of justice and morality that is based on a denial of relationship and connection and that is dependent on an uncompromising superego, females are more capable of empathy.

In this society, which assigns primary responsibility for parenting to women, men and women develop into incompatible people. Both males and females desire a return to the original emotional nurturance they experienced as infants, but the male's sense of separateness, brought about by being parented by a person of a different gender, causes most men to be incapable of providing this sort of nurturance. Women, on the other hand, are conditioned to give it as well as to desire it, but they rarely receive it from men. And whereas men form dyadic relationships, the triadic model—formed in females during the Oedipal period—is followed by women as they extend their affection also to their children and maintain close ties to their mothers or other women friends.

Although Chodorow noted that all known sex-gender systems have been male-dominated, her feminist position and her attention to historical and material conditions have led her to a theory that, with modification, may have the potential to account for change. Women's roles are historical and social products, and the nature of women's mothering is not transcultural or universal, Chodorow argued, pointing to contradictions within the process that reproduces mothering. The forms of the tensions and strains created by these contradictions are, she argued, dependent partially on internal developments within the sex-gender system and partially on external historical conditions, particularly on changes in the organization of production. A fusion of these forces can lead, as it has in our time, to widespread and even explicitly political resistance to dominant patterns. Chodorow noted particularly the recent attention given to males involved in primary parenting, speculating that

> equal parenting [by males and females] would leave people of both genders with the positive capacities each has, but without the destructive extremes these currently tend toward. . . . Men would be able to retain the autonomy which comes from differentiation without that differentiation being rigid and reactive, and women would have more opportunity to gain it. People's sexual choices might become more flexible, less desperate.[23]

The notion of equal parenting constitutes a basic challenge to our social, economic, and ideological organization, but the more positive development of gender proposed by Chodorow would depend on significant social, economic, and ideological changes—changes that might be welcomed even by those who feel that Chodorow's theorizing stops short.

Chodorow's documentation of the emotional primacy of women for other women has tantalized some feminist theorists who want to push her theorizing further, to account for a range of female friendships. They feel she fails to acknowledge and theorize the range of important female relationships, as well as the practical impediments to these relationships imposed by a society in which heterosexuality is dominant (witch burning, male control of law, production of narrative texts—like Hollywood films—driven by a celebration of heterosexual romance, etc.).[24] Noting that Chodorow comes "close to the edge of an acknowledgement of lesbian existence," Adrienne Rich has critiqued Chodorow's assumption that heterosexuality is the norm, describing Chodorow as "stuck with trying to reform a man-made institution—compulsory heterosexuality—as if, despite profound emotional impulses drawing women toward women, there is some mystical/biological heterosexual inclination, a 'preference' or 'choice' which draws women to men."[25] Janice Raymond pushed the critique further, arguing that Chodorow's theories actually—though not consciously—boost "hetero-reality" by failing to emphasize the importance of women's relationships with women and by subtly encouraging women to "live for men."[26] Raymond argued that male parenting will actually enhance male supremacy by giving men more power than they already have rather than encouraging an acknowledgment of female friendships; power is at stake here, and political considerations are primary. And Rich pointed in a profitable direction for adapting Chodorow's work by suggesting that "heterosexuality, like motherhood, needs to be recognized as a *political institution*."[27]

Like all dominant political institutions, heterosexuality receives constant ideological (and sometimes compulsory) reinforcement. In the bulk of Hollywood films, heterosexual relationships and men's relationships with other men dominate, with women represented only in terms of their relationships with men or in terms of their conflict or competition with other women. But in a significant minority of films—even very successful films—women's emotional attachments to other women are prominent, and teasing out this tendency in Chodorow's theorizing produces a potentially emancipatory approach to interpreting these female-oriented films. Understanding the possibilities for resistance empowers more than a simple understanding of victimization; we must, in fact, understand the conditions of victimization and the possibilities for agency under oppression.[28]

Carol Gilligan's research and theorizing productively complement Chodorow's, as do the critiques of her work; her emphasis on discourse is of particular value for film theory and criticism. Analyzing interviews with people on the topic of morality, Gilligan found distinct differences between the way males and females talk, differences strikingly similar to those found by Chodorow. Gilligan described two distinct perspectives, two modes of thinking, two different experiences of self. One, the male, is rooted in objectivity and impartiality, is premised "on a fundamental separation between other and self," and is characterized by reciprocity, the need to receive in response to one's giving. The other, the female perspective, is based in a blurring of boundaries between self and other, allows feelings to influence thought, and is characterized by response and connectedness. Addressing psychoanalytic theorizing, Gilligan argued that Freud's desire to eliminate contradictions within his theory "blinded him to the reality of women's experience" and to the asymmetrical personality development of males and females. He lived in a society "where women's lives were not considered to inform human possibility," and he worked with a notion of theory construction limited by a "conception of objectivity in science that led to a series of enforced separations," the analytic situation characteristic of the masculine perspective.[29]

Some of Gilligan's critics contend that other significant factors—like occupation—can account for the distinctions she attributed to gender, and some are uneasy with linking these characteristics to sex differences. Joan Tronto, for instance, argued that Gilligan's equation of "care" with "female" has not been adequately supported and is fraught with philosophical peril.[30] Claudia Card, focusing on Gilligan's contrast between a female ethics of responsibility and a male ethics of rights, argued that Gilligan may have mistaken a misplaced female gratitude to men for their "benefactions"—which females could, in fact, not refuse—for a discourse of caring. Like Rich and Raymond, who objected to Chodorow's primary emphasis on psychological reasons for the reproduction of heterosexual dominance, Card wants Gilligan's analysis of discourse expanded to include attention to the material—and often violent—realities women live, realities in which they may seek male approval not for its own sake and not because they "care" about maintaining relationships but because they feel the approval is necessary for their security (for protection against violent assault, for job security, etc.). Card suggested that such action and the discourse that naturalizes it actually entrench that need. In addition, she fears that Gilligan's focus on improving the quality of connectedness (a concern attributed to the female) may, politically, be self-defeating; separation can be more empowering than destructive relationships with men, and the discourse of connectedness works against that separation by naturalizing female concern with relationships.[31]

In addition, some critics consider Gilligan and Chodorow essentialists, but in fact neither Gilligan nor Chodorow actually argued that the differences described are essentially gendered; the differences and the discourses that reinforce them are, however, very real and most often gender-connected in our society. Gilligan, for instance, reported that males and females describe themselves differently—females in terms of relationships, males in terms of separation—but she did not argue that these distinctions are absolute. Rather, she contended that once we see them, we may begin to see the existence of feminine traits in men and vice versa. Whatever the perils of these gendered differences, they are differences that are socially constructed and discursively reinforced. Theorizing such as that done by Chodorow, Gilligan, Rich, Raymond, and Card allows both the expansion of psychoanalytic theory to explain gender differences in social rather than biological terms and the theorizing of gender construction and representation in terms of hierarchies of power.[32] It may help us move toward a materialist psychoanalysis.

Stories of Mothers and Daughters

During the 1950s, Ross Hunter recognized the potential profits from the audience that had previously supported the "women's films" in the 1930s and 1940s, and he polished Universal Studios' young contract players and refurbished old ones to provide an update of this previously popular genre. His exploitation of the female matinee audience brought Universal a growing share of the fragmenting American audience,[33] and other studios followed suit. Some of the films, in fact, must have appealed to more than just matinee audiences, since they reached *Variety*'s success-story lists. This regenerated form, still organized around a woman's point of view—her problems, her desires—attempted to depict a reality so realistic that its viewers would feel that they had learned something as they escaped into darkened theaters during the middle of the day. And the reality the films pictured was that of a capitalistic and patriarchal social system—but a system in which women used their limited power to resist total male domination.

Although patriarchy had preceded both capitalism and nation states, these forces had aggravated the power of men over women and their labor, thus increasing the inequality in divisions of labor and destroying the family as a group whose members had unified interests. Nevertheless, the interdependence of men and women was maintained, and while both the capitalistic state and capitalism itself produced and benefited from the privatization of the family-kin group, this institution maintained an unpredictable and problematic dominance. The various film melodramas of the 1950s—maternal melodramas, patriarchal melodramas, lover-centered melodramas—lay bare the family's internal contradictions more explicitly than any other film genre. As Geoffrey Nowell-Smith explained:

> Melodrama can thus be seen as a contradictory nexus, in which certain determinations (social, physical, artistic) are brought together but in which the problem of the articulation of these determinations is not successfully resolved. The importance of melodrama . . . lies precisely in its ideological failure. Because it cannot accommodate its problem, either in a real present or in an ideal future, but lays them open in their shameless contradictoriness, it opens a space which most Hollywood forms have studiously closed off.[34]

The female-oriented film melodramas of the 1950s call attention to gendered identity construction during a period when precisely what it means to be a woman—and, as a result, what it means to be a man—were becoming controversial issues; if only for this, these films deserve attention. In fact, they prove fascinating for many reasons. Four female-oriented melodramas made *Variety*'s lists of top money-makers during the 1950s: *Magnificent Obsession* (1954), directed by Douglas Sirk, produced by Ross Hunter for Universal Studios, and based on a 1935 film adapted from Lloyd C. Douglas's novel and directed by John Stahl; *Picnic* (1956), adapted for Columbia Pictures from William Inge's stage play and directed by Joshua Logan (also a Broadway director); *Peyton Place* (1958), adapted from Grace Metalious's controversial novel and directed by Mark Robson for Twentieth Century-Fox; and *Imitation of Life* (1959), directed by Douglas Sirk (for Universal), a remake of the 1934 film of the same name directed by John Stahl and adapted from Fannie Hurst's best-seller. I reserve discussion of this last film until the final chapter and add to this section the discussion of a film made to capitalize on the phenomenal success of *Magnificent Obsession*: *All That Heaven Allows* (1955) was directed by Douglas Sirk and produced by Ross Hunter with the same cast, the next best thing to a sequel.

These female-oriented melodramas center on communities of women and children, and the absence of a patriarchal figure motivates the narratives. To achieve integration into the (heterosexual) social order, the female protagonist, who has lost the adult male in a triadic relationship, must acquire a mate and participate in a heterosexual dyad. For social reasons, she must create the dyad; for personal reasons, she strives to create or recreate a triad. Steve Neale noted that men are crucial to genres like the war film and the western, even as the genres go out of their way to incorporate "the direct representation of woman, no matter how 'contrived' or 'clumsy' this may seem in terms of the logic of a given narrative." But though melodramas and musicals tend to feature female characters, they almost always also include men as central figures. "Indeed, men are crucial to these genres, more so, perhaps than women to war films and westerns."[35] The female-oriented melodrama cannot end with its female protagonist continuing a life independent and alone (read: without a man). But although the solution provides her with a mate—completing a family unit, filling the place of the absent patriarch, and concluding the narrative—the solution may be obtained only through the action of a female character, generally the protagonist, and is achieved only through a fantastic narrative rupture, which heightens the solution's artificiality and exposes the contradictions it so transparently attempts to overcome.

The often improbable happy endings in female-oriented family melodramas have caused critics to ridicule the genre and its audience, leading to the notion that the films do function simply and solely to reinforce dominant ideology, to champion the heterosexual dyad. Of course, they do, and it would be surprising if they did otherwise, but the narrative contortions necessary to produce the deus-ex-machina endings expose contradictions rather than resolve them. Neither Freudian nor Lacanian theories of psychoanalysis can provide a theoretical framework capable of explaining these plots, but the newer psychoanalytic models presented by Chodorow and Gilligan can, although this work has received little attention from feminist film theorists and critics. However, literary critics like Janice Radway have found these models quite helpful; Radway sees in literary texts plot patterns based in the gender differences described by Chodorow and Gilligan.[36] Chodorow and Gilligan describe socially constructed gender-linked differences in modes of thinking and communicating that do not present the male as normative, and these identity differences and the resulting modes of interpersonal interactions correspond remarkably closely to the representations of gender in the female-oriented melodramas of the 1950s.

Chodorowian theory explains the communities of women and children on which the female-oriented melodrama is focused, whereas Freudian and Lacanian theories do not. Chodorow argued that one way women fulfill the needs not met by a dyadic relationship is "through the creation and maintenance of important personal relations with other women," relationships generally ignored in male-oriented narratives and, indeed, in male-oriented theories. Chodorow observed that women "tend to have closer personal ties with other women" than men do with other men and that women "spend more time in the company of women than they do with men." She argued that these relationships "are one way of resolving and recreating the mother-daughter bond and are an expression of women's general relational capacities and definition of self in relationship."[37]

The plot of the female-oriented melodrama begins as the community of women and children is invaded by a young and virile male "intruder-redeemer" who identifies the problem—the female protagonist's lack of connectedness to a male—and enables its solution: their coupling and integration into the larger community as the core of a family unit. This narrative feature lends credence to the readings that argue family melodramas operate simply and straightforwardly to reinforce a repressive patriarchy, but a reading that focuses on the needs of the female protagonist—needs that, Chodorow argued, include the completion of a triadic relational model—requires an expansion of theory. The completion of a triadic model does participate in the reproduction of a patriarchal sex-gender system. Indeed, contemporary American patriarchy is precisely the status quo Chodorow described. But unlike Freud and Lacan, Chodorow did not describe the situation as inherent, inevitable, or unchangeable. Neither did she describe the masculine (or the feminine) as normative. She sees an asymmetrically organized sex-gender system that privileges the male and the masculine but that also includes rewards for females, rewards that encourage, even necessitate, female participation in a system that represses women.

The female-oriented melodramatic narratives are clearly organized around the female, but the male is indeed central; he is crucial for the film's conclusion and for the female's entry into the larger social order. However, in the plot of the female-oriented melodrama, unlike that of the social problem film, it is not the male's individual action that precipitates closure. A contradictory combination of female independence (the willingness to confront social norms) and dependence (the need for male companionship) provides a common thread throughout these films. Toward the end, the narrative is ruptured by a marginally believable accident, an unexpected death, or something similar that enables the female protagonist (or, in one case, her surrogate) to act on her desires for the intruder-redeemer, even if she must challenge prevailing social standards, which are shown, of course, to be secondary to the requirement to couple.

In *Magnificent Obsession* (1954), Helen Phillips (Jane Wyman) cannot initially accept the affection of Bob Merrick (Rock Hudson). Beyond the fact that she considers him indirectly responsible for her husband's death, she finds his socioeconomic position unacceptable, and he *is* younger than she. Although wealthy, he doesn't work for his money and squanders his inherited wealth on boats, cars, and pretty women. Helen's friend Nancy (Agnes Moorehead) and her stepdaughter, Joyce (Barbara Rush), show their disdain for Bob more openly than Helen, the perfect lady, ever will. Nancy and Joyce speak for the community; Bob, they believe, is beneath serious consideration. His high-flying, freewheeling life-style had resulted in an injury in a boating accident, which required emergency medical attention in the form of treatment with a special apparatus. The area hospital owned only one of them, and while it was being used on Bob, Helen's husband, a highly respected doctor and the hospital's administrator, also needed it; he died. Bob was hospitalized. Attempting to sneak out of the hospital, he meets Helen, falls in love, and accidentally causes her to be blinded. She flees to the Swiss Alps for medical help. Bob assumes an alias and follows, hoping to fill the void left by her husband's death. While wooing Helen in the Alps, he reveals his identity and his love during a romantic evening of dancing and dining. Helen flees again, worried that people would pity *him* for having a blind wife.

In the follow-up film, *All That Heaven Allows* (1955), Ron Kirby (Rock Hudson, again) proves socially unacceptable as a suitor for Cary Scott (Jane Wyman, again) not only because he is younger but also because he is of a lower social status. Cary's friends in the country club set—even her "best" friend Sara Warren (Agnes Moorehead, again)—think the relationship is almost unspeakably indiscreet. Sara cloaks her criticism with "concern" for Cary's happiness, but basically she cannot see how Cary could be happy outside the upper-middle-class socioeconomic environment. Ron's college education means little, since he works with his hands and is neither wealthy nor upwardly mobile. But in each film, the male figure offers the female protagonist tenderness and the possibility of secure emotional nurturance. This, for the bourgeois widow, is such a basic need that the couple eventually overcomes peer and family pressure. Both the male and the female characters, however, do still maintain close ties to others, creating triadic relationships. The intruder-redeemer is, in this respect, more "feminine" than "masculine."

In *Magnificent Obsession*, Joyce and Helen's friendship has grown into a mother-daughter relationship; Joyce even comments, "You're the only mother I've ever known." But when Helen decides to protect Bob by running away, she leaves without Joyce, refusing to interfere with Joyce's natural development and her growing attachment to a young lawyer. Nevertheless, she takes Nancy with her, dependent not only on Nancy's eyes but also on her friendship. And in *All That Heaven Allows*, Cary maintains and develops outside relationships as she develops her relationship with Ron. Cary and her daughter, Kay, remain close, even as Kay falls in love and begins to pull away from Cary. Cary, of course, allows Kay's coupling. It parallels and highlights her own, as Joyce's does for Helen, but it is Kay's tearful reaction to community pressure that inspires Cary to refuse Ron's proposal. When Kay finally announces her own engagement, Cary realizes her mistake and her impending loneliness. She has, however, maintained female companionship. Sara severely tested her and Cary's relationship with her opposition to Ron, but Cary then developed an attachment to Alida Anderson (Virginia Grey), the wife of Ron's friend Mick (Charles Drake). Female relationships provide support, even in narratives equipped with strong, tender, gentle males, but the final male-female coupling is the ideological payoff. No woman is complete, the rhetoric of these endings pronounces, without a man.

Constance MacKenzie (Lana Turner) in *Peyton Place* (1958) tries desperately to convince herself that she doesn't need a man; she even shuns other adult female companionship, funneling all her affection to her daughter, Alison (Diane Varsi). She rebuffs the advances of Michael Rossi (Lee Philips), routinely at first and then even more vehemently after she hears his liberal ideas about sex education in the public schools. Hurt by a sexual relationship at an early age, Constance reacted by overvaluing both its cause, adultery, and also its result, her daughter, and by turning inward. When the truth is revealed, Constance's prudishness and her strictness with Alison are revealed as pathological. Chodorow explained that "hypersymbiotic" mothers, reacting to a trauma, become extreme in consider-

ing their daughters extensions of themselves. Normally fluid ego boundaries seem to disappear entirely as these mothers refuse to allow their
daughters to separate from them, to individuate. In this narrative, when
Alison learns her mother's secret and realizes that her obsessions are
pathological, she flees. Constance must then face the fact that her attempt
to be socially acceptable through celibacy was further from the "norm"
than her illicit love affair had been. To be included in the social order, she
must recognize her need for a man. She accepts Michael, but the film
doesn't end there. As part of the dramatic courtroom scene that resolves a
subplot, Constance finally admits to herself and to the community that
her narcissistic self-absorption was destructive, and she is rewarded with
the construction of a triad; Alison returns her affections.

Each of these films depicts a protagonist who, initially tempted by
narcissism, rejects her autonomy and enters into the social order not by
becoming a mother but by creating a relational triad. The fourth film,
Picnic (1956), differs in that its protagonist is not a widowed (or abandoned) mother but the mother's eldest daughter. Madge Owens (Kim
Novak), who lost her father at an early age, has become sexually mature,
and her mother, Flo Owens (Betty Field), plots the daughter's entrance
into the adult community. This mother too is hypersymbiotic, even going
so far as to push Madge into a relationship with a rich young man, Alan
Benson (Cliff Robertson), hoping that it will result in a marriage. Madge,
however, isn't sure that this is what she wants. Her mother, fascinated,
quizzes Madge about her sexual activities with Alan. Such mothers, Chodorow explained, use their daughters for their own autoerotic gratifi-
cation.

Madge's intruder-redeemer arrives on a freight train—obviously without financial resources. Hal Carter (William Holden) was Alan's former
fraternity brother, a result not of his socioeconomic status but of his
athletic prowess; now broke, Hal hopes Alan can help him. Their relationship is strained and eventually broken by Hal and Madge's obvious attraction to each other. Over the period of a single day—before, during, and
after a classically small-town Labor Day picnic—Hal and Madge meet, fall
in love, and consider a life together. Her mother tries to prevent her
individuation. Madge, blonde and firstborn, resembles her mother, but
her younger sister, Millie (Susan Strasberg), possibly because she is
darker, tomboyish, and bookish, has been spared hypersymbiotic atten-

tion; she has developed more normally and is a more independent thinker than Madge. Millie encourages Madge's individuation and plots a future for herself as a writer in "the city," the very move Alison makes in *Peyton Place* when she separates from her mother.

Madge's relationship with her mother is strained, pushed to the breaking point. In *Picnic*, as in *Peyton Place*, the daughter responds by breaking away from her mother; the result is rupture rather than a more normal continuity in the mother-daughter relationship. As her mother tries to prevent her individuation, Madge herself can respond only by overreacting. She must establish her separateness in a masculine manner, by rejecting her mother. Alison's separation in *Peyton Place* results in health: her mother grows from it, and they are allowed to reunite. But in *Picnic*, the consequences are unclear: the protagonist must leave her mother and her primary community to move with her man, Hal, into the larger social order.

Not just any man can enable such a move. Each of the male leads is, in a very real sense, an intruder-redeemer, but instead of creating order from chaos and then leaving, as he does in westerns and detective films, the intruder-redeemer in the female-oriented melodrama functions to identify a problem within the existing structure: the incomplete triad of the female protagonist.[38] He solves the problem by mating with her, sometimes removing her from her primary community, and as a result, they are both integrated into the social order. In the masculine genres, the intruder-redeemer enters a disrupted community from the outside, restores order, and then leaves—alone, riding into the proverbial sunset. Of these four leading men, Hal most closely resembles the intruder-redeemer of the masculine genres. He enters a community from the outside, exerts a strongly masculine presence, and exits at the end of the film. But he doesn't leave alone. His opponent, a hypersymbiotic mother, precludes his staying in the community, so the couple moves on to another. In the female-oriented melodramas, this character type does not restructure the community he enters, and he doesn't leave alone. In fact, he usually doesn't leave at all.

Michael Rossi comes from the outside to Peyton Place. He sweeps into town—a fresh breeze of virile, mature masculinity—and becomes principal of the local high school, chosen over a spinster schoolteacher who has been there forever. His ideas are new, and his looks outshine any in town.

The primary impediment to his integration into the community is his marital status; he is single. And Constance is the only real candidate for marriage in all of Peyton Place. She rebuffs his attentions, and he plans to leave, to go on to a larger school (and a community with more available women, we suppose), but when Constance finally goes to him, pledging her love, he decides to remain and they couple, integrated together into the social order. Both Ron in *All That Heaven Allows* and Bob in *Magnificent Obsession* live within the same geographical area as their female protagonists, but their differing socioeconomic status has prevented previous contact. Ron and Bob each intrude into the primary community of the female protagonist to remind her of what she has lost and to show her what she can have—another man. Ron, a Thoreauvian individualist, contrasts vividly with Cary's resolutely upwardly mobile son, Ned (William Reynolds), and her usual escort, Harvey (Conrad Nagel), a bland but pleasant hypochondriac who assures her that she will be secure if they marry. But security isn't all that Cary wants.

When Ron and Cary finally unite, it is in a country millhouse that he has restored for her. He takes her out of her primary community, away from the big, fancy house and the country club friends who have been shown to be superficial, but his primary community is populated by warm and close friends who are happy to see him settle down. Ron is the only one of the four male leads who seems to have a close male friend, but even this relationship is not exactly one of equals. Mick and Ron were army buddies, but Mick always followed Ron, and as his wife, Alida, tells Cary, Ron led Mick away from the rat race of big-time capitalism toward the satisfaction of walking "to his own drummer." Ron's separateness, his refusal to bend to communal expectations, is drawn explicitly. In many ways Ron is like the male heroes of many romance novels; he denies connectedness and simultaneously looks to a dyadic heterosexual relationship but also presents a certain femininity, a gentleness and a potential for nurturance. Describing a major category of the male heroes of romance novels in *Reading the Romance*, Radway drew on Chodorow to describe "the ideal male partner" as one "who is capable of fulfilling both object roles in this woman's triangular inner-object configuration." Radway described this ideal:

His spectacular masculinity underscores his status as her heterosexual lover and confirms the completeness of her rejection of her childlike self. At the same time, his extraordinary tenderness and capacity for gentle nurturance means she does not have to give up the physical part of her mother's attentions because his "soft" sexual attention allows her to return to the passive state of infancy where all of her needs were satisfied and her fears were erased at her mother's breast.[39]

The male intruder-redeemer must, in effect, adopt a triadic relational model, becoming a "sensitive man" and offering the protagonist a relationship in which she can be nurtured. Cary, in *All That Heaven Allows*, clearly longs for such a man, and Ron may be able to make Cary happy with a dyad. He may be the completely satisfactory lover that the conclusion of the film encourages the viewer to believe.

In *Magnificent Obsession*, Bob, whose life-style has set him apart from the more respectable residents of Brightwood, attempts to bridge the social and emotional gap that separates him from Helen, but this only results in the accident that blinds her. He pursues her around the world, but when she flees, he temporarily puts pursuit aside. Years later, he receives a call from her friend Nancy and rushes to her bedside in a small clinic outside Santa Fe. By then, his transformation is complete. Now a hard-working and productive member of the community, a doctor (who performs the delicate operation necessary to return Helen's sight), he provides the dual personality requisite for our hero. He is both the strong individual and the caring man. His reunion with Helen and their subsequent commitment to each other allow them integration into the social order. The abstract desert setting where the film ends leads to the expectation that they will return to a world somewhere between the ones they each initially inhabited. They will be met by Joyce, her husband, and their baby. The film ends with interlocking triads, Joyce now both daughter and mother.

In the widow-oriented version of the genre, the romantic subplots often involve the children of the female protagonist as they too attempt to make the transition into the symbolic and social orders. The happy ending to Joyce's romance prefigures Helen's happy ending, and Joyce's baby now occupies the third place in her triad, freeing Helen to Bob, much as

Kay's engagement frees Cary from the responsibilities of motherhood and reminds her of her potential loneliness, enabling her reunion with Ron. An interesting departure from this pattern occurs in the one daughter-oriented film. The romantic subplot in *Picnic* involves Rosemary Sidney (Rosalind Russell), an "old maid schoolteacher," and her date Howard Bevans (Arthur O'Connell), a "bachelor storekeeper." Rosemary yearns for the entry into the social order that has eluded her for many years and viciously lashes out at Hal, jealous of the opportunity he provides for Madge. She sees Howard as her last chance and desperately grabs for him, bewildering Howard, who has been quite content as a bachelor storekeeper. The frantic tone to this romance vividly depicts a woman's need to have a man in order to "fit" into the patriarchal bourgeois social order. Their happy ending is accidental, as are most in female-oriented family melodramas.

Most of the women's films of the 1930s and 1940s ended tragically, but in the 1950s, the (eventually unsuccessful) return to an emphasis on woman as wife-companion, exemplified by the suburban housewife, required a different ending, a "happy ending" that provided the female protagonist with a male companion, a husband, a strong and capable patriarch to whom she could submit. But often, this required outrageous plot manipulation. Ron's fall from a cliff at the end of *All That Heaven Allows* results in a concussion; overwhelmed by love, Cary rushes to him, and the passive Cary, previously unable to act against the social pressure of her family and friends, is now able to have her man anyway. A greater force has intervened, as it does when Nancy acts against Helen's wishes and calls Bob to Helen's bedside in *Magnificent Obsession*. In *Peyton Place*, a dramatic rape-murder subplot culminates in the messy public trial that provokes Constance's awakening and her public confession of parental inadequacy. The beautiful Madge in *Picnic*, always her mother's pawn, breaks away from her family, her community, and her future as Mrs. Alan Benson in a barely more credible move to embrace the romantic ideal and to reject the practical. Madge has no salable skills and little intellect; on her own, she would almost certainly be confined to positions like the sales job she already has at the local five-and-dime. Yet she risks economic and social security to follow a man she met the day before. Indeed, the narrative itself calls attention to the rupture as it gives us the emotionally satisfying but illogical conclusion to what was previously presented as an impossible situation, and action is closed before repercussions can occur. But this satisfaction is temporary. The existence of sequels and indeed the existence of the genre itself indicate our society's ongoing concern and fascination with the contradictions within our ideological reproductive cycle. And when we look beyond these female-oriented films to other, male-oriented family melodramas, we find a rather different approach to the problem.

Think, for instance, of Georgie in *The Country Girl*, Lola in *Come Back, Little Sheba*, and both Stella and Blanche in *A Streetcar Named Desire*. They are isolated from other women and are denied motherhood. Chodorow's theory fails to account for these narratives. When women do come together in male-oriented family melodramas, their usually temporary unions result in antagonism or competition. In *God's Little Acre*, *Some Came Running*, and *The Man with the Golden Arm*, the strong females are in competition for the same man. In *Cat on a Hot Tin Roof*, Big Mama only criticizes her daughter-in-law Maggie for her childlessness and offers no sympathy. In *A Streetcar Named Desire*, Blanche appears to want to exploit her sister, and although Stella seems sympathetic to Blanche, her loyalty is to her husband, Stanley, who is driven wild by their reunion and blocks any possible friendship. The male organizing sensibility in these films excludes female friendships, and women are defined only in relation to men. The films, produced—by men, of course—for a "general" or male-dominated audience and centered on a male character, present a portrait of the family romance quite different from the one presented in the female-oriented melodramas; the picture in male-dominated melodramas is closer to the traditional Freudian or Lacanian privileging of the masculine, where women are defined as *not* male, as the radically Other.

Chodorow's theory of identity development illuminates elements within the female-oriented films, but her theory does not account for significant differences across even the melodramatic genres. No psychoanalytic theory does, not even Chodorow's, and without an expanded psychoanalytic model, we cannot understand the differences among the genres. For instance, even though their endings privilege the couple and emphasize the importance of the male, the female-oriented melodramas present female characters defined not simply in relation to men but in relation to other women as well. They also define men differently, as more nurturing and less individualistic than in other forms. The family romance plays itself out in more than one way—ways that can be seen and recounted

from radically different points of view. Psychoanalytic theories that privilege the masculine are too limited to begin to examine even the range of
family romance(s). To understand the role of film texts in a hegemonic
ideological process, we must be able to recognize struggle, to see resistance (where it exists) as well as dominance, and we must be able to
recognize the exceptional. The exceptional is evident not just at the level
of subject matter and theme; it is also evident in the cinematic enunciative
patterns that govern narrative presentation and guide interpretation.

Enunciative Patterns: Seeing and Being Seen

Christian Metz developed a theoretical framework for analyzing
cinematic systems of signification, assuming a homologous relationship
between verbal and filmic communication.[40] Working from this framework, the film analyst Raymond Bellour, in the late 1960s and early
1970s, incorporated what Bertrand Augst called "semio-psychoanalysis"
into his methodology for textual analysis, pushing beyond earlier studies
of cinematic enunciation inspired by linguistic and literary models. Bellour concentrated on a specific enunciative function, "the look" or "the
gaze," in his effort to examine the way in which cinematic discourse involves the spectator while simultaneously concealing the traces of its enunciation.[41] This emphasis on "the gaze" ties his method to Lacan's psychoanalytic theory; the initial realization of the separation of the self and
the other comes at the "mirror stage" when the child looks into a mirror
and recognizes himself as a distinct and signifiable entity. Lacan argued
that this subjectivity is later organized through the intervention of the
phallus, enabling entry into the symbolic. The structure privileges "the
gaze" and also—through Lacan's emphasis on the threat of castration—
determines its content, woman, who is said to represent lack and castration.[42]

In the cinema, however, the gaze cannot be entirely identified with
Lacan's mirror stage; it is more complex. Jean-Louis Baudry suggested
that the spectator identifies at the level of the camera itself, but Metz
qualified this, arguing that, like the child who sees his own image in a
mirror, what the spectator sees as an "other who turn into *I*, is, after all,
the image of his own body; so it is still an identification (and not merely a

secondary one) with something *seen*."[43] Simultaneously, the spectator identifies with the seeing camera and with the characters on the screen. Quite frequently, these seem to converge, as the camera becomes complicit with a character's point of view. The optical point-of-view shot, at the eye level of the character, effects a complicity between the spectator's point of view and that of the "seeing" character. In the popular and conventional "shot/reverse shot" (involving two characters), the character for whom the spectator has "stood in," and whom the spectator has seen *with*, becomes the object of the look of the second character, providing the image with which to identify (and the process begins anew as the spectator "sees" with the second character), effectively and unnoticeably suturing the spectator into the film and its language.[44]

Bellour's pioneering work on Hitchcock's films provided the model for much of the subsequent analysis of the representation of gender in narrative film. His analyses are complex, and his methodology is implicit, requiring an extremely attentive reader, but the results are impressive. He details the pattern and interaction of textual codes, shot by shot, explicating the intricate composition of cinematic sequences and revealing the nature of cinematic enunciation (in, primarily, mainstream Hollywood films). His analysis of a segment from *The Birds* is the most succinct and accessible. Bellour focuses on the segment that chronicles Melanie Daniels's initial trip to the Brenner household. His shot-by-shot analysis follows three filmic codes that compose the segment: framing (close/distant), camera movement (still/moving), and point of view (seeing/seen). He shows the tension between symmetry and asymmetry in the codes that advance the narrative and shows how they are fundamentally tied to the representation of sexual difference. His analysis of point of view, the most important of these three codes, traces the movement of its control. Initially, Melanie is the seeing agent, and the spectator's attention shifts between Melanie—seeing—and what she sees. At the point when she is finally seen by Mitch Brenner, Melanie's control is lost, she becomes the seen object, and she is symbolically punished for her aggression by the first attack of the killer birds.[45]

This, Bellour argued, is typical of the "classic realist text." Hitchcock's perverse textual organization is only an extreme of a highly conventionalized system and, as such, Bellour believes, is exemplary of the structured voyeurism that participates in and supports an inequitable symbolic and social system. The argument for the normalcy of the male gaze (referring both to the gaze of the characters and that of the spectator) and the inevitability of punishment for any female brazen enough to assume the agency of the gaze has become central to feminist film analysis. In 1975, in "Visual Pleasure and Narrative Cinema," Laura Mulvey observed, "Traditionally, the woman displayed has functioned on two levels: as erotic object for the characters within the screen story, and as erotic object for the spectator within the auditorium, with a shifting tension between the looks on either side of the screen."[46] Bellour concurred, describing American cinema's dependency "on a system of representations in which the woman occupies a central place only to the extent that it's a place assigned to her by the logic of masculine desire."[47]

In 1980, with an appendix to *Genre* entitled "Genre and Sexuality," Stephen Neale objected, pointing out that the "the direct object of scopophilic desire (the desire to take pleasure in seeing) need not necessarily be female—it can be and often is, male." He qualified the stance by pointing out that "the two objects of the look, male and female, tend to be inscribed and represented differently in this respect." In most cases, they differ, for instance, in the "degree of eroticism with which they are explicitly marked," with the look at the male tending to be de-eroticized and rendered "innocent" as he turns into

> a relay point in the looking structure, the point at which the looks are turned toward their ultimate destination, the woman. The erotic component in the look thus tends constantly to be displaced away from the male and on to the female—on to that which is already ideologically defined and accepted as an unproblematic sexual object. In this respect patriarchy does not so much institute the woman as sexual object in the cinema as offer the female body as an accepted and acceptable image on to which to deflect the erotic component in the scopophilic drive.[48]

However, even this is generically determined. In melodrama, Neale finds "an eroticization of the body of the male."[49] His observation, as we will see, is accurate. Representation of the human body is specified generically, and the male as well as the female can serve as the object of scopophilic desire. For instance, in the western, a "male" genre, the body of the (male)

hero functions as the erotic object, situated dynamically, oscillating between the natural landscape and the civilized town or homestead. Recognizing its dominance, Neale denied an exclusive attention to the male in
the western. He also pointed out that the male characters in the "female"
genres—melodramas and musicals—are feminized. They are allowed to
acquire attributes usually attributed to (reserved for?) the female. Here
they too can be depicted suffering and waiting; they too can be the objects
of erotic desire. The spectator's relation to the film text is manipulated
differently from genre to genre, but this important point seems to have
slipped by many feminists, who remain fascinated with the way cinematic
enunciative patterns victimize the feminine.

In 1981, Laura Mulvey published some "afterthoughts" on her 1975
manifesto. Standing by the arguments she made earlier, she added to them
in an attempt to account for the double problem of the female spectator
and the female character who may occupy the center of a text. In her
analysis, Mulvey followed a Freudian analysis of female development, tracing the female through an early masculine phase and a later phase in
which femininity represses masculinity. Women's involvement in popular
narratives, she argued, depends on transsexual identification, on the acti-
vation of the fantasy of action available only to the masculine, and on a
repression of their "correct" femininity.[50] Her position here is problematic in that it reasserts Freud's assumption that the male and the masculine
constitute the norm whereas the female and the feminine are aberrant. In
addition, it maintains a deterministic view of cinematic enunciation.

With *Women's Pictures* in 1982, Annette Kuhn did little more than
explicate the party line. The limits to this approach are intimately bound
up with its advances. Premised on the assumption that meanings are actually produced in and through the film text itself, this approach made it
clear that the meanings of film texts are not transparent. Kuhn explained
that this method is also founded on the assumption "that part of the work
of ideology is to conceal its own operation, and that this operation can
have its own independent effects within cultural productions." Understanding film texts, then, requires deconstructing them (breaking them
down) and reconstructing them in such a way that "what was previously
hidden is now brought to light." The primary advance this affords the
analysis of gender representation is that, as Kuhn explained, it "would aim

to expose the processes whereby woman is constructed as a myth, as a fixed signifier, within textual practices of meaning production."[51] This fixity, on the other hand, is itself problematic.

Basic to this shortcoming is the rigidity of the notion of the "classic realist text." First, this notion obscures differences in cinematic enunciative practices, ignoring the possibility that such practices may be, to an extent, generically and historically specific. Second, it assumes that the text governs its own reading, that the spectators are unconscious puppets centered by the cinematic apparatus and the film text. As Dave Morley has pointed out, "This runs counter to two of the most important advances previously established by structural linguistics: the essentially polysemic nature of signs and sign-based discourses, and the interrogative/expansive nature of all readings."[52] Although a text may—and most frequently does—privilege certain readings, it does not control its own readings by infallibly reproducing the primary psychoanalytic processes, as Bellour and the proponents of what Morley calls "screen theory" would have us believe. Indeed, filmic codes can be used not only to support or to challenge dominant ideological positions but also to play contradictions against each other.

E. Ann Kaplan published *Women and Film* in 1983 and, with it, resisted the notion that films can and do work in significantly different ways. Kaplan believes that films "center" their spectators and that they do it in such a way as to limit access to a "masculine" spectator. Articulating the mainstream feminist film studies position, Kaplan argued, "In Hollywood films, then, women are ultimately refused a voice, a discourse, and their desire is subjected to male desire." Directly taking on the basic question "Is the gaze male?," Kaplan gave the sophisticated version of a resounding "Yes!" by stating: "The gaze is not necessarily male (literally), but to own and activate the gaze, given our language and the structure of the unconscious, is to be in the 'masculine' position. It is this persistent presentation of the masculine position that feminist film critics have demonstrated in their analysis of Hollywood films."[53]

She argued, additionally, that although women can receive and return a gaze, only the male gaze "carries with it the power of action and of possession" and that "all dominant images are basically male constructs." As she searches for a nonsignificatory locus to challenge the discourses she sees necessarily excluding women (which she finds in Motherhood, with a capital *M*), she precludes the possibility that any sort of real feminine discourse might have existed in mainstream American cinema. Although Kaplan ends *Women and Film* urging us to transcend patterns of opposition that include "male/female," "dominant/submissive," and "active/passive," she follows Julia Kristeva in arguing that "it is impossible to know what the 'feminine' might be, outside of male constructs."[54] It is not possible, using this theoretical framework, to recognize in Hollywood films the discourses that speak of and to women, and not only does Kaplan's theory block such vision, but also her choice of films (as we might suspect) supports her conclusion.

Begging a limitation of space, Kaplan included analyses of only three classic Hollywood films, all from the 1930s and 1940s, none from the 1950s. Since she wanted to explicate specific filmic patterns, such as the manipulation of "the gaze," she examined only films in which the codes operate as she predicted they would. The films of the 1950s, she argued, "are in a sense an anomaly, a decade unto themselves." Although they "show earlier codes straining at the seams," in them fear of sexuality "overflows."[55] This is precisely why their omission calls into question the adequacy of Kaplan's assumptions concerning the nature of cinematic enunciative practices. Indeed, a pattern does appear to exist; indeed, the gaze has been used most frequently to objectify the representation of the female, but a close analysis of scenes from two female-oriented melodramas from the 1950s (which compose the next section of this chapter) will show that universalizing this finding is inadequate. It leads to the belief that cinematic enunciative practices are essentially gender-bound when in fact this is untrue. Their uses have historically been dominated by masculine discourses and have historically operated to repress the feminine (and the female), but such use has not been successful in eliminating feminine discourses in even the most pervasive categories of mass-produced, mass-consumed texts. In actuality, mechanisms such as the gaze have been used in ways unaccounted for by that version of film theory and analysis based in semio-psychoanalysis, which was initiated in France and England in the early 1970s and which came to pervade American film studies by the late 1970s.

By 1984, when Mary Ann Doane, Patricia Mellencamp, and Linda Williams published the state-of-the-art anthology *Re-vision*, they included articles positing the female spectator and acknowledging (at least on a theoretical level) the variety of discourses that intersect women's existence. Much feminist film theory and analysis had pushed beyond the sort of textual analysis that assumes that the text can and does, inevitably and negatively, ideologically center its spectator(s), but there remained (and still remains) a distressing tendency to assume that the enunciative practices of mainstream cinema operate monolithically and repressively in their maintenance of patriarchy. Regrettably, *Re-vision* still contained remnants of this position. The editors introduced the essays by noting that "they provide a number of different entries and suggestions for breaking the hold of a monolithic construction of sexual difference,"[56] but the first few sentences of Kaja Silverman's contribution indicated just how strong the notions of the classic realist text and the gaze as male still held:

> It is by now axiomatic that the female subject is the object rather than the subject of the gaze in mainstream narrative cinema. She is excluded from authoritative vision not only at the level of the enunciation, but at that of the fiction. At the same time she functions as an organizing spectacle, as the lack which structures the symbolic order and sustains the relay of male glances.
>
> It is equally axiomatic that the female subject as she has been constructed by the Hollywood cinema is denied any active role in discourse.[57]

Even though this position and the analyses based on it are both formidable and enlightening, there are significant limitations in the work done in this mode. Two of the editors, however, contributed essays that made some headway in breaking through the restrictions that feminist film theory, so new, had already imposed on itself (axiomatic!).

In her essay, Mary Ann Doane focused on the "women's films" of the 1940s. Agreeing with Claire Johnston that we cannot simply rediscover women's history and insert it unproblematically into a traditionally written history, Doane argued that "to retrieve and reestablish women as agents of history is to construct one's discourse upon a denial of the more problematic and complex aspects of subjectivity and sexuality." Working through a psychoanalytically informed analysis—and limited thereby—Doane contributed two key innovations. She attempted to address, as psychoanalytic criticism had not generally done, the sexual specificity of the intended spectator, and she examined the influence of generic conventions on enunciative practices. She traced three distinct but related registers as they are "characterized by a certain violence which is coincident with the attribution of the gaze to the female." She found that in the women's films, space is deployed, the uncanny (the strange) is activated, the body of the female is de-eroticized by the medical gaze and medical speech, and female sexuality is displaced or replaced—all in the service of immobilizing what Hollywood conceived of as a female audience. In these women's films Doane does indeed see a female spectator, but in this genre she finds "the continual inability to sustain a coherent representation of female subjectivity in the context of phallocentric discursive mechanisms" and a denial to women of "the space of a reading."[58]

In another essay in *Re-vision*, Linda Williams addressed the question of gender representation in the horror film. She assumed, from a Lacanian view, the female as a biological freak (lacking, castrated) in the gaze of the male, whose "horror" must be defused. In her biological difference, the female, like the monster, possesses a power in difference. Both the female and the monster, Williams suggested, threaten the male through their nonphallic sexuality. Both the male and the female characters in horror films maintain the agency of the gaze, but their gazes are significantly different. The male's gaze is conventional: punishing the object through a sadistic voyeurism or fetishistically overvaluing it, either way mastering its threat. The female does this and more; in her gaze, the female character recognizes in the monster a freakishness similar to her own and sympathetically identifies. Thus, Williams posited, "in the classic horror film, the woman's look at the monster offers at least a potentially subversive recognition of the power and potency of a non-phallic sexuality."[59] However, because this threatens the male, the female is punished violently. And Williams's analysis did not stop here. She traced a change in the horror film genre and with it a change in the use of the female gaze in horror films.

With the emergence of the "progressive" horror film, which exposes the perverse structure of seeing that operates in the genre by making the structure explicit, has come "the deepening of the woman's responsibility for the horror that endangers her. . . . the identification between woman and monster becomes greater, the nature of the identification is more negatively charged, and women are increasingly punished for the threatening nature of their sexuality." Increasingly, the woman's point-of-view shots are replaced by shots from the point of view of the unseen, killing monster, and the female victim's mutilated body "is the only visible horror." The sort of sympathy engendered by enunciative practices that allow identification with the female victim is being eradicated. That potential subversion available through the female look in earlier, classic horror films is replaced by repressive titillation. Williams concluded that although "the horror film may be a rare example of a genre that permits the expression of woman's sexual potency and desire, and which associates this desire with the autonomous act of looking," most recent horror films operate "only to punish her for this very act, only to demonstrate how monstrous female desire can be."[60] Williams's work here made two significant advances. She examined the gaze of the female character and the way this potentially influences the spectator's reading of a horror film, though she made no argument concerning the sexual specificity of the spectator. Second, she traced the use of the gaze as it changes through the evolution of a genre, not assuming that genres are static.

In the fall 1984 issue of *Cinema Journal*, Williams published an article that is even more interesting—both because of the theoretical and critical work it represents and because of the furor it incited. In the wake of Williams's article, the "Dialogue" section of *Cinema Journal* became a site for struggle among feminist film theorists, a conflict ultimately represented by an interchange between E. Ann Kaplan, who held firmly to a Lacanian position, and feminist critics who challenged her position, seeking to open up feminist film studies. The struggle took place in the form of competing readings of *Stella Dallas*. Summarizing several of the rounds will help to situate the reading I present in the last part of this chapter. In the initial article, " 'Something Else Besides a Mother': *Stella Dallas* and the Maternal Melodrama," Williams pointed out that "a female 'look' " is central to the film and argued that its "mere existence" makes the film worthy of special scrutiny. Williams referred to Christine Gledhill's assertion that discourses of concern to women are inscribed differently in texts consumed by primarily female audiences, and she argued that what we, as feminists, need is "a theoretical and practical recognition of the ways in which women actually do speak to each other within patriarchy." Maternal melodramas "have reading positions inscribed into their texts that demand a female reading competence," a competence derived from the "social fact of female mothering." This, she maintained, is the case with the

1937 film version of *Stella Dallas*, which was directed by King Vidor and starred Barbara Stanwyck. Williams drew on Chodorow's analysis of the connectedness of the mother-daughter bond to explain "the multiple and continuous female identity capable of fluidly shifting" between identities of mother and daughter, and she pulled from Luce Irigaray, Adrienne Rich, Julia Kristeva, and Jane Gallop to describe how women's ability to recognize themselves in the bodies of other women allows them to understand just what it is that melodrama does: speak beyond the capacities of representation.[61]

Williams described the film, *Stella Dallas*, as characterized by multiple and conflicting points of view that act to prevent identification with a single character. The ending is crucial for Williams's argument: the audience looks at Stella, who is looking through a window, watching as her daughter gets married. Stella, failed but triumphant, is locked out of the upper-class world in which her daughter is getting married. Stella's overriding ambition had, in fact, gained her daughter's entry into this world, even though she knew that she herself would never fit in. During the film, point of view does not remain stable but shifts back and forth between Stella's and other characters' points of view. E. Ann Kaplan had suggested that this technique undercuts and, thus, punishes Stella, but Williams countered this with the argument that the female spectator would tend to view the ending as she would the rest of the film, from a variety of points of view. According to Williams, Stella presents "the heroic attempt to live out the contradiction" between being a woman and being a mother. Indeed, she argued, "the female spectator tends to identify with contradiction itself."[62] Female spectator positions are, according to Williams, inscribed in the text. The socially constructed female—formed, according to Chodorow, through a process of double identification—constantly juggles identification, and the divided spectator identifies with the woman whose very triumph is in her own victimization.

Kaplan was the first to respond to Williams, in the very next issue of *Cinema Journal* (Winter 1985). She insisted that Williams was correct that Kaplan assumed a "monolithic position for the female spectator" but incorrect in her claim that the film does not insist on a closure of the contradictions it raises. Additionally, Kaplan distinguished between the "historical spectator" and the "hypothetical spectator" inscribed by the text, through the film's strategies, and she argued that *her* description was of the latter, indicating that her description of the film was superior. She also took issue with Williams's theorizing on the socially constructed differences between male and female spectators, taking the highly formalist position that the female spectator "cannot simply identify differently than the male spectator in relation to the camera's look." She added, "I do not see how the individual spectator can prevent being constructed by the film's mechanisms."[63] Obviously, Kaplan and Williams saw the same film, and their descriptions are not contradictory, but what they made of what they saw distinctly differed. They are themselves proof that historical spectators bring with them discourses that, regardless of the film's construction, influence their interpretation.

Next on the scene were Patrice Petro and Carol Flinn, who in the Fall 1985 issue responded to both Williams and Kaplan with what amounted to a critique of Kaplan's Winter 1985 entry. Petro and Flinn initiated their salvo with the observation that Kaplan's stress on a monolithic female spectator position operated to close down the possibilities for feminist film criticism, whereas Williams's essay operated to open up possibilities. They headed for the jugular by pointing out the chief contradiction in Kaplan's argument: she implied that socially constructed readers actively *produce* meanings while, on the other hand, she maintained that films *dictate* their own readings. They note Kaplan's adherence to the latter position and her implication that resistant readings can be made only by spectators familiar with feminist theory.

They correctly explained Kaplan's and Williams's differing positions in terms of differing basic assumptions. Williams seeks out moments when a female voice is heard in the text, assuming that that is indeed possible, whereas Kaplan holds firm to her position that this is impossible. Petro and Flinn located the difficulties in Kaplan's position by pointing to her location of the text within the novelistic tradition as a realist text, essentially Oedipal in its narrative logic and centered in its mode of address. Williams, they contended, had more accurately placed *Stella Dallas* as a maternal melodrama, examining its melodramatic features—its style, its polarization of opposites.[64] The film, they argued, simply cannot be understood in terms of traditional realist categories.

Kaplan replied once more, in the same (Fall 1985) issue of *Cinema Journal*. Her constant access to the "Dialogue" forum tends to privilege her position, but her opponents are persuasive. In this entry, she began with an attempt to clarify the categories she had laid out in her previous entry; she explained the two kinds of subject positions: "that which the film offers" (which she had called the "hypothetical" position) and "that which the subject brings" (a socially constructed spectator). She maintained, "There is a delicate negotiation in any film reception between the hypothetical spectator offered by the film and the reading formations of the viewer." She was apparently still missing—or, by not explicitly acknowledging, was dismissing—Williams's original point that there are female spectator positions inscribed in, and perhaps even privileged by, the film text *Stella Dallas* and that the social and the psychoanalytic are *not* two different phenomena. Kaplan maintained her position that a Hollywood film is incapable of critiquing the dominant modes of representation, ignoring the argument that those dominant modes are themselves not monolithic, that they can speak for, with, and to women, and that this is especially the case among texts produced for a predominantly female audience. Kaplan obviously saw little variation, even generic variation, in the enunciative patterns of Hollywood films; they are monolithically patriarchal. She did acknowledge that Hollywood films may express contradiction and even resistance—but only narratively or thematically, never through variations in enunciative practices. She wrote, "It cannot question the *terms of woman's imaging*."[65]

I seek to challenge precisely this rigid position with the readings I present later in this chapter. Whereas Kaplan claimed that *Stella Dallas* is ultimately patriarchal because it fails to open up an "alternate 'feminist' space," I argue that she is missing the point. It is not at all likely that mainstream texts will open up a *feminist* space, but it *is* true that they open up for the expression of *feminine voices*. Kaplan would obviously reply with the argument that the feminine is determined by patriarchy, and to an extent, this argument is correct. Marginalized groups are partially—*but not entirely*—determined by the relevant cultural center. They—or *we*— must take responsibility for our participation in the signifying systems in which we participate. As I argued earlier, we must be able to see resistance where it exists.

One more episode in this ongoing "dialogue" merits discussion. In the Summer 1986 issue of *Cinema Journal*, Christine Gledhill offered some pertinent thoughts on melodrama and *Stella Dallas*; Kaplan, predictably, responded, in the same issue. It is here that Gledhill described the three major modes of modern cultural perception/expression—realism, melodrama, and modernism. She discussed melodrama's peculiar "dual ability" to see how things are and how they aren't and melodrama's simultaneous insistence on the realities of everyday life and its insistence on attempting to communicate that which is beyond the power of language. Melodrama, she argued, does not step outside patriarchy but "works from the inside out." Gledhill also addressed the feminist fetishizing of the gaze, arguing that there is far more to melodrama than simply point-of-view shots. Additionally, she argued that feminists have tended to reduce the complexity of the gaze: "A look does not of itself produce meaning nor can the 'look' of the camera fix meaning." Indeed, as we will see, the gaze can mean more than one thing, and the gaze can be associated with a strongly feminine perspective.[66]

In her reply, Kaplan pulled out the feminist bogeyman—essentialism, the dread danger of considering anything essentially female or male. She charged that, when Gledhill called attention to the misogyny of male critics who conflate women's concerns with bourgeois ideology, she ran the risk of essentialism; Kaplan questioned the wisdom of valorizing women's socially constructed sphere. In Gledhill's defense, it is important to note that, in the version of "Developments in Feminist Film Criticism" included in Re-vision, she argued that constantly bringing the sexual difference implied in the figure of woman back to the patriarchal same—as Kaplan does—is an essentialist approach; she concluded with a long discussion of the essentialism dilemma. Referring to the unofficial women's discourses with which they negotiate dominant institutions and their contradictions, Gledhill argued: "To reference this social effectivity when such discourses provide material for fiction—as in the woman's film, melodrama, or soap opera for instance—is not a matter of playing off the fiction against some putative 'objective reality' or 'pure feminine discourse.' Rather it gives more weight to the 'reality' of the production of discourses."[67]

It is, in fact, Kaplan and not Gledhill who continues to create and recreate an essentialist discourse, arguing in this particular entry in the *Cinema Journal* "dialogue" that she views "all popular and mainstream texts as taking shape within the patriarchal feminine and as therefore unable to sweep aside the existing language order to give woman any kind of subjectivity."[68] If such an essentializing claim is correct, then changing such mainstream cultural texts would be of little value—from this claim, a logical conclusion, but not one I think we can take seriously. What we must take seriously is recuperating those feminine voices structured into mainstream texts and understanding how these texts have participated not just in the reinforcement of patriarchy but also in the maintenance of alternative ways of seeing and living in our world as they provide the pleasures of looking *with* women. I present the following analyses of the enunciative strategies used in segments from *Picnic* and *All That Heaven Allows* as a step in that direction.

Picnic, clearly organized around the female protagonist, Madge (Kim Novak), begins with the arrival of her intruder-redeemer, Hal (William Holden). Quickly, he is established as virile but destitute—and painfully conscious of his lack of socioeconomic status. An aerial shot of a train opens the film, followed by shots of a train yard and grain elevators, reminiscent of Italian neorealism; this places Hal in the Midwest. Humiliated by the conductor's derisive comments, he climbs from a freight train. He washes up in a nearby river, seminude, and his erotic potential becomes obvious. He walks up to a two-story, white frame house and shyly asks for work, and his poverty is confirmed. Mrs. Potts (Verna Felton), with white hair and a petite but dowdy figure, tells him that nobody works *today* (Labor Day), and he seems desperate. Mrs. Potts, archetypically grandmotherly, chides Hal, "You stop being embarrassed and come in and have some breakfast." As she feeds him, attention shifts to the house next door, where the other members of this female community are introduced, and two "seeing/seen" exchanges—on which the rest of the film is based—are set up.

Madge is introduced in contrast to her tomboyish younger sister, Millie, who is sitting, leaning against the exterior of the house, reading a book and sneaking a cigarette (figure 4-1). Madge, drying her hair, leans out of a second-story window over Millie and drips water on her sister's book (figure 4-2). Flo Owens (Betty Field), their mother, enters, and Millie quickly hides her cigarette. Madge mentions cutting her hair, and Mrs. Owens is shocked. Madge's role as erotic object—even for the other female characters—is established. Rosemary Sidney (Rosalind Russell) enters the scene wearing rollers in her hair and a housecoat and rubbing cold cream into her face, hardly an attractive figure. At this point Hal, shirtless again, begins to work in Mrs. Potts's backyard; the nurturing Mrs. Potts

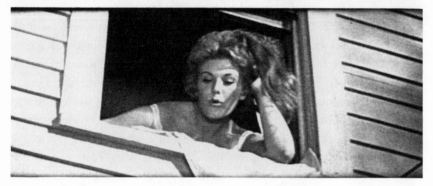

has volunteered to wash the shirt, calming Hal's fears that his seminudity will offend someone. After all, she notes, he is a *man*. Suddenly, a medium close-up of Hal standing behind the barrel he's burning trash in makes him appear totally naked; not a stitch of clothing shows. Cut to Rosemary, strolling in the Owens's backyard, who sees him and practically gawks (figure 4-3). Cut to Hal, who sees her, looks slightly embarrassed, then nods and smiles (figure 4-4). Cut back to Rosemary, upset that she was caught in her voyeurism (figure 4-5). She rebuffs him with an unpleasant facial expression and remarks: "Workin' over there naked as an Indian. Who does he think is interested?" *Her* obvious interest in his physique and her practically unchecked voyeuristic sexual desire combine with her physical unattractiveness to set up the possibility of jealousy.

The second seeing/seen sequence follows directly. Madge emerges from the Owens's house wearing a low-cut dress that, cinched in at the waist and flowing into a full skirt, accentuates her figure. As she arranges her hair, she immediately becomes the center of attention for Millie, the pa-

4.3

4.4

4.5

perboy Bomber, and the camera (figure 4-6). Having clearly dismissed
Millie by commenting on her masculinity, Bomber chases Madge around
the yard, until a deep voice orders, "Be on your way, lover boy," and Hal
strides into the frame, still shirtless (figure 4-7). Bomber, intimidated,
leaves. Repeated medium close-ups of Madge establish her as Hal's erotic
equal, and an exchange of point-of-view shots builds sexual tension,
heightened by their timid salutations and her averted gaze. Both are si-

4.6

4.7

4.8

multaneously agents and objects of seeing (figures 4-8 and 4-9). The camera has quickly established both as erotic objects for its—and the spectator's—gaze. Hal carries on a conversation with Millie, as he bounces a basketball, until Mrs. Owens comes outside and interrupts.

Cutting between Hal and Mrs. Owens heightens Hal's sexuality even further (figures 4-10 and 4-11); Mrs. Owens's sexuality is implied, both

4.9

4.10

4.11

become embarrassed, and Hal turns to leave, shooting a basket and trotting toward Mrs. Potts's backyard (figures 4-12 and 4-13). Mrs. Owens tries to herd her daughters inside, away from the intruder who obviously threatens her while attracting Madge. But this attempt to separate Hal and Madge is frustrated as Mrs. Potts enters and (naively?) calls Madge over to introduce her to Hal, as a friend of Madge's boyfriend, Alan

4.12

4.13

4.14

(figure 4-14). Once again, a series of medium close-up shots and reverse shots between Hal and Madge builds tension, as Mrs. Potts discreetly retreats. Madge loosens her hair as she approaches and coyly brushes it while they talk. They make inconsequential conversation as they are both shown simultaneously seeing and being seen, and the medium close-ups become close-ups, intensifying their involvement (figures 4-15 and 4-16).

Mrs. Owens again intervenes, calling Madge home. Hal realizes the

4.15

4.16

4.17

mother's disapproval. Madge presses against the fence post, fondling one of a number of phallic symbols scattered throughout the film. She gives Hal a desirous look, then turns and walks away (figure 4-17). Hal watches her retreat, leading the spectators to assume that perhaps his point of view will be privileged (figure 4-18). But as Madge opens the screen door at the back of the house, *she* turns to watch *him* (figure 4-19). A long shot through the screen door shows Hal striding through Mrs. Potts's yard

4.18

4.19

(figure 4-20). The final shot of the sequence shows Madge watching Hal and finally closing the door to end the sequence (figure 4-21).

Hal and Madge have been established as the film's primary objects, and the exchange of point-of-view shots has established them as equals. Madge's control of the final gaze is maintained throughout the film. Unlike *The Birds*, in which punishment is meted out to Melanie for daring to control the look, this film consistently returns control to the female, and although Madge is frequently the center of attention, she is also frequently the agent of the gaze and, as such, the positive and unabashed expression of feminine desire. Feminine control and desire are established similarly in *All That Heaven Allows*. This film also begins with an aerial shot. The camera pauses on a steeple against a clear, blue sky; the steeple clock reads noon. As the credits roll, the camera pans down and across a small town. The streets are quiet but active. An occasional car passes, and a few people stroll along the tidy sidewalks. The camera settles on a woman pushing a baby carriage and follows her progress, finally moving beyond her. It settles on a curve in the street, and the woman walks back into the

4.20

4.21

frame as a blue station wagon—the hallmark of the suburban matron—enters the frame. The first cut moves to a closer shot of the station wagon as the car pulls to a stop. The second cut gives a low-angle shot of Agnes Moorehead getting out of the station wagon, and the camera follows her movement as she crosses a well-tended yard, glances at a man trimming trees (figure 4-22), and approaches a two-story, white frame house.

In the fourth shot, the camera dollies in slowly on Jane Wyman as she exits from the house carrying a tray of dishes to the patio table, set for lunch and complete with flowers. Wyman wears a tailored gray suit; Moorehead is in blue. Both wear calm, cool colors for a quiet and conservative life-style. The camera pans left to become a two-shot of the women conversing. The spectators learn that Wyman is playing the widow Cary Scott, and Moorehead is playing her friend Sara, who can't stay for lunch. Eye-level, the camera pans with them as they walk left, hand in hand, to Sara's station wagon (figure 4-23), and the camera stops on the male figure as he walks away, carrying a ladder to his wood-paneled station wagon (figure 4-24). He looks toward the women at about the same time

4.22

4.23

that Cary explains to Sara that she's not a "club woman"—"Sometimes I wonder, but it's just not for me." What *is*? This man? What is the significance of his gaze? Cary is now established as part of the country club set, but not an active part. She is somehow different from its other inhabitants.

4.24

Cut to a two-shot, panning with the two women who are walking close together, as close female friends can. As they reach the station wagon, Sara mentions that she has to find a date for the evening for her husband's business associate. At the word *date*, the first shot/reverse-shot sequence begins. An over-the-shoulder close-up of Cary, from Sara's point of view, shows Cary's undisguised interest in the prospect (figure 4-25). The high-angle reverse shot, from Cary's point of view, shows Sara as she rejects Cary's implicit suggestion and explains the ways of the world (figure 4-26): "Oh, look, now, he's forty, which means he'll consider any female over eighteen too old. We might as well face it. I've got to be off. Oh, how about joining us at the club tonight, for dinner?"

Reverse to a low-angle, over-the-shoulder close-up of Cary, who lowers her eyes and declines, obviously disappointed (figure 4-27). Cary's height advantage, emphasized by the high and low shots, implies another advantage, and Sara's visual inferiority is compounded by her callousness. She rubs salt in Cary's wound by offering to call Harvey. "At least," she says, "he's available." A medium two-shot returns them to equality, and Cary's silence serves as her acceptance (figure 4-28). They say good-bye. This exchange establishes Cary as the central character, again privileging her with a height advantage as Sara steps down from the curb and Cary is

4.25

4.26

given the reaction shots. Cary is the sympathetic character, and she re-mains as Sara leaves.

The camera pans with Cary as she walks back to the house, carrying a big box of dishes Sara has returned. As she passes the man, he turns around and offers help; the camera movement stops on him. The width of his shoulders is impressive, and when he turns around, the spectator sees

4.27

4.28

Rock Hudson, dressed in khaki work clothes, plain, practical, and earthy. He takes the box, and they walk out of the frame (figure 4-29). A quick cut to an extreme low angle of the two as they walk past and out of the frame (figure 4-30) contrasts with the earlier, naturalistic framing, and the camera holds momentarily on the limbs of a tree against the sky, the heavens. This unusual shot comments on their union. Already, their social

4.29

4.30

and sexual differences are established, but these stars had coupled just the year before in *Magnificent Obsession*, overcoming similar problems.

Then the camera pans, moving to catch up with them as they walk to the patio. She offers him some coffee, and he puts down the box. And a cut to a medium two-shot in Cary's territory, the patio, shows Cary and her substitute companion at opposite sides of the screen. She offers him

4.31

lunch, and he responds briefly, "A roll and some coffee will do." But when she moves to sit, he pulls her chair out for her. Cut to a closer shot as he moves left (momentarily obscuring Cary) and sits, settling into a comfortable, over-the-shoulder shot of Cary, from his point of view, still privileging her centrality (figure 4-31).

She initiates conversation but he isn't responsive, so she offers him a roll. As he takes one, she politely shoves the tray back toward him, offering another. When he takes it, she breaks into a smile, pleased that he has allowed her to nurture. She continues to try to initiate conversation, but his answers are frustratingly short and ambiguous. This take is long and stable, and music rises as she patiently chatters on. Finally, she elicits his identity, and after she finds out that he is Ron Kirby, the son of the former nursery owner, we finally get a reverse shot of Ron as he informs her that his father died three years earlier (figure 4-32). Reverse to an extreme close-up over-the-shoulder shot of Cary as she realizes he has been coming to her house for several years and she hasn't even noticed him before (figure 4-33). Reverse again to a shot, slightly less close, of Ron as he smiles and starts to talk about something he really cares about (figure 4-34): "This may be my last year. At agricultural school, I got interested in *trees*. So I started growing them." Cut back to Cary as she politely asks about trees, and then back to Ron as he explains that one of the trees in

4.32

4.33

her yard is a goldenrain tree and gets up to snip off a small branch for her
(figure 4-35). The camera moves with him as he moves back into an over-
the-shoulder shot of Cary; he explains the legend that the tree "can only
thrive near a home where there's love" (figure 4-36).

The music rises as their conversation begins to take on a personal di-

4.34

4.35

mension, and their mutual attraction begins to become evident. But before the conversation can go very far, he rises, moving out of the frame to
return to work as she looks at and fondles the clipping (figure 4-37). As
the sequence ends, she smiles and looks offscreen after Ron (figure 4-38).
Smiling again, she looks down, introspective (figure 4-39), and the pic-

4.36

4.37

ture dissolves to the goldenrain tree clipping in a crystal vase in front of a window. It is evening, and the camera pulls back to include a mirror in a bedroom lighted only by lamps. Cary looks first at the clipping and then at herself in the mirror as she applies makeup (figure 4-40). The camera pulls back even farther, to include her body in what becomes an over-the-

4.38

4.39

shoulder shot of Cary looking at herself, realizing her still active sexual desire and her need for love (figure 4-41).

The use of the mirror is an indication of the melodramatic stylization that is to follow, and it functions to intensify Cary's inward gaze. Desire, in this film, is self-conscious, and this is made evident by Sirk's use of

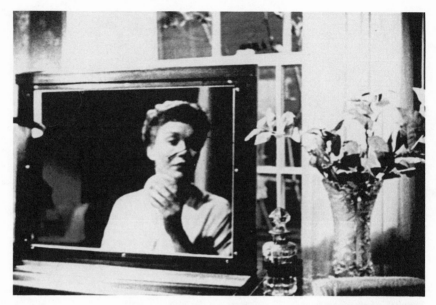

4.40

4.41

highly stylized sets and extremes in camerawork. And though the social and economic implications of desire are just as great in *Picnic*, there is little opportunity to suppress that desire. The director, Joshua Logan, and the cinematographer, James Wong Howe, shot most of *Picnic* in the naturalistic Hollywood style that erases the traces of enunciation. But in an artifi-

4.42

4.43

cial, stylized, after-dark sequence, the two manipulate camera angles, movement, and lighting to bring previously unexpressed tensions to the surface.

While Madge is presented to the town as Queen of Neewollah (Halloween spelled backward), the exchange of looks between her and Hal as she floats down the river as queen assures that their relationship will develop, that indeed she will leave the less virile Alan (figures 4-42 and 4-43). A trivial turn of events allows Madge to escape the community's attention, and she goes to "check on" Millie, who is dancing with Hal. Hal is trying to teach Millie a new dance step, and Millie despairs of learning it. Suddenly, Madge appears in a low-angle medium shot, descending the steps onto the pier and twisting her body—clothed in a low-cut, hot-pink dress—to a jazz rhythm (figure 4-44). She exchanges medium close-ups with Hal as they once again have desirous eyes only for each other (figures 4-45 and 4-46). A two-shot of Hal and Madge separates them by the entire width of the cinemascopic screen (figure 4-47). The camera moves with them as they dance toward each other, the distance emphasized by a

4.44

4.45

4.46

boat, clear in deep focus, floating behind them. He takes her hand; they circle; the boat passes. The camera stops as they pause, and a cut to Millie shows her watching them (figure 4-48).

In the next shot of Hal and Madge, their arms frame the top of the screen, and Madge's torso dances across the screen left to right, in front of Millie and offscreen. Hal's torso reenters briefly—emphasis on his buttocks—and the camera moves in on Millie who, looking miserable, grabs

4.47

4.48

4.49

Howard's bottle. A high-angle long-shot of Hal and Madge dancing (figure 4-49) is followed by a low-angle close-up as they move in close to each other. They pause with the music, the camera stills, and as they resume movement, the camera follows. They gaze at each other, and he puts her hand on his chest (figure 4-50).

Cut to a medium low shot of Mrs. Owens and Mrs. Potts as they arrive and look down at the couple from an overhanging bridge (figure 4-51);

4.50

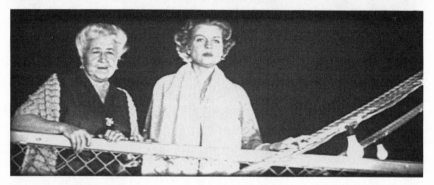

4.51

the women's presence increases the number of Hal and Madge's spectators and emphasizes the couple's status as erotic objects for the other characters and for the film's spectators. A high-angle shot from the bridge reinforces Hal and Madge's centrality (figure 4-52). In a medium two-shot, the spectators are given additional information (backstory); Mrs. Potts remarks to Mrs. Owens: "Aren't they graceful? You used to dance like that, Flo." Mrs. Owens's lost youth and the impending frustration of her ambitions for Madge combine to make her look both sad and desperate. Although Hal and Madge and their relationship are central to the film, the responses of the other characters are also important. The occasional omniscient camerawork allows the spectator room and time to reflect. Finally, with a low-angle close-up, the camera returns to Hal and Madge, gazing into each other's eyes (figure 4-53).

Soon, a series of cuts between Howard and Rosemary, Hal and Madge, and Millie, who appears sick but still looks on, increases the tension. Rosemary—tipsy, annoyed by the attention everyone is giving to Hal and Madge, and jealous of the attention Hal gives to Madge—begins making

4.52

4.53

a spectacle of herself by forcing her date Howard to dance, by kicking her legs up high and exposing her bright-red petticoat (hidden desire) (figure 4-54), by declaring that all men have to show their legs, and by pulling up Hal's trouser legs (figure 4-55). She then forces Hal to dance with her (figure 4-56). Long-shots, close-ups, and medium close-ups follow this progress and finally dissolve into a close-up of Madge, gazing into the water, looking sad and just a little bewildered (a Kim Novak specialty) (figure 4-57).

A long close-up of Hal and Rosemary involves the spectator in the excruciating scene as Rosemary becomes sexually aggressive and Hal tries to pull away, reversing traditional gender roles. She holds on to his shirt until it rips. Dramatic music emphasizes the tension, and a cut to a long-shot punctuates the violence of her action, Hal's status as erotic object, and his embarrassment (figure 4-58). Another series of quick cuts brings most of the characters together and escalates the tension even further. Millie gets sick, and Madge tries to help her. Rapid reversal from an extremely low to an extremely high angle disorients the spectator as Millie

4.54

4.55

4.56

pushes Madge away, repeating: "Madge is the pretty one! Madge is the pretty one!" (figure 4-59). Rosemary attacks Hal, accusing him of being a worthless bum whose youth is fading, and caps her neurotic and jealous viciousness by lying, accusing Hal of feeding Millie liquor (figure 4-60). Howard defends Hal, the passive Madge—her gaze unfocused—looks even more bewildered, and Rosemary's attack continues until a spotlight and all eyes turn on them; they are a spectacle (figure 4-61). Alan enters

4.57

4.58

4.59

and assumes it is Hal's fault. Hal exits, but Mrs. Owens blocks Madge from following.

The sequence would seem to have no closure; all the characters quickly flee. But it has established the two situations that can terminate the film in a happy ending. Rosemary is forced to realize the extent of her neurosis, the hopelessness of her life as an old maid, and Howard's availability. Hal and Madge realize the depths of their passion, and they now know that

4.60

4.61

4.62

their satisfaction can come only from a union. Their many point-of-view shots pull the spectator into their desire, and the numerous two-shots cement them as a couple.

Several sequences later, the film closes, with all participants properly and primly clothed. Rosemary, no longer seeing or seen, leads the bewildered but accepting Howard away to be married; she wears a tailored dress with a hat and gloves, and he wears a suit and tie (figure 4-62). Hal

4.63

4.64

4.65

arrives to see Madge one last time before he hops the freight train to Tulsa. He wears his leather bomber jacket over a work shirt. Not even Madge's body is on display; she wears a prim skirt, blouse, and sweater. Hal and Mrs. Owens once more struggle for control of screen space—and, of course, Madge—in a shot/reverse-shot sequence as Hal finally pulls Madge away from her mother, who has literally clung to Madge's back (figures 4-63, 4-64, 4-65, 4-66, and 4-67). But he must leave to catch the

4.66

4.67

4.68

train, and the final decision is Madge's (figures 4-68, 4-69, and 4-70). She breaks away from her mother and heads toward the house (figure 4-71). Her decision is made obvious by a two-shot of her mother and Mrs. Potts gazing after her (figure 4-72).

Mrs. Potts, to an emotionally moving musical accompaniment, speaks the movie's final message: "I got so used to things as they were—everything so prim. The geranium in the window, the smell of Mama's medi-

4.69

4.70

4.71

cine. And then *he* walked in! And it was different! He clomped through the place like he was still outdoors. There was a *man* in the house! And it seemed good." Early morning has brought the return of naturalistic lighting, and the film is once again free from extreme-angle shots. The small community, though disrupted, is freed from overt sexual tension. Madge, modest in a pastel-blue tailored suit, boards a bus (figure 4-73), and an aerial shot of the bus indicates that its path will intersect that of the freight

4.72

4.73

train Hal is on (figures 4-74 and 4-75), and the film closes. Desire has been channeled into the socially acceptable; two marriages are set, and even filmic chaos is calmed.

Chaos, in *All That Heaven Allows*, is internalized. The looks between Cary and Ron not only initiated their relationship but also fueled Cary's desire to reemerge as a sexual being, despite her husband's death. Although she is attracted to Ron, she has doubts, which are cued by recurring looks of introspection. One particularly poignant inward gaze occurs during the winter, as the snow and cold parallel her sexual isolation after she has turned down Ron for the sake of her children. What frequently functions as a voyeuristic operation in genres like the detective film instead becomes a cue to Cary's internal chaos. The camera shoots through a window at which Cary stands, looking out. She watches caroling children pass by on a sleigh, and then she gazes into dark emptiness, a teardrop falling down across her cheek (figure 4-76).

In the next scene, her children return home for Christmas. While her son, Ned, is out of the room, her daughter, Kay (whose pressure was what

4.74

4.75

finally moved Cary to reject Ron), tells Cary that she is going to be married. The sterile black-and-white room is broken by the red of Kay's dress and the roses that have replaced Cary's usual white ones. The red of Kay's dress symbolizes her sexual initiation; Cary's roses are a small reminder of her sexuality. Cary wears black (mourning—but for whom?) and is privileged with a close-up reaction shot as she crumbles when Kay refers to Ron, "But that was different; you didn't really love him, did you?" Before they can carry on, Ned enters, and soon the children's present for Cary does too. It is the television set Cary previously said she didn't want, decorated with a red bow, offering a substitute for an active life (the widow's best friend). The salesman marvels that with simply the touch of a finger, "You'll have all the company you want," but what the camera shows is a full-frame close-up of the television screen reflecting Cary, who looks at her reflection, distraught (figure 4-77). The introspection that initiated the sequence ends it, but now she is even losing the children she had sacrificed so much for.

But, as the luck of the family melodrama would have it, the gods inter-

4.76

4.77

vene to provide a happy ending. The camera focuses once again on the steeple. This time it is dark and snowing; and the clock reads midnight. Cary strolls through her living room, now warmed by a fire. Its colors have altered; now they are the warm browns and oranges that have consistently been associated with Ron. And the gray suit Cary wears no longer seems so cold. Alida brings the news of Ron's accident, which she con-

4.78

fides to Cary in the close-up two-shot generally reserved for lovers or close female companions (figure 4-78). Males are rarely filmed in this manner; their individuality is preserved by visual isolation.

The next morning, Ron awakens to a low-angle shot of Cary (figure 4-79); the shot is reversed to a high-angle over-the-shoulder shot of him from her point of view (figure 4-80). Cut to a straight two-shot of them gazing at each other as she responds to his question, "Yes, darling, I've come home." He is feminized, and they are equalized. The music rises, and the camera pans up to include a young buck in the snow outside the millhouse window (figure 4-81).

Finally, the camera pans up, away from their mutual gaze, and the deer bounds away. Thus the film ends, the audience dismissed from Cary and Ron's intimacy and assured that Cary will no longer be plagued by long introspective looks into mirrors or darkness. Their relationship is renewed, and they can look together into the "natural" world. Although the conflict that generates this and other such narratives emphasizes the family as the locus for ideological struggle, endings like this one visually and narratively affirm the heterosexual couple—and the family—as the locus for interdependence. This sort of happy ending also closes *Magnificent Obsession*, *Peyton Place*, *Imitation of Life*, and many of the male-oriented melodramas, but *Picnic*'s closing shot operates differently. Whereas both *All That Heaven Allows* and *Picnic* open with omniscient aerial shots,

4.79

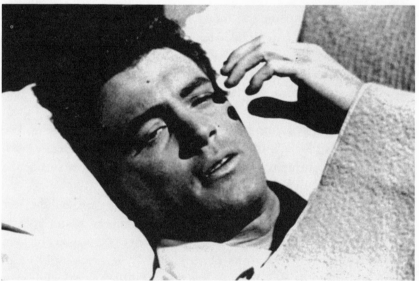

4.80

Picnic returns to the air in its conclusion, perhaps indicating an openness and definitely encouraging the spectator's withdrawal from the scene of the story. Cary and Madge have both escaped repressive situations, but Cary has found her solution, and the more youthful Madge still heads toward hers.

4.81

Manipulation of the spectator's gaze can encourage an identification with or valuation of characters, their actions, and their relationships. When characters operate as the object of the viewer's gaze, they function as either the agent or the object of seeing. The manipulation of these possibilities creates tension and moves the narrative. In reading these sequences, for instance, we have seen that the exchange between two characters' point-of-view shots can either establish or intensify a relationship. Dependent on establishing the stable male-female relationship that will enable resolution, the female-oriented melodramas use the basic convention heavily. Frequently used in all genres as a strategy for filming a conversation, the shot/reverse shot is particularly important in implicating the viewer in the development of a relationship, since in the cinema, showing is far more effective than telling.

Within this strategy, however, there are possible modifications. For instance, the quality of the character's gaze is important. Compare the different looks Cary gives Sara and Ron. During the conversation about the date, Cary's responses to Sara range from interest to disappointment to acceptance. All of this is dependent on the acting, the quality of the gaze; the dialogue is minimal. Cary's looks toward Ron also vary, but they are sexually cued and quite different from the looks she gives Sara. Initially she displays polite interest, but as Ron begins to accept her hospitality and to reveal the personal details of his life, she becomes more interested. Not only does the quality of her gaze change, but the quality of the spectator's gaze changes as well; the shot of Ron from her point of view moves from a medium close-up to a close-up. The shot also moves from an over-the-shoulder shot to a full-face shot of Ron as the spectator is sutured into the story, standing in for Cary. The same strategy for intensification is used in *Picnic* when Hal and Madge have their first two-person conversation.

Cary's and Madge's hopeless, unfocused gazes signal introspection, another possible quality for the gaze. But such a quality vanishes as the heterosexual coupling is cemented and the formation of the couple or family is complete. Some of the strategies that deliver the isolated gaze are relatively genre-specific in the response they encourage. In *All That Heaven Allows*, when the camera peers in through a window of the Scotts' house and focuses on Cary, the function of the shot is to encourage not a sense of voyeurism but our identification with the isolated character. Such shots function very differently in other genres. For instance, in a detective film a shot like this can encourage scopophilic desire by heightening the sense of an investigation. A snaking camera movement might also function this way in a detective film, but in *Picnic*, it functions to enhance the intensification of Madge and Hal's relationship as they move across the dance floor. The camera moves with them and pauses with them, cementing their devotion to each other.

Yet another filmic strategy that affects gender representation is the manipulation of the two-shot to develop a sense of closeness between two characters. For instance, as Hal and Madge move together during the dance sequence—across the entire width of the screen—their relationship intensifies and becomes more sexual. A close-up two-shot also indicates intimacy and is commonly used to indicate heterosexual romance or female friendship. The female-oriented melodrama depends on close female relationships, and their maintenance is as important as the creation of the primary male-female relationship; the reunion between Constance and Alison in *Peyton Place* makes this point forcefully. But close male companionships are rare in this subgenre. Of these films, only *All That Heaven Allows* presents one, the relationship between Ron and Mick. But their two-shots (during a hunting scene) maintain a safe distance between the two men, who remain in medium-shots and never move in close. Although certain male-oriented melodramas depict strong male friendships, in the female-oriented variety, males generally serve two primary functions: they provide erotic objects, and they enable the female protagonist to couple. A shot-by-shot analysis of cinematic enunciation enables an understanding of how this is effected.

This sort of analysis can be used to explicate the filmic conventions used to develop situations and relationships and is, as a result, quite useful in an analysis of gender representation. It shows us how specifically filmic devices attempt to involve viewers in the narrative. Here it has shown too that the use of these conventions may vary according to genre, leading to the conclusion that cinematic codes do not function consistently across the whole of cinematic discourse, as Bellour and the *Screen* writers contended. Representations of gender and its rhetoric vary, even within a single text and certainly across an entire genre. No single approach adequately describes these discourses, but an analysis of cinematic enunciation enables a clearer understanding of the struggle over the meanings of gender.

5

Race, Class, and Gender

Race, Class, and Feminist Film Studies

Film theory and criticism, like any other scholarly arena, has not developed in a vacuum and has been conditioned by historical factors; as the direction of British cultural studies was altered by the contemporary women's movement and by the presence of feminists at the Centre for Contemporary Cultural Studies, film studies was similarly influenced. A significant number of women have been involved in film studies, and feminists have been among the most active of film theorists and critics; analysis of the cinematic representation of gender has become an area that even the most conservative of film scholars cannot entirely ignore. However because of cultural studies' Marxist heritage, because scholars of color were present at the Centre for Contemporary Cultural Studies, and because cultural studies scholars have focused on understanding the turmoil in British society since World War II—turmoil that has included racial unrest—British cultural studies scholars have also concentrated their attention on race and class. Until very recently that move has not been paralleled in mainstream film studies—even within the realm of feminist film studies, an interpretive community predominantly female *and* white. Some film scholars in the United States have consistently been concerned with issues of race and class, in addition to issues of gender, and this trend is—fortunately—gathering strength, but the mainstream of feminist film studies has not yet embraced it.[1] Some space at the annual conference of the Society for Cinema Studies has been reserved for a discussion of the relation of film to race and class, but in the past few years, *Cinema Journal*, the SCS organ that has frequently published feminist work, has included only a very few articles with a central concern for either race or class.

Jane Gaines has called attention to the dearth of film criticism linking race and gender, pointing out that the "voice" of academic feminist film criticism is a white voice; analysis of the gaze has ignored the fact that it is not just male but also white precisely because feminist film studies has been overwhelmingly dominated by whites. "Cinema aesthetics and the aesthetics of racial distinction," she argued, "are one and the same."[2] Falling prey to the very tendency toward universalizing that plagues most psychoanalytic theory, many white feminists have theorized gender without regard to the diverse inflections that result from the intersection of gender with race, class, national origin, educational background, and age.[3] Recently, exceptions have begun to appear. Deidre Pribram's recently published anthology of articles by feminists working in the United States, *Female Spectators* (1988), included two articles that specifically address the intersection of race and gender, though these were late additions made at the request of the British editors of Verso Press's Questions for Feminism series. Jacqueline Bobo's analysis of African American women as cultural readers focused on the responses of African American men and women to *The Color Purple* and shows how their readings can be understood as subversive, and Alile Sharon Larkin, a filmmaker, has written about African American women's struggle to regain control of their own images. The (often indirect) interaction of the editorial board in Great Britain with the critics, theorists, and filmmakers—most of whom work in the United States—who produced *Female Spectators* indicates the early stages of the growing but still embryonic influence of British cultural studies on American film scholarship.[4]

The lack of attention to class among film scholars is particularly paradoxical because most contemporary film theorists and critics—and certainly most feminists working in the area—are influenced by Marxist theory, if only through the pervasive influence of Althusser's theories in film studies.[5] Still, although Marxist-socialist feminists constitute a distinct interpretive community within the broader spectrum of feminism and feminist film studies, they have unfortunately remained marginalized in the United States. Describing that spectrum allows me to place the work of the Marxist-socialist feminists who have produced the most important recent work on the intersection of gender, race, and class in film texts, to illustrate the need for more work in this vein, and to lay the groundwork for the readings that follow. The categories I describe are, like most categories, overly general, mechanistic, and often—especially at their boundaries—sloppy, and they change in response to historical necessity and political strategy. Nevertheless, they are categories often used to distinguish among feminist theories and are, in fact, useful, especially because they indicate the diversity of feminisms—primarily the white feminisms that have dominated feminist film studies—and offer ways of distinguishing among them.

Feminisms are, for a variety of purposes, classified in different ways, and for my purposes even some of the categories I use are problematic. I draw most closely from the categories delineated by H. Leslie Steeves, who drew her major categories (liberal, radical, traditional Marxist, and socialist) from Alison M. Jaggar but complicated them with categories delineated by Jean Bethke Elshtain. Elshtain divided feminists into four different categories (liberal, radical, Marxist, and psychoanalytic), and Steeves drew on this for subcategorization, conflating Marxist and socialist feminists (retaining some distinctions between them) and dividing this category into feminists who are influenced by psychoanalytic theory and who focus in detail on texts and feminists who "add class oppression to their primary focus on gender oppression."[6] Steeves places my work in both of these subcategories. In addition, I draw on—and critique—E. Ann Kaplan's distinctions between essentialist and antiessentialist feminisms.

To explicate: Kaplan argued that "feminism is by definition a *political* and *philosophical* term" and that politically distinct feminisms include bourgeois feminism, Marxist feminism, radical feminism, and post-structuralist feminism. She subdivided these four categories into two philosophical categories: "essentialist" and "antiessentialist." Essentialist feminisms, Kaplan contended, assume "a basic 'truth' about women that patriarchal society has kept hidden. . . . they offer an alternate way not only of *seeing* but of *being* that threatens patriarchy." She contended that radical feminism, Marxist feminism, and bourgeois feminism are essentialist and that only post-structuralist feminists are antiessentialists, who "attempt to understand the processes through which female subjectivity is constituted in patriarchal culture" and who "do not find an 'essential' femininity behind the socially constructed subject."[7] It is in Kaplan's overlay of these philosophically and politically distinct categories that problems arise.

For instance, radical feminism is often described as an essentialist feminism; Kaplan, Steeves, and Jaggar all position separatist radical feminism as a feminism that assumes that biologically innate differences between the sexes are the root of women's oppression and that posits the establishment of separate female communities as the solution to women's problems. However, radical feminists like Adrienne Rich (who posits compulsory heterosexuality as a political institution) and Janice Raymond (who constructs a philosophy of female friendship) are distinctly antiessentialist.[8] As Raymond argued:

It is my contention that the positive dimensions of women's "otherness" are grounded in the culture that women have constructed with and for each other throughout history and in all cultures. I would base women's "otherness" specifically in the culture of female friendship—a culture that has a vitality, élan, and power of its own but that resides in no essentialist feminine nature. Women have no biological edge on the more humane qualities of human existence, nor does women's uniqueness proceed from any biological differences from men. Rather, just as any cultural context distinguishes one group from another, women's "otherness" proceeds from women's culture.[9]

Clearly, separatist politics and a focus on female communities do not lead to an essentialist philosophy.

Radical feminist scholars working within the academy have been active in speech and literary studies, concentrating on showing the existence of a women's language and literary tradition, and radical feminists have also pursued audience research focused on the readings produced by distinct female communities.[10] This research, however, has not yet focused significantly on class and race. Radical feminists compose a minority interpretive community within film studies, and their criticism concentrates primarily on analyses of the work of experimental (often lesbian) filmmakers,[11] though—as I have shown in chapter 4—a focus on female friendships and female communities allows a more adequate understanding of certain film texts than do approaches that ignore this important realm of female experience.

Liberal feminism (in Kaplan's terms, "bourgeois feminism") is the feminism that has had the greatest effect in the United States. An "essentialist" feminism, it is characterized by the insistence that prevailing bourgeois ideas are adequate but are inequitably applied and that individual action can be effective in combating inequity; liberal feminists believe equal opportunity is possible within the existing capitalist socioeconomic systems. Some liberal feminists have focused on the ways gender intersects with race and class in the perpetuation of inequities, but they see this perpetuation as the result of irrational prejudices. Liberal-bourgeois feminists privilege rational mental development and insist that it is the responsibility of the state to provide equal opportunities to all in pursuing mental growth and professional success and that rational arguments and legal struggle can bring this about; currently, issues concerning equal pay and employment dominate the liberal feminist agenda. Until recently, liberal feminists have tended to uncritically accept male-biased methods in their research, which in film and media studies has consisted primarily of the "images of women" studies, including quantitative and qualitative content analyses of media texts.[12] The recent publication of a second, updated edition of Molly Haskell's *From Reverence to Rape* indicates the continuing presence of a liberal feminist interpretive community in film studies, though it is no longer the dominant feminism in this arena.

Traditional or orthodox Marxist feminists, who consider class oppression the primary source of women's oppression, can be distinguished from socialist feminists, who argue that additional categories—such as race, sexual preference, and cultural background—must be considered. In fact, few contemporary Marxist feminists could be classified as traditional, and the category seems to exist primarily for the purpose of analytic distinctions rather than for the description of actual critics and theorists. Jaggar preserved the distinction but argued that socialist feminists, who became recognizable as a group in the 1970s, actually apply "the central principles of Marxism more consistently than did Marx himself."[13] Kaplan described "pre-Althusserian" Marxist feminists as essentialists in order to distinguish them from their antiessentialist Marxist feminist counterparts, and though the distinction is valid, it hardly does justice to our current situation. Steeves conflated Marxist and socialist feminists into one category and wrote about them all as socialist feminists, but as noted above, she found that socialist feminist communications scholars break down into two groups: textual analysts who are influenced by psychoanalytic theory and researchers (textual analysts and others) who focus on class oppression as well as on gender oppression. Most feminist film scholars fall into Steeve's first subcategory. Few insist on constant attention to class and race. Jane Gaines and Julia Lesage are notable exceptions.

Gaines has consistently drawn on Marxist theory to explain the symbolic use of the representation of woman in the exchange of representational commodities. She has also evaluated the use of psychoanalytic theory in streamlining "a Marxist problematic which dealt awkwardly with the social individual," acknowledging the socialist feminist attempt to think simultaneously about the individual and the collective, about "the (real, historical) subject" and its place in a society divided by race and class.[14] Lesage, consistently concerned with both class and gender, has drawn on Antonio Gramsci's description of ideology as a hegemonic process to help her explain distinct differences between film texts and to explain their participation in the reproduction of a class society *and* in resistance to oppression. Hegemony, she explained, is a term used "to describe the complex ways that the dominant, most powerful class (in our era the bourgeoisie) maintains control over ideas." The dominant class writes history, imposes norms, and controls our institutions, some of which "comprise generally agreed upon systems for conducting personal affairs, and these shape women's lives directly, namely the institutions of marriage, the family, and heterosexuality." In the 1980s, she argued, no one should be surprised to find that "all these institutions foster an ideology that promotes the outlook of white middle class males." The "hegemonic female fantasy" works to extend that outlook, and most of our narrative arts "are devoted to working out the conflicts and contradictions of the bourgeoisie in terms understandable and acceptable to its male members."[15] Lesage has also drawn on Frantz Fanon's description of the mental colonization of people in economically colonized countries to show

how women too are mentally colonized, how they accept values and practices that support another group and actually contribute to their own oppression. Fanon also described mental decolonization, the shedding of the colonizer's values and practices, and Lesage drew on this description to show how women can begin to resist oppression.[16]

Ideology has come to be understood as inherently linked to the reproduction of oppression through the reproduction of gender, patriarchal relations, and social class. Traditional Marxist cultural criticism, which focused primarily on "high art," concentrated on placing texts within their social, historical, and economic context. This does, of course, enrich an understanding of the various systems of codes that make up any text, but recent attention to mass-media texts and recent developments in Marxist theory have productively complicated our understanding of culture and our methods for analysis. Until fairly recently, Marxist analysis of cultural documents denigrated the products of what was referred to as the "culture industry," considering them simply and solely tools used by the ruling class to enforce an ideology on a naive, powerless, and somewhat willing public.[17] Based on a rigid and hierarchical notion of ideology, this position ignored the complexity of "entertainment" forms and the sophistication of their audiences. When Marxists did begin to turn their critical attention toward entertainment texts, their analyses generally ignored questions relating to sexual difference.

With advancements in Marxist theory, in general, and socialist feminism, in particular, the traditional Marxist emphasis on the economic as determinant has been displaced, and now it is seen as one force in interaction with others. This displacement aids analysis of gender representation by, for instance, allowing us to see patriarchy as autonomous and not linked to a particular mode of production; although patriarchy tends to support capitalism, it preceded capitalism and exists even now in conjunction with other modes of production. Retaining the Marxist emphasis on the economic and on class relations, Marxist feminist theorists have rejected the traditional Marxist notion that the family determines a woman's class position and have called attention to the struggles over gender definition within this institution, which—as Heidi Hartman noted—is a primary site for struggle. Sometimes, in fact, the family serves as the site for struggle among classes and races, and any serious analysis of the struggle over the meanings of gender must attend to the inflections of the related, but not parallel, struggles over race and class, tracing the interaction of residual, dominant, emergent, and preemergent ideologies.

Coming to Manhood in Male-Oriented Melodramas

Many films seem to ask for a particular kind of analysis. Some, for instance, depict men attempting to establish adult relationships with their fathers, and psychoanalytic theory offers valuable tools for reading the representations of this relationship. But the psychoanalytic focus on interpersonal relationships obscures the ways films like these present and inflect the overlays of ideologies related to social class, race, and gender and their interactions. Explicit attention to the intersections of residual, dominant, and emergent ideologies enriches an analysis of how these films participate in defining and redefining gender. Of particular interest are popular 1950s male-oriented films that focus on the transition to manhood. Several young actors consistently played "anguished youth," symbolizing for many an initial awareness of a "generation gap." James Dean's performances in *East of Eden* and *Rebel without a Cause* gave depth to the anguished youth and exposed his dependence on the family. That the adaptation of John Steinbeck's story was produced when it was does not seem at all accidental; *East of Eden*, though set in 1916, poignantly displayed 1950s youth while American women and men struggled through the process of redefining gender and generational differences in the face of increasing materialism (and continuing racism). Bourgeois success could once more, in the postwar 1950s, be expressed through the acquisition and display of the material, and with women bringing in a second income, more and more families entered the middle class. But combining traditional family values and gender definitions with materialism proved difficult.

The protagonist in *East of Eden* (1955), Cal Trask (Dean), sets himself apart from his family and his peers, believing himself to be different, or "bad." He investigates the rumor that his mother is alive and is the proprietor of a nearby brothel; his father had always told him that she was dead. He believes that he has inherited her "badness," but the film reveals a different and far more touching explanation. His righteous and religious father, Adam (Raymond Massey), shows Cal little compassion and prefers his other son, Aron (Richard Davalos), so constantly that Cal's unspoken pleas for affection seem pathetic. But Cal is imaginative and a hard worker; he shows signs of becoming quite a capitalist. Seeking his father's approval, Cal follows business reports in newspapers and contributes new ideas to Adam's farming operation. When Adam loses most of his money on an experimental business venture, Cal sees his chance. He secretly borrows money from his mother and gambles on agriculture futures and an impending war. When he makes enough money to replace what his father lost, Cal proudly offers it to him as a birthday gift, hoping that his monetary offering will bring favorable attention. But when Adam learns how Cal made the money, he refuses the gift, refusing to profit from war. Oblivious to the pain he inflicts, he rebukes Cal by comparing him with Aron. Adam, incapable of compassion, embodies contradiction. On an intellectual and public level, Adam deplores violence and agonizes over his work with the local draft board, but on a personal and familial level, he is blind to the violence he himself inflicts.

Cal retaliates against Adam's insensitivity by revealing their mother's profession to Aron and by taking him to see her. Aron is revealed as the weaker son; he gets drunk, brawls, and laughs in his father's face as he leaves to join the army. Adam suffers a stroke and collapses, the extent of his paralysis unclear. Cal plans to leave home, but the sincere and charming Abra (Julie Harris)—Aron's and now, possibly, Cal's girlfriend—pleads with Adam, "You have to give him some sign that you love him, or else he'll never be a man" (and becoming "a man" is, of course, what the film is about). Adam responds, haltingly asking Cal to get rid of the obnoxious nurse and to care for Adam himself. As the film combines residual political, religious, and economic values with a cruel and inflexible character, it clearly valorizes advanced capitalism by associating capitalism with the sympathetic underdog, Cal, whose compassion and flexibility win out over rigidity and strict adherence to traditional values and practices. The film closes with Cal sitting quietly at his father's bedside; the residual fades away as Adam accepts Cal's love and care.

The interrelationship of love and money permeates the film. Cal's mother, Kate (Jo Van Fleet), owns one of the finest brothels on the West Coast; she sells "love" and admits that she's one of the best businesswomen around, but people look down on her because her profession isn't respectable (and, after all, she is a Working Woman and a Woman Alone).

Her affluence is evidence of her success and of the market for her "product." And that product is only *rented out* by prostitutes, whereas in marriage it is *sold*; the feudal flip side (after marriage) is that a woman is then *owned* by her husband. This message becomes explicit as Kate is revealed as the key to understanding Adam. When she explains to Cal why she left them, she says, "He wanted to *own* me." Although Adam isn't interested in making a profit, he deals with people as if they were property, to be owned and controlled. Kate, a Working Woman, embodies American woman's growing independence, her refusal to be man's property, but her position as a madam connects independence with prostitution. That Working Woman—now a mother and a Woman Alone—embodies contradictory American ideologies of labor and gender in the 1950s. Cal also resists Adam's control but still desperately needs his love. This particular contradiction, indicative of Cal's basic confusion, manifests itself in Cal's attempt to buy his father's love with a monetary gift.

Cal's "bad" self-image also exhibits an economic and racist aspect in the women with whom he associates. Obviously attracted to the blonde and virginal Abra, he most frequently associates with darker, speechless young women of a lower social class, perhaps of a different ethnic origin. Only when his father finally proffers his affection and Cal begins to become "a man" does Cal feel free to offer his kiss to Abra; only then is it appropriate for him to care for a white, middle-class woman. The choice of a mate is central to a number of male-oriented melodramas, including some of the anguished youth variety. Montgomery Clift took the anguished youth away from the family and into the "adult" world in *A Place in the Sun* and *From Here to Eternity*, and in each film, social class is crucial to coupling. George Eastman, in *A Place in the Sun*, ruins himself by trying to cross class boundaries, and Robert E. Lee Prewitt, in *From Here to Eternity*, aspires to marry a woman who aspires to marry up. Marlon Brando's working-class immigrant Stanley Kowalski, in *A Streetcar Named Desire*, marries Stella, a woman who was raised for a higher class status but whose family's actual economic situation determined hers and made her "suited" for Stanley. Her sister, Blanche, however, resists her assignment to the working class, and when she arrives at the Kowalski household, differing attitudes toward class lead to tension. Stanley, proud of his class origins, is offended by Blanche's attitudes, and the film sides with him, associating her resistance with prostitution, as *East of Eden* does with Kate. Stella, however, never becomes bitter, willingly allowing her class position to be determined by her husband.

Another passive, sweet woman is portrayed by Olivia de Havilland in the even more successful (though not so well remembered) *Not as a Stranger* (1955). She plays Kristina Hedvigson, an attractive but unsophisticated Minnesota Swede whose closest friends still retain their Scandinavian accents; she wants "what all women want," a husband and a family. A nurse, she works in the hospital where the male protagonist, the bright but self-righteous medical student Lucas Marsh (Robert Mitchum), studies. Ambitious and rigidly idealistic, Luke works harder than his classmates, adding part-time jobs at the medical school to his already busy schedule, but he cannot make enough money to get by. The prudent and conservative Kris has a substantial savings account, whereas Luke—because his drunken father has squandered the money saved by Luke's mother for his education—is on the verge of being expelled from medical school for nonpayment of tuition fees. Luke soon meets and woos Kristina, against the advice of his best friend, Al Boone (Frank Sinatra). But Kris has money saved, and Luke needs it. Al's confrontation with Luke outlines the class—and the related ethnic—conflicts that will follow:

A L

This is not the sort of dame you marry!

L U K E

I'm marrying her.

A L

Look, a doctor's wife . . . went to the right school. Her folks belong to the country club, she's charming, she was brought up that way. This dame ought to marry a farmer.

L U K E

That's the way it is, Al. I want to marry her. It's my part of the bargain.

A L

You're cheating her right from the start, Luke. You don't even love her.

L U K E

Well, she'll never know. She'll never find out.

AL

I think it's a dirty, stinkin' thing to do. You're takin' advantage of a poor squarehead who's afraid of being an old maid. You're lettin' yourself be *kept*.

Even Luke, who self-righteously looks down on the other medical students who plan for an expensive life-style, realizes the truth of what Al says. He knows that the life-styles of most doctors include partners born and educated in the upper or middle class; he also knows that he is taking advantage of the woman's insecurity and is robbing her of the "true love" that 1950s films teach us are at the heart of any "good marriage." And he knows that Al's derogatory attitude toward agrarian Scandinavian immigrants is not uncommon among his peers. His knowledge and attitude cannot be concealed forever. Still, he marries Kris.

After Luke graduates, Kris quits her job, and they move together to a small town so that he can pursue his romanticized (and residual) ideal. He dreams of becoming a heroic and altruistic country doctor, giving all things to all the rural patients whom his specializing, money-grubbing urban medical-school compatriots will not be treating. With these doctors, the film presents a negative view of the emerging medical practices of specialization and high fees and the ideology of medical treatment they imply. Between the long hours Luke works and the increasing amount of time he spends with the wealthy and beautiful but decadent and sexually aggressive widow Harriet Lang (Gloria Grahame), Luke hardly communicates with Kristina. Kris desperately wants a child, but Luke does not, more concerned with being a perfect doctor than with being a husband and father. Even when Kris learns that she's pregnant, she can't find a way to break the news to him. One night Luke stays out very late, with Harriet, and when he arrives home, he finds his former classmate Al waiting outside for him. Al informs him that Kristina is pregnant but is unable to tell him herself. Kris knows that he has been with Harriet and confronts him:

From the beginning, you never thought I was smart enough, or attractive enough or woman enough to be your wife. You came crawling in here now because your friend told you I was going to have your child. Stop pretending! I'm sick of it. . . . I don't need you to have this child. You had to have money, so you married me. Well, you made it. You're a doctor. You don't need me now. And I don't need the little you got to give me. I don't want to live with you, Luke. Please, get out of here!

He leaves, in shock. Just that evening he had broken off with Harriet, realizing how much he cared for Kristina.

Two weeks later, after no reconciliation, Luke is further traumatized by the death of his good friend Dave Runkleman (Charles Bickford), the older doctor whose practice he had just begun to take over. Worse even, he had failed to save his friend, who died from a heart attack. He wanders the streets, finally coming to his home. He has no one to turn to but Kris. He walks through the rain to the front door and begs for her help. In tears, they embrace. Luke's realization that he could fail coincides with his acceptance of guilt for being "kept." In pursuit of his lofty idealism, he had himself taken advantage of another person, an honorable and loving person who would indeed make a good wife and mother. His actions, the film shows, are clearly reprehensible, but repenting for flirtation with the upper class and accepting a quiet, middle-class life can absolve a man from even the shame of having been kept by a woman. The film also depicts a family structure that demands that a woman quit working outside the home in order to care for her children, sending the message that it is acceptable for a woman to work before she is married but that, when she begins a family, she should retire from the work force. The sexy widow Harriet Lang embodies yet another cluster of cultural assumptions. Most obvious is the notion that sexually aggressive women do not win. Physically coded for sensuality (sexuality), she wears tight clothing, often smokes, always carries a drink, and moves to call attention to her body, especially when she dances. She uses sex to get what she wants, violating patriarchal order. But although ultimately punished, she lives on *her* terms. She is the female excess that patriarchy cannot entirely encapsulate. She floats from one unattractive man to another and loses her only handsome and virile suitor, Luke. The film ties positive values to working hard, and Harriet also embodies the notion that with wealth comes decadence, in contrast with Kristina's middle-class stability and propriety, which even the upwardly mobile professional, Al, comes to respect.

This film seems to beg for more than just attention to class and ethnicity. It fairly cries out for a bit of psychoanalytically informed attention, and combining psychoanalysis with ideological analysis shows the several readings inscribed in the text, as well as the limitations of interpretations based in a single psychoanalytic theory. The advantages of a comparative approach become clear. A Freudian explanation of this narrative might focus on Luke's replacing his mother—his provider and nurturer—with Kristina. The film's ending might be read as Luke's acknowledgment of Kristina's mothering role. Kristina herself might be understood in terms of her "narcissistic" desire for a child. Certainly, for Freud, women exist only in relationship to men; for each other, they are—as are Kristina and Harriet—rivals, enemies. A quite different, but still credible, reading can be posited: a feminine voice can be heard even in this male Oedipal drama, and hearing it can lead toward a different reading of the film. Whereas Kristina's desire to mother would be interpreted by a Freudian as simply narcissistic, a Chodorowian would interpret it as her socially conditioned inclination toward a triadic relationship. Her pregnancy and her reconciliation with Luke, at the end, cement the triad. The weakness in this reading is that Kristina is *not* the film's center; Luke is, and the story—*his* story—is told from a masculine perspective, one that represents Kristina only in relation to him. The Chodorowian approach helps to account for the presence in the text of a weak but perceptible "feminine voice," but male-oriented melodramas tell different sorts of stories than do female-oriented melodramas, and in them, that voice is weak. Conflicting voices *within* the film encourage conflicting readings *of* the film, and comparing the readings encouraged by differing theories offers a way to reveal, by identifying textual heteroglossia, ideological struggle. In *Not as a Stranger*, the female voice speaks even as the male dominates, and the struggles that result in the playing out of the Freudian family romance may also convincingly be read using Lacanian theory. The final scene can be read as Luke's move into adulthood. When his symbolic father, Runkleman, dies, despite Luke's efforts to save him, Luke realizes that he is vulnerable, imperfect, alone in the world: fatherless. He must now take responsibility for himself and for the family he has (unwittingly) begun. He finally enters the Symbolic, after an extremely extended adolescence.

Frank Sinatra, a supporting actor in both *From Here to Eternity* and *Not as a Stranger*, plays the lead in another film about a male's belated entry into adulthood. *Some Came Running* (1959) places Sinatra as Dave Hirsh, a wandering ex-soldier and novelist who unexpectedly wakes up in his midwestern hometown, Parkman; his buddies poured him onto the bus the night before. Dave finds that he is, also unexpectedly, being trailed by a sweet young woman, Ginny Moorhead (Shirley MacLaine), who insists that he asked her to come along. Dave settles into a local hotel and deposits a substantial sum in a local bank, the rival to a bank that his brother, Frank, serves as a director. Frank, the local jeweler, quickly finds out and comes to visit; it rapidly becomes evident that Dave's hypocritical brother, his only remaining family, is not happy to have him there, and his sister-in-law, Agnes, objects even more. Dave, it seems, included unflattering and thinly disguised portraits of them in a very successful novel, and in addition, he tends to lead what they consider an inappropriately rowdy life. Dave soon meets people from all the socioeconomic strata in Parkman. Most important to the plot are a hard-drinking gambler extraordinaire, Bama Dillert (Dean Martin), and an upper-middle-class college literature professor, Gwen French (Martha Hyer). Dave and Bama become fast friends and drinking partners, and Dave moves into Bama's apartment. Theirs is, in fact, the only friendship in the film. But their rowdy activities are used to place them outside traditional class lines. Dave, as a novelist, an artist, may be considered outside traditional boundaries and may actually be expected to imbibe frequently (the legacy of Hemingway and others of his ilk), but drinking heavily places Bama, who has no apparent artistic abilities or inclinations, in the sort of non-class characterized by Luke's gutter-crawling father in *Not as a Stranger* and by Doc, the abusive binge-drinker in *Come Back, Little Sheba*. Heavy drinking signifies an outsider, and Dave, abandoned by his brother as a child, sees the world only in terms of separation. Bama, another radical individualist and wanderer, is his comrade; they are outsiders together. They reinforce the notion that the Man Alone is resistant to "settling down," that by *nature*, man is a loner, but loners together at least seem friends.

Once she gets beyond Dave's macho facade and prompts him to talk about his writing, Gwen also shows promise as a friend, but she *is* a woman, and instead of developing a friendship, Dave tries to court her. Gwen is intrigued but hesitant, evidently a novice at courtship. Ginny, meanwhile, has gone to work in a local brassiere factory and continues to pursue Dave. Ginny and Gwen can be seen as two sides of woman. Both are the stereotypical Woman Alone; each is, in her own way, desperate, but their desperation is inflected by class. Their differences are clearly defined and accentuated through the use of costuming, acting, language, and character traits; neither is entirely "whole." Ginny wears clothes that place her as a stereotypical prostitute, and her weak, high voice combines with a limited vocabulary to pale in contrast with Gwen's mellow voice and sophisticated control of English. Literacy is presented as clearly related to class; Gwen teaches literature, but Ginny doesn't even seem to read very well. The two are contrasted almost as animal and human. Ginny sometimes sits like a puppy at Dave's feet, displays little intelligence, and expresses her emotions freely; she even has to remind Dave that she *is* human. Gwen is very intelligent but represses emotion. Ginny, working class, pursues Dave, while Gwen, upper-middle class, is pursued. But even though Ginny is sexually aggressive, she is also naive, unlike Harriet in *Not as a Stranger*, and she can be forgiven. Still, connecting female sexual aggression with working-class *or* wealthy characters functions to place it outside the norm. Dave's male sexual aggression is "normal."

Gwen is mind to Ginny's body. An attractive blonde, Gwen wears conservative pastel shirtwaists, and her hair is usually restrained and upswept. Often, she wears glasses, masking her beauty and signaling her intellect. Both women, however, are fetishized as spectacle. Ginny's costuming is so outrageous as to call attention to her physical body. And when Gwen is first introduced, the actors are blocked and the camera is positioned so that when she walks into Frank and Agnes Hirsh's living room, she is the center of all characters' eyes, as well as the object of the spectator's gaze. Dave flatters her brain to get to her body, which she finally reveals as attractive by removing her glasses and hairpins, letting her hair flow, sexily. Dave gazes at her, but she does not return the gaze. He kisses her (of course); she resists, weakly.

When Ginny finds out about Gwen's link to Dave, she goes to talk to Gwen, to ask her if she is going to marry Dave. In her skimpy, frilly clothes, Ginny looks ridiculously out of place in a college setting. The class and educational differences between Gwen and Ginny make the confrontation excruciating. Ginny's pathos and Gwen's pained composure make both characters sympathetic, and neither can be dismissed, but the rhetoric of these performances associates self-control with the middle class, and lack of it with the working class. Ginny mentions that she accompanied Dave and Bama on a gambling trip, and this undermines her "morality." It also undermines any faith Gwen had in Dave. Ginny breaks down, sobbing that she loves Dave but doesn't think he loves her. Gwen tells Ginny that there is nothing between Dave and herself, promising to say nothing to Dave of Ginny's visit.

Gwen then rejects Dave's attentions, asking him in a tone somewhere between order and plea: "Leave me alone. Stay away from me." Dave responds by proposing to a surprised but delighted Ginny, who promises to make him "a really good wife." Bama, who, like Al in *Not as a Stranger*, has a clear sense of social stratification, objects, arguing that Ginny's sincerity cannot make up for her lack of social skills and education. But Dave stands by his decision, having realized that Ginny is, indeed, human, even if working class. She is also desperate for family, and this Dave—the next thing to an orphan—appreciates. But, just as they marry, Ginny's jealous ex-boyfriend, a Chicago hood, shows up in Parkman with a gun, and in a surrealistic segment, replete with swirling lights and swelling music, the hood chases and shoots at them. Ginny jumps in front of Dave, saving him at the cost of her own life and proving that nobility is a trait not determined by social class.

The film ends as Ginny is buried in a serene cemetery that overlooks a peaceful river. Gwen attends, Dave stands apart from everyone, and Bama, for the first time, risks losing luck and takes his hat off in honor of a woman he had finally come to respect. Although both the working class and the well-educated upper-middle class are portrayed sympathetically, the film's rhetoric supports the notion that one should marry within one's own class. Ginny's good nature in the face of adversity and her devotion to Dave were admirable, but the film indicates that Dave's almost condescending acceptance of Ginny would eventually make their union problematic. The emerging notion that love is enough to make a marriage work—presented positively in *All That Heaven Allows*—is, in this film, shown to be naive. Ginny, moving up across class lines, dies in the end. Gwen's quiet life-style differs from Dave's, but their class and educational orientations are almost identical; she is the "right match," but he had to learn that lesson traumatically. Still, although the film's message preaches the inadvisability of interclass marriage, the fact that the issue is central to the narrative indicates an American concern with the issue in the 1950s.

"Dynastic Melodramas"

The representation of difference is enhanced by setting in a film melodrama variation that combines multiple generations and marital couplings within a single family domain. These "dynastic melodramas" are generally set in the Deep South or in Texas, regions charged with special symbolic significance in our culture. Texas, in our American mythology, serves as the space for the meeting of symbolic opposites, a primary reason it has been so consistently used as the setting for westerns, which depict the meeting of civilization and wilderness. In Texas, the South and the West meet. This setting allows for the depiction of extremes—of morality and of wealth. The Deep South serves a similar function but is enriched by the must of many generations and antebellum decay. Dynasties grown old have weakened, and patriarchs search for the strength that will assure their families of immortality.

Giant (1957) begins in the rolling hills of Maryland, where the tall, handsome Texas rancher Jordan "Bick" Benedict (Rock Hudson) meets and is captivated by the lovely, aristocratic Leslie Lynnton (Elizabeth Taylor).[18] They marry, and she leaves the East (home of "old money") and returns with him to "his country"—his ranch, Reata, in Texas—only to find some of their basic values in conflict. What follows is a history of contemporary Texas, told from a white, upper-class point of view. Raised with the tradition of noblesse oblige, Leslie is shocked at the way Jordan and the other white folks—even the working-class Jett Rink (James Dean)—treat Chicanos, or "those people," as Jordan refers to them. Leslie, determined to become a Texan, decides to change what *Texan* means. She continues to be gracious to those "beneath" her, and by the end of the film, twenty-five years (and over three hours) later, her son, Jordie Junior (Dennis Hopper) has married a Chicana, and Jordan has been beaten fighting for the young lady's right to be served in a redneck diner. In the wake and spirit of the Supreme Court's decision in *Brown* v. *Board of Education of Topeka, Kansas* (1954), this film overtly champions an emerging ideology of racial equality by presenting the Chicano characters as noble, honorable, and patriotic, but the less positive undertones are unavoidable. Young Angel (Sal Mineo), the "first Reata baby" born after Leslie's arrival, is Reata's first World War II casualty, an implicit acknowl-

edgment of the classist and racist nature of the American military in wartime but one that is glossed over by the "honor" of his sacrifice.

Ideologies of class are represented quite differently. Working-class
whites don't receive the same treatment, as if somehow their class status is
both inherent and indicative of a lack of will. Jett Rink rides the crest of
Texas wealth's transition from cattle ranching to oil drilling, having struck
oil on the small piece of Reata willed him by Jordan's sister, Luz (Mer-
cedes McCambridge). The old aristocracy (all of three generations old)
becomes overshadowed by the nouveau riche (an ideology that works to
naturalize the still youthful aristocracy), but of course, the nouveau riche
can't handle money or liquor. As the ranching West and its romance fade,
the upstart "white trash" enriched by oil money are displayed as tasteless
and bigoted. The aristocracy only gains in stature.

The western hero is civilized by the Anglo-Southern lady and even
comes to share with her the control of the dynasty he is committed to
perpetuate, calling into question the dominant ideology of gender difference. Leslie frequently challenges Jordan's ideas not only about Chicanos
but also about women, finally confronting him and his friends in a dramatic scene where she accuses the gentlemen of dating back 100,000
years, "You ought to be wearing leopard skins and carrying clubs!" Because of her class and marital status, she "gets away" with her uppity
display, but both male and female must ultimately compromise. The preemergent ideologies evidenced in Leslie become fully emergent in her
children; the next generation exhibits a slightly more egalitarian orientation. The Benedict twins switch sex roles; the daughter rejects finishing
school in Switzerland, heading off instead to Texas Tech, "a man's school,"
to learn animal husbandry, while Jordie Junior goes "back East" to become a doctor, respectable but hardly the "masculine" rancher his father
had wanted. The third child, a daughter, trades, like her mother, on her
beauty and charm, but the changing times are signaled by her decision to
independently seek her fortune as an actress rather than as some man's
wife. Still, men are shown to need feminine manipulation. In the final
scene, Jordan moans self-pityingly: "I'm a failure. Nothin's turned out like
I planned." Leslie reassures him that his gallant effort to defend his Chicana daughter-in-law, an effort during which he ended up on the floor of a
hamburger joint "in the middle of the salad," made him her hero. His

response reaffirms the mystique of women, "If I live to be ninety, I'm never gonna be able to figure you out."

Set in an oil town in Texas, *Written on the Wind* (1957) contrasts the "still intact" with a decaying and crumbling society. The director Douglas Sirk retrospectively claimed that the film was a piece of social criticism, of the rich and spoiled and of the American family. After *Magnificent Obsession*, Sirk recounted, there was "a certain dialectic at work" in casting Rock Hudson. "That very beautiful body of his was putty in my hands. . . . I used him as a straight, good-looking American guy."[19] In *Written on the Wind*, Hudson played one of the two intact characters who are contrasted with two divided characters. As he had in *Magnificent Obsession* and *All That Heaven Allows*, Sirk presents Hudson as the tall and dark but open, civilized, and handsome American hero of the period. In *Written on the Wind*, Hudson portrays Mitch Wayne, the son of a "twentieth century Daniel Boone" and the companion of Kyle Hadley (Robert Stack), the tortured and decadent son of an oil tycoon. Kyle's female counterpart is Marylee Hadley (Dorothy Malone), his sister, and the second stable, intact character is Lucy Moore (later Hadley) (Lauren Bacall).

This film associates idle wealth with moral decay and hard work with righteousness. Of middle-class origin, the Hadleys have been moved by their wealth into a class for which they were unprepared, served by the African American servants (residual remnants of southern slavery) who serve the family as they watch it slowly decay. Jason, the patriarch, is absorbed with running Hadley Oil and too busy to indulge in decadence—but his offspring turn to vice as their aspirations are unfulfilled. Kyle—"the weakest of us all," as Marylee describes him—cannot fill his father's shoes and is tormented by the fact that Mitch can. Marylee, perhaps the strongest of the four, assumed all her life that she would marry Mitch, but he has continually spurned her; she turns to booze, jazz, and one-night stands. Mitch and Lucy's middle-class stability highlights the Hadley siblings' decadence.

Both Kyle and Mitch fall in love with Lucy within the first few sequences; she is the perfect modern woman of the 1950s. Employed in the Hadley corporation's New York office and with vague ambitions in the advertising field, she knows, nevertheless, that she "will probably walk down the aisle and end up in a suburb, with a husband, mortgage, and children," accepting residual but still very active notions of wife-and-motherhood. Kyle makes other plans; along with his decadence comes a sense of style and pathos Lucy finds irresistible. They marry, Lucy quits her job, and they return to Hadley, Texas, and the family estate. Mitch stoically hides his love, planning to leave Texas for the oil fields of Iran, a possibility also mentioned as the son Ned's future in *All That Heaven Allows* (and humorous, in retrospect, to the 1990s spectator, as is Rock Hudson's status as the spectacular heterosexual lover). Mitch and Lucy never question their social or economic positions; they fit perfectly within capitalism and the nuclear family. Even if they are the least interesting of the four characters, the ideological power of their happiness and success reinforces the value and values of the middle class. Still, theirs is not the only ideology presented; dominance is not unchallenged. Kyle and Marylee remain the more fascinating and dynamic characters of the film, and even though they "lose," they gain sympathy.

The film climaxes when, after an unfruitful year of marriage, Kyle learns that he has "reproductive difficulties." When Lucy finally does become pregnant, Kyle imagines grounds for jealousy. During an ensuing suicidal battle with his lifelong friend Mitch, Kyle manages to get himself shot to death. This initiates the film's protracted and ideologically explicit conclusion. Kyle, in the world of the film melodrama, had only two choices. Weak in soul and economic potential, he could reform or die. His reformation was short-lived, and his return to vice could culminate only in death. Mitch and Lucy, both strongly committed to "the American way," ride off together in the film's final shot (because, rumor has it, Hudson's contract stipulated that the last shot must include him). But the emotional impact of the conclusion comes in the penultimate shots where we see Marylee sitting, in a tailored pastel-blue suit, at her father's desk and beneath his portrait, fondling his model oil derrick. This image contrasts radically with the Marylee of the earlier part of the film, "borrowed" almost intact from the *film noir* thriller. Dorothy Malone's costuming and acting, constantly accompanied with a jazz melody, bring the melodrama's heroine into question. Contrasted with Lauren Bacall's Lucy, Malone's classic *femme noire* negatively defines female propriety. Costumed primarily in low-cut, tight-fitting outfits in stark or bright colors, Marylee exudes a sexuality checked only by the long arm of her father's law. Lucy, on the other hand, always controls her sexuality, knowing and fitting her "appropriate" role.

Marylee's aggressive sexuality threatens bourgeois social order, and she is punished when, in the wake of Kyle's death, Lucy turns to Mitch and begs him: "Take me away, Mitch. Take me out of this house." Marylee is left with only an incestuous spiritual coupling with her now dead (and literally absent) father, a coupling made explicit as she sits before his portrait and strokes the toy derrick he holds in the painting. Her happy ending substitutes poorly for the coupling with Mitch she has so actively desired throughout the film. Her "reward" for flaunting prevailing social definitions of sexual difference places her in a merely figurative couple and at the pinnacle of a thriving oil business. Although this image of woman was rare in the 1950s, it was ideologically more acceptable than the position in which she was first depicted, in a bar on the "wrong side of town" with an oil-field worker (who was, of course, beneath her social class). But her transformation from nymphomaniac to prim and proper businesswoman would seem to negate the power of her personality and is, finally, unconvincing. Readings proliferate: does Marylee's masculine tailored suit represent the power she now has? Or is it symbolic of her sexual repression and victimization? It seems unlikely that her formidable will could be so easily frustrated, even if that is what is necessary for a happy ending. Marylee's loss is the dominant ideology's gain, but it is achieved only by placing her in a potentially powerful position. Still, the conclusion pictures the rich as an unhappy, immoral lot, and Marylee is doomed to isolation, the last member of her family.

In *Written on the Wind*, the patriarchal dynastic impulse is minor; of the younger men, only Mitch Wayne is strong enough to run a business and a family at the same time, and he is unwilling to buy Hadley Oil with his sexuality. In *Giant*, Jordan Benedict simply assumes dynasty, noting its relationship to the economic when he explains to Leslie: "Honey, I want you to understand this. I run Reata at all times. . . . That's the way it is. Everything on it is run by me. That's the way it's always been, too. . . . That's the way my father ran this outfit, and that's the way my grandfather ran it. All of it! He kept it together for his son, and my father kept it together for his. And I'm keeping it together for mine." He confronts a temporary dynastic crisis when Jordie decides to become a doctor, but this wrinkle doesn't dominate the plot, as it does in *Cat on a Hot Tin Roof* and *The Long, Hot Summer*, both adaptations from works by two of the South's most famous sons, Tennessee Williams and William Faulkner.

Horace Newcomb has suggested that American television has consistently used the South, particularly Appalachia, "for that liminal ground on which to criticize its own values, to challenge the 'acceptable' way of life with other attitudes."[20] The South also serves this function in film. In the late 1950s, when the structure of the family and sexual divisions of labor were shifting, both *The Long, Hot Summer* (1958) and *Cat on a Hot Tin Roof* (1958) employed the southern setting to champion a residual ideology. Annette Kuhn wrote that the family is "a terrain on which the forces of history are acted out, played out, exhausted." She argued that its form can be understood through an analysis of patriarchy, a term she used in reference to "concrete relations of property and power between men and women." In more detail, she explained, "Patriarchy—the rule of the father—is a structure written into particular expressions of the sexual division of labour whereby property, the means of production of exchange values, is appropriated by men, and whereby this property relation informs household and family relations in such a way that men may appropriate the labour and actual persons of women."[21]

During this period, the 1950s, the power of patriarchy was experiencing a significant challenge, and in the films of this period, residual as well as dominant and emergent notions of sexual difference and family structure waged their battle. The southern dynastic melodramas provided grounds for overt expression of the value of the patriarchal dynasty. The patriarchs in these films find themselves with grown children who don't exhibit the potential for heading the family. In *The Long, Hot Summer*, Will Varner (Orson Welles), in the manner of the old-fashioned patriarch, controls everyone and everything around him. His patriarchal conception of the world requires a strong male figure at the center of the family constellation, and his problem is that neither of his offspring is a suitable heir. His son, Jody (Tony Franciosa), is sniveling and inept and knows it. His daughter, the strong-willed schoolteacher Clara (Joanne Woodward), can't inherit control, of course, because she's a woman, and women in this world are only property.

Varner's luck changes when he hires the intruder-redeemer Ben Quick (Paul Newman) to run his store in town. Ben proves himself an adept capitalist and then proves his aptitude for patriarchy when he tames and weds the headstrong Clara, promising Varner grandsons. Personal relations here are integrally related to the economic, based on the assumption that women are interchangeable products whose function is to have babies. The meddling and ultimately ineffectual Big Mama (Judith Anderson) in *Cat on a Hot Tin Roof* states this explicitly, "That's what marriage is for—family." She is even more to the point when she directly addresses her daughter-in-law Maggie (Elizabeth Taylor): "Do you make Brick [Paul Newman] happy? Something's wrong. You're childless and my son drinks." Maggie's function, after all, is to produce babies, but the truth is that that is just what she wants to do. After three years of marriage, she is still not fulfilling her function, and the dynasty is in crisis.

Both of his sons have failed Big Daddy (Burl Ives). Gooper (Jack Carson), ambitious but ineffectual, has proved his sexual prowess by producing five children, and a sixth is on the way, but Gooper hasn't the strength Big Daddy feels is necessary for taking the family helm. A former athlete, Brick shows promise, but he can't seem to grow up. He drinks, appears tormented, and won't sleep with his wife. However, as it becomes clear that Big Daddy is dying, Brick confronts his troubles. It turns out that he believes himself responsible for the suicide of his closest childhood friend, Skipper, and he believes that Maggie had an adulterous liaison with Skipper shortly before his friend's death.

As Production Code restrictions loosened, film melodrama became able to exploit this sort of scandalous material. *Cat on a Hot Tin Roof* presents previously taboo subject matter but uses it for an ultimately conservative end. As Big Daddy confronts Brick about his weakness, Brick struggles to enter manhood. The truth comes out. Maggie never did sleep with Skipper; she is as pure as the driven snow. Her desires are traditional; all she wants is a husband's love and his children. The film climaxes in a one-on-one confrontation between Brick and Big Daddy. In a basement surrounded by "art" objects Big Daddy bought on junkets to Europe, Brick attacks his father's materialism and the trappings of wealth: "You can't buy *love*. . . . I don't want *things*." After considerable demolition of *things* and vehement accusations, they achieve an unprecedented closeness. Physically and emotionally drained, they help each other up the stairs to the living room and to Maggie's announcement, "A child is coming, sired by Brick out of Maggie The Cat." It can't be true, but it makes Big Daddy happy, so Brick summons Maggie to their bedroom, and she responds enthusiastically, "Yes, sir!" Maggie's willing submission to his authority enables Brick to assert himself as heir apparent, just as it enables the film to strongly reaffirm patriarchal notions of gender and dynastic family structure.

Another dynastic melodrama, *God's Little Acre* (1958), presents a picture of the rural poor. This film, like *A Streetcar Named Desire*, is set in the South, but their differences are as instructive as their similarities. *Streetcar* draws its characters from the decayed aristocracy and from recent immigrants; *God's Little Acre* presents a southern farm family and contrasts it with the residents of a nearby small town, populated primarily by unemployed factory workers. Ty Ty (Robert Ryan), the slightly mad head of the dirt-farming Walden family, is obsessed with the notion that gold is buried on his rural Georgia farm. He and two of his sons have dug sizable holes all over the farm, searching for the gold his grandfather told him was on the land while ignoring the possibility that this "gold" is perhaps metaphorical and neglecting the farm so much that Ty Ty is forced to ask his cotton-broker son Jim Leslie (Lance Fuller) for money. This unites the family for the first time, even bringing Ty Ty's daughter Rosamund (Helen Wescott) and her husband, Bill (Aldo Ray), from Peachtree Valley. When Ty Ty, his daughter Darlin' Jill (Fay Spain), and his daughter-in-law Griselda (Tina Louise) visit Jim Leslie's house in Atlanta, their poverty is accentuated. Jim Leslie has married a wealthy widow and now owns a fancy house furnished with expensive knickknacks. During the excruciating encounter, Jim Leslie flirts outrageously with Griselda and makes it clear that he is not happy to see Ty Ty. But, feeling guilty that he is ashamed of his past, he gives Ty Ty money anyway.

The subplot for which the film gained notoriety involves Bill, Ty Ty's son-in-law, and Griselda, Ty Ty's daughter-in-law. They lust after each other in scenes as torrid as any in this period. Their adultery and the jealousy it evokes in Griselda's husband, Buck (Jack Lord), increase tension, but the film's climax addresses a specifically economic issue. The rumor circulates that the closed factory in Peachtree Valley will not reopen and that many of the unemployed factory workers—including Bill—will be permanently destitute. Bill vows to reopen the factory himself: "When the power's on, the valley hums, there's meat and potatoes on every table, people remember funny things to laugh at. When the power's off, the valley's dead. . . . You see why I've got to turn on the power? I've been talking about it too long. It takes a *man* to turn on the power, not just a talker." His wife, Rosamund, in desperation, turns to Griselda: "You love him, same as I do. You gotta help him." But even Griselda can't dissuade him. He enters the factory, turns on the power, is cheered by a crowd of workers, and is killed, shot by the company's guard. An individual *man* may act, but he cannot, alone, challenge the power of capitalism.

Bill's funeral brings the family together for the last time, and in its aftermath, Buck's temper flares. Ty Ty protects first Griselda and then his prodigal son Jim Leslie from Buck's jealous wrath. Ty Ty pleads with his children: "We're gettin' further and further away from the happy life. All of us oughta sit down and think a little about livin' and how to do it." He even admits that money doesn't matter: "All you boys seem to think about is the things you can see and touch. Well, that ain't livin'. It's the things you feel down inside you. That's what livin's for." He promises never to dig another hole "except to plant seeds for things to grow" and goes back to his farming, restoring narrative order.

Within the film, various ideologies compete. Although it presents a negative picture of murderous capitalist bosses, their power and the sanctity of private property are naturalized, and Bill's death shows the consequences of active resistance to capitalist injustice. And though the film acknowledges the problems of the unemployed, it encourages passivity and resignation. Indeed, although the film is premised on a search for gold, its message promotes the notion that quality of life is not dependent on money, a frequent theme in this period of increasing materialism in America. The one character who does achieve material success, Jim Leslie, is presented as despicable; he gained his moderate wealth by being a "kept" man and has never repented. For though sin is basic to the film melodrama, repentance works. Griselda, in the film's final segment, brings water to the men who are now back working in the fields. The conclusion shows woman in support of man, the breadwinner. Griselda's return to the domestic absolves her from the shame of her earlier wandering. The film's conclusion supports the patriarchal ideology that places woman's realm as the domestic. Her products are use-values. Man's realm is the economic, his products the exchange-values so important to capitalism.

It is not surprising that these films never seriously critique capitalism and that their messages often reinforce patriarchy; neither is it surprising that the narratives participate in American racism, symbolically annihilating people of color, since the films are almost entirely populated by whites, with the few African Americans and Chicanos in service positions. Popular cultural forms function to preserve social institutions and to disseminate information about them. These forms do, however, also function to allow discussion and to negotiate change, and it is important to note the low-level critiques made within them. Most of these male-oriented melodramas privilege the middle class, the class whose support for capitalism is most crucial, and they champion hard work. The Judeo-Christian warning that it is easier to pass a camel through the eye of a needle than to get a rich man into heaven combines with the Protestant work ethic to reinforce an American dogma—"work is honorable; wealth is decadent." These films frequently present unflattering pictures of the wealthy, as *Written on the Wind* does, and encourage acceptance of class boundaries and the restrictions they imply. When the films depict the crossing of class boundaries, as in *Giant* or *Some Came Running*, they emphasize the difficulties it entails.

Ambition is problematic; while upward mobility was becoming an increasingly common goal in America, these films meted out punishment to those ambitious characters who attempt to circumvent hard work. When George's dream in *A Place in the Sun* leads him to contemplate murder, his rich friends abandon him. Cal, in *East of Eden*, is rebuked by his father for participating in high capitalism through wartime speculation in commodities and thereby making money from the misery of others. But because Cal's intentions were honorable, he is rewarded in the end and allowed to return to his father and to work on their farm. Money can't buy happiness, the films preach, and selling sexual favors also draws punishment. Luke, in *Not as a Stranger*, learns that the consequences of the latter are painful, but most of the characters who sell "love" are female, and in this respect, social class has a distinct influence on the representation of gender. Many of the working-class women in these films support themselves selling "love" via forms of prostitution. Blanche in *A Streetcar Named Desire*, Alma in *From Here to Eternity*, and Kate in *East of Eden* are all involved in some form of "the world's oldest profession." These women work because they must, but "work" takes place in the public sphere, and in these films, few women venture into this sacred arena.

Those women who do work outside the home generally fit into three categories. Those who are young and unmarried and intend to leave their work when they marry, returning to the domestic sphere, compose the first group. Kristina quits nursing as soon as Luke finishes his internship in *Not as a Stranger*, and she resists his suggestion that she return to nursing rather than begin a family. Clara, surely, will not return to teaching at the end of *The Long, Hot Summer*, and even career-woman Lucy, in *Written on the Wind*, assumes that she will leave the work force for a suburban family life. She goes instead to a Texas mansion, but leaves it with Mitch, presumably to fulfill her earlier ambition.

The two other groups suffer social stigmata: members of one group are doomed to spinsterhood, like Gwen in *Some Came Running*. The only "respectable" middle-class woman that remains employed, Gwen also remains unmarried. She is the stereotypical naive intellectual. She wears unflattering glasses and arranges her hair to increase the severity of her appearance. She dresses conservatively to mask her sexuality, and she is flustered when Dave flatters her. Marylee, in *Written on the Wind*, also suffers from spinsterhood, though she is far from sexually naive.

Members of the third group seem "loose," sexually suspect. Even the working-class women who must work in the public sphere, like Ginny in *Some Came Running* and Alice in *A Place in the Sun*, are suspect. But most of the female characters in these male-oriented family melodramas—and, indeed, in many of the female-oriented films—are not employed outside the home. Even the headstrong Leslie in *Giant* accepts the admonition that women don't belong in business or politics (though her daughters reject it). Even though this prohibition may be at the root of Marylee's problems in *Written on the Wind*, its removal doesn't thrill her. The issue of women working outside the home is rarely raised in explicit terms. Women's problems are still unnamed, and the film melodramas address them in emotional rather than intellectual terms. The rhetoric of these popular films emphasizes the domestic as woman's natural arena and the workplace as a poor and undesirable substitute. The issue is, however, raised, and no matter what the rhetoric of the narrative pattern, the fact remains that we do see some women outside their traditional sphere.

Imitating Life

The 1959 version of *Imitation of Life* turns around the issue of women working outside the home, but even here, the sociological nature of the issue is ignored. The problem is privatized, and another problem— one *with* a sociological tag, "racism"—draws attention away from the film's ultimate stakes: gender definition and family structure. *Imitation of Life* presents the social debate over sexual difference through an interplay of narrative and filmic events, best understood in its complexity. Though it may be unreasonable to expect a reading of any text to amalgamate historical, sociological, structural, psychoanalytic, semiotic, and ideological analyses, this particular film offers an uncommon richness. But no single approach can account for the complexity and ambiguity of this film, and a dialogue among various approaches makes clear the materials this film offers for meaning-making and the ways in which it both challenges and privileges prevailing notions.

When the film is placed in its sociohistorical and industrial contexts, it becomes clear, for instance, that the film carried little risk for Universal Studios. Ross Hunter's recognition of a market for the revival of the "weepies" had already paid off, so a fairly sizable market seemed certain. And the conservative nature of this narrative pattern enabled the inclusion of controversial subject matter concerning race relations and mothering, which insured the attention of the press and, as a result, an even larger audience. In addition, Hunter combined money-makers. Already, Douglas Sirk had proved himself as a master stylist of the wide-screen melodrama, and several of the films he had directed for Universal in the 1950s had hit *Variety*'s yearly Top Twenty Moneymaker charts. The story itself had twice before seen success, originally in Fannie Hurst's best-selling novel (1932)[22] and then in a film adaptation directed by John Stahl (1934). Elaborately and expensively costumed, the star in the 1950s version, Lana Turner, brought to the film not only her star persona but also the intrigue of her personal life, which paralleled some of the subject matter of the film—a lover slain by a rival, her daughter. Booked "day-and-date" in black, white, and integrated theaters, *Imitation of Life*, Douglas Sirk's last Hollywood film, ranked fourth in domestic earnings in 1959 and became Universal Studios' highest-grossing film to that time.[23]

Simultaneously hailed and condemned as one of the best or worst tearjerkers of its time, *Imitation of Life* tells a popular story. Its basic plot line resembles two popular kinds of narratives. Like a certain variation of the women's picture, it depicts a housewife's rise to financial success and her subsequent realization that money can't buy happiness, only family can. And like the even more popular male-oriented social problem film, it purports to be about an identified sociological problem while it derives its emotional power from chronicling the rebuilding of a shattered nuclear family: two single mothers—one white, one African American—meet and join forces as they raise their daughters in a female community. White Lora Meredith (Lana Turner), attractive and thirtyish, aspires to act on Broadway; African American Annie Johnson (Juanita Moore) just wants to mother. Lora's driving ambition obscures her mothering and blocks her romance with a photographer, Steve Archer (John Gavin, a Rock Hudson look-alike). Her ambition, bolstered by Annie's support, also provides Lora with the stamina to achieve stardom, and this success boosts the two women and their daughters from poverty to affluence.

Midway through the film, a flashy montage moves through eight years of Lora's seemingly untroubled rise to the pinnacle of success, but the glitter of success begins to lose its attraction as Steve Archer returns to the story. At this point, none of the major characters are happy. Lora's daughter, Susie (Sandra Dee), goes to a boarding school but wants to see more of her mother. Annie's daughter, Sara Jane (Susan Kohner), wants to be successful—and white. Annie wants Sara Jane to accept her blackness and to be happy with a middle-class (but African American) life. Even Lora wants more. Her career in stage comedy isn't enough; she wants to perform in serious stage dramas and in movies, and she wants love. Her long-term relationship with a playwright, David Edwards (Dan O'Herlihy), doesn't satisfy her. As if by magic, Steve shows up for Lora's dramatic debut in a play considered controversial for its stance on racial problems. Now a commercial success himself, Steve too still has artistic aspirations and still wants Lora, who is now tempted by an exciting and important film role.

Meanwhile, Sara Jane is beaten unmercifully by her white boyfriend, Frankie (Troy Donahue), who has learned that she was only "passing" for white, and Annie's health begins to fail. Lora goes to Italy for filming, Susie falls in love with Steve in Lora's absence, and Sara Jane runs away to become a white show girl. Lora returns, and Annie—through a detective hired by Steve—finds Sara Jane, only to be thoroughly rejected. Lora finally accepts Steve's marriage proposal, unknowingly breaking Susie's heart. Annie dies, even as Lora declares, "I won't let you," and is mourned with a dramatic and ostentatious funeral. As Annie's body is being loaded into a horse-drawn carriage, Sara Jane returns, sobbing, and throws herself onto the flower-covered casket. Lora pulls her away and into a limousine, and the film ends with Lora finally in a mothering role. As she comforts Sara Jane and holds Susie's hand, Steve looks on approvingly.

Several discourses crisscross this narrative; several stories are told. The most obvious one concerns race. In an interview more than ten years after the film's release, Sirk described his aims in making *Imitation of Life*:

> After I read the outline, I made one change, socially—an important one, I think. In Stahl's treatment of the story, the white and the Negro women are co-owners of a thriving pancake business—which took all the social significance out of the Negro mother's situation. Maybe it would have been all right for Stahl's time, but nowadays a Negro women who got rich *could* buy a house, and wouldn't be dependent to such a degree on the white woman, a fact which makes the Negro woman's daughter less understandable. So I had to change the axis of the film and make the Negro woman just the typical Negro, a servant, without much she could call her own but the friendship, love and charity of a white mistress. This whole uncertain and kind of oppressive situation accounts much more for the daughter's attitude.[24]

Sirk's notion of the "typical Negro" reflects an implicit racism, an insensitivity to the black woman's character, and a naiveté about the relation of class, race, gender, and labor. As Marina Heung pointed out in her fine reading of the film—one of the few recent *Cinema Journal* entries to consider race, class, *and* gender—"For white women, work is viewed as a problem, a matter of weighing crucial alternatives, while for black women, it is a natural signifier of their assumed status in white society."[25] Still, Sirk's retrospective emphasis on racial problems and his dramatic emphasis on Sara Jane's plight—the contrast of her brightly colored costumes with the icy or pastel costumes worn by Lora and Susie and the increased pacing and intensity of the scenes focused on Sara Jane—indicate a certain degree of social consciousness. Sirk does appear to have been an uncommonly self- and socially-conscious director. He had worked in German theater after World War I, "when everybody's thinking was political,"[26] and had brought with him to America and Hollywood a taste for social criticism. He gravitated toward melodrama, a genre particularly appropriate for social commentary, and although race is clearly an ideological issue in this film, its emotional impact obscures the class and gender questions that accompany it.

The relatively recent critical resurrection of Sirk's films has focused on his ability to subvert generic conventions, and that was apparently his intention when he directed this film. But his emphasis, and that of many critics, on the racial angle in *Imitation of Life* places the film as a social problem film, which, as with the films I discussed in chapter 3, obscures its participation in the social debate over notions of gender and family, as well as the genre's implicit involvement in this process. An analysis of the film's narrative structure shows that, as in the social problem films of the period, family is what is at stake in this maternal melodrama. Sirk's stylization and the depiction of motherhood that results from his plot changes indicate an appreciation of the problem at the film's core. Unlike most film melodramas, this film directly addresses the relation of mothering to women's work in the public sphere. Tracing the differences between this film and John Stahl's 1934 version illustrates the film's rhetoric as it displays the intersections between ambition, sexuality, and motherhood.

Ambition proves a necessity for Beatrice Pullman (Claudette Colbert), Lora's counterpart in the depression-era version, and success drops from the heavens. Widowed with a child, the still young and attractive Bea pounds the sidewalks in her late husband's position as maple-syrup salesperson; her entry into the work force was necessitated by her sudden poverty and by her responsibility to her daughter. She doesn't actively seek advancement but doesn't flinch when opportunity presents itself, first in the form of her maid's pancakes (they open a restaurant) and later in the form of advice from a customer, who encourages her to move into mass production. Bea's ambition and almost accidental success do not violate the traditional notion that woman, the nurturer, should sacrifice herself, suppressing sexual desires for the good of her daughter.

On the other hand, in the 1959 version Lora exhibits her personal ambition from the very beginning. No viable romantic interest arises for Bea until well into the narrative, but Steve is there for Lora from the very

beginning. Indeed, the first shot of Lora is from his point of view (figures 5-1 and 5-2); his camera frames her (figure 5-3), so successfully turning her body into a commodity that his pictures result in her first commercial acting job. The fairly standard shot/reverse-shot sequences that develop their relationship as the two exchange looks visually encourage the specta-

5.3

tor's involvement in their growing relationship. But during a luncheon with the intruder-redeemer Steve, Lora tells him of her theatrical ambitions, "I've never wanted anything else." She adds, almost as an afterthought, "Except Susie, of course," indicating that marriage and motherhood had intruded on her ambition rather than composed it. Their luncheon date is cut short by news of an audition; Lora leaves hurriedly, emphasizing her "unfeminine" ambition.

When success doesn't fall from the heavens for Lora the way it did for Bea and when Steve, a photographer who wants his work to hang in museums, finds work with an ad agency, he jumps to what he considers the "logical" conclusion, "Then I guess you'll have to marry me." An analysis of the film's enunciative practices exposes how a few low-angle close-ups emphasize Steve as an erotic object (figure 5-4). But as Lora steadfastly refuses to give up her ambition, he loses this status and becomes instead monolithic and menacing. She is offered her first big break, by a sleazy agent (Robert Alda) who earlier made a pass at her, but Steve doesn't want her to even go to the audition. They quarrel in the narrow hallway of her apartment building as Lora tries to leave (figure 5-5):

STEVE
I'm not asking you not to go down there, Lora. I'm *telling* you.

5.4

5.5

LORA

What makes you think you have that right?

STEVE

'Cause I love you. Isn't that enough?

She has tried to explain that she wants "something *more*," that she has already satisfied the need for primary relationships described by Nancy

5.6

Chodorow. She has a child, and even now, Annie and Sarah Jane round out their small community.

As Lora actively and vehemently rejects the "opportunity" to marry and "settle down," she powerfully takes control of the film. She asserts, "I want to *achieve* something," and tries to get by him, but he argues back, trying to keep her from leaving, "What you want isn't *real*." A woman *choosing* to work outside the home poses threat enough, but choosing *acting* as a career damns her more quickly than anything else. Although a public revelation of the massive numbers of women working outside the home and of the increasing domestication of the American male occurred in the late 1950s, popular prejudices were not rewritten overnight, and it is not unreasonable to charge that choosing acting as the profession for the protagonist in this version was an explicitly antifeminist move. This first reference to the artificiality of the life to which Lora aspires slips by, however, as she is privileged by a series of over-the-shoulder close-up reaction shots from Steve's point of view (figure 5-6). By this time, he receives no reaction shots, and the only view of him is of his back; he seems overpowering and large. She struggles against his confinement, desperately striving for "something I've wanted all my life, since I was a child." Finally, she gains control, he exits, and the question of women's work outside the home becomes established as central to the narrative.

Foreshadowing the contemporary feminist movement, Lora repeatedly

5.7

5.8

rejects offers of marriage because it is clear that, in the 1950s, marriage was defined in terms of "settling down," which would end her career. Even David Edwards, the playwright-lover who comes to write all his plays around Lora, intends with his proposal that she renounce her theatrical career, and Lora questions the nature of their long-standing relation-

5.9

ship. He wants what has been both a romance and a business partnership to turn into a marriage, but Lora, by this time a fixture on Broadway, tells Annie that she knows "something is missing" (figure 5-7). She refers to the glamorous life, but she knows also that she doesn't love Dave. A business alliance was once the most adequate basis for marriage, and it was the basis of Bea's youthful marriage in the earlier film version, but even by the 1930s, this had become a residual ideology. Certainly by the 1950s, romance and love were, at least on the silver screen, the only reasonable motive for getting married. This brief scene between Lora and Annie follows the time-spanning montage and sets up everything that follows, especially the eventually consummated relationship with Steve. It also prefigures Lora's move to "serious drama" and pushes her career in another, more demanding direction.

Whereas, in the earlier version, Bea's ambition was presented as altruistic—and necessary, in light of a depression-time economy—Lora's is presented as narcissistic; her artistry is presented as selfish vanity. Joan Crawford's fiercely ambitious title character in *Mildred Pierce* (1945) had worked only to benefit her daughter, but by the early 1950s, film melodramas were not representing middle-class white women working outside the home at all. When some middle-class working women finally found representation in the mid-1950s, they worked only until married (*Written on the Wind; The Long, Hot Summer; Picnic*). By the end of the decade, white middle-class working mothers had once again become a cinematic option, but rarely was their working a central issue. For example, Constance MacKenzie in *Peyton Place* worked because she had no man to support her and her daughter, but Constance's work does not pull her away from her daughter. And even though she sent her daughter away to boarding school, Bea, in the earlier film version of *Imitation of Life*, showered affection and gifts on a grateful and appreciative daughter. The later, revised version presents the female community as faulty; female solidarity threatens patriarchy, and this film works to defuse that threat. Lora gives little thought to motherhood and pays minimal attention to Susie, frequently bypassing visits with Susie when presented with opportunities to further her career. And Susie resents it.

Sweetly, Susie informs Steve, and the audience, that she doesn't *mind* the way her mother dresses, but the cloying innocence of her voice makes her anger clear, and her soft, pastel-colored costumes present a dramatic and judgmental contrast to Lora's vivid image. The film participates in the discursive struggle over "mother" as Susie's jealous comments attempt to freeze a residual meaning of the term while Lora's passionate commitment to her acting career functions as an attempt to dislodge "mother," expressing an emerging ideology. But the film challenges the emergent; Sirk's use of color and his manipulation of Turner's icy performance present a very different "mother" than Stahl did in his "realistic" representational style. In one scene, Lora wears bright-orange capri pants that emphasize her sexuality, and in another, she shows up for Susie's graduation wearing flashy sunglasses, a turban, and a sexy, slinky ice-blue dress (figure 5-8). Never does she look the asexual matron. Lora's actions as well as her image have separated her from her daughter—and from her "natural" role as nurturer. Lora has assumed the "masculine," breadwinning role in this four-woman community.

Their "family" maintains, with its racial inequity, the structural inequity common to the dominant, nuclear family. The white women are, like males generally, privileged, whereas the African American women, like females, occupy a lesser position. Although Annie and Sara Jane are central to the narrative, the film maintains a rigid class distinction between African Americans and whites. Lora gives Susie expensive clothes and a horse, and Susie is sent to an exclusive boarding school, while Sara Jane remains behind and is expected to help Annie around the house. Annie, the constant nurturer, is everyone's source of support and advice. Juanita Moore's physical bulk and constantly conservative costuming give Annie's character an asexual but powerfully maternal image. Lana Turner's Lora is overtly (and inappropriately) sexual, lacking in maternal qualities; sexuality and motherhood are defined as mutually exclusive. Annie acknowledges the legitimacy of Lora's sexuality and encourages her relationship with Steve but never overtly expresses her own desires. She devotes herself to caring for Lora, Susie, and Sara Jane. Annie provides a constant source of nurturance for Susie; she is always there when Susie needs adult guidance, allowing Lora the freedom to pursue her career. Annie also nurtures Lora and provides guidance for her too when her narcissistic self-absorption threatens Lora's relationship with Susie. But though "mother love" would seem personified in Annie, she too proves inadequate.

Nancy Chodorow pointed out, "Women's mothering includes the capacities for its own reproduction."[27] But although Annie's mothering potentially reproduces itself in Susie, Annie has considerably less success with her own daughter, Sara Jane, whom she seems incapable of understanding (figure 5-9). Chodorow did acknowledge the importance of historical conditions in the development of sex-gender systems, noting that changes in the economy have sharpened the contradictions within the family. In this film, the very possibility of reproducing mothers and mothering is at stake. At a time when women were entering the work force in unprecedented numbers, this film pits both residual and emergent notions of family structure and gender against the dominant ideology, which prevails in the narrative solution. In *Imitation of Life*, those generic elements that support dominant ideology and those that—intentionally or unintentionally—subvert or challenge it interact to produce a message as inherently contradictory as the ideological process it participates in.

This sort of "subversion," however, leaves intact a narrative structure that supports the very social system against which Sirk's favorite character, Sara Jane, wants to rebel.[28] Race is not the only barrier in her path; she faces another crucial social inequality. Sara Jane, repulsed by her mother's plans for her, rejects not only blackness but also hearth, home, and submission to constricting notions of propriety. Annie, a pragmatist (and something of a fatalist), wants Sara Jane to accept her racial identity. It is a sin, she tells her daughter, to be ashamed of who you are. This does not

5.10

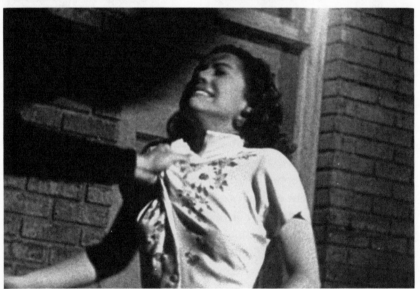

5.11

preclude a desire for Sara Jane to improve her "station" in life. For Annie, this means that Sara Jane should attend church functions, go to a respectable black college, and "graduate" into white-collar work as a teacher or a librarian. The assumption that Sara Jane will work is a given for Annie, and the respectable middle class is her goal for Sara Jane, but Sara Jane

5.12

wants more. She wants the markers of success and class status that Lora
has received. Race functions as a class marker in this film, and whereas the
issue of women's work outside the home becomes central for middle-class
white women, women of the working class—in this case Annie and Sara
Jane—have worked outside their homes since the advent of the industrial
revolution. Annie has managed, to some extent, to combine her home and
her workplace, and perhaps it is the very domesticity of her work that
prevents Annie from understanding the ideological changes that distance
her from her daughter and that complicate for her the reproduction of
mothering described by Chodorow. Neither hearth nor workplace, per se,
is among Sara Jane's goals. She wants the unquestioned social status that
accompanies white affluence, but her efforts produce only an "imitation of
life."

Initially, Sara Jane plans to achieve her goals through a liaison with her
upper-middle-class white boyfriend, played by the blond Troy Donahue
(figure 5-10). But when he discovers her secret and brutally turns against
her (figure 5-11), she sells her sexuality on the stage (figure 5-12). Pos-
sessing none of the inhibiting attitudes that initially hampered Lora's
career progress (another of the film's racist premises), Sara Jane will sell it,
if that's what it takes to get ahead. This too is a significant change from
the earlier film version of *Imitation of Life*, which was made just as the

restrictions of the Production Code were beginning to be enforced. In the earlier film, Sara Jane's counterpart, Peola (Freddie Washington), took "respectable" work as a cashier, not as a scantily clad singer or chorus girl. Neither did she have a romantic relationship, much less a relationship with a white man. Sexuality was not an issue for Peola, and neither was the ambition that characterizes Sara Jane's rejection of blackness.

Lora is Sara Jane's vision of success, but Lora is not just white. She is also the antithesis of domesticity. Annie represents a residual ideology, a value system that relegates women to the domestic sphere and insists that, for women, family takes precedence over all else. Early in the film, Steve too champions this position, and his inflexibility moves Lora, representative of an emergent notion of woman, to reject him. Sara Jane, rejected by her white boyfriend, abandons the idea of marrying success (and whiteness) and goes after it on her own, as Lora had, but the flagrant sexuality of her entrance into show business shows a disregard for traditional values far greater than Lora's. She is punished by her mother's death.

Annie's death ruptures the narrative, providing a motivation for dramatic changes and enabling a sad but "happy" ending. Lora too is shaken by Annie's demise, but by it she is narratively enabled to assume a modified (modernized?) version of Annie's role. Steve's return provides the strong masculine presence necessary for Lora's miraculous transformation. She now embraces family and appears to provide the nurturance she has so long needed herself. The often improbable happy endings in film melodramas have led to the notion that the films function simply and solely to reinforce dominant ideology. Of course they reinforce dominance, but the narrative contortions necessary for the production of these deus-ex-machina endings expose the improbability of actually achieving the "happiness" the endings depict. And they leave many questions unanswered. The resolution of *Imitation of Life* is, as is common to the genre, both pat and ambiguous. Can Lora really give up her acting career? Can Steve yield enough to accept her success? Will Susie's move to Colorado really soothe her pain? Will Sara Jane accept her blackness and social class? Will she become respectable? Can individual action actually solve any of their problems?

Race is not the only focus in the film; gender and class limit as surely. Lora has achieved success in comedy and serious drama on the stage and has completed a significant film, but because she is female, these achieve-ments are not considered positively but actually count against her. In his 1959 *New York Times* review of the film, Bosley Crowther described Lora as a woman who has "concentrated on a self-aggrandizing career,"[29] a judgment not likely to have been applied to a man or a male character. Crowther is, I admit, a straw man, but his attitude is not less damaging than that of Sirk and the screenwriters, Eleanore Griffin and Allan Scott, whose clichéd dialogue provides Lora with no adequate response to accu-sations that she has neglected her daughter by pursuing a career. Indeed, the rhetoric of the film insists that this was inevitable. Perhaps her prob-lems are not racial, but they are certainly social, and individual moral choice will not solve them neatly, as the dramatic and emotionally moving resolution to this film encourages its audience to believe.

This narrative closure definitely reinforces dominant ideology, encour-aging belief in the power of the individual and ignoring the necessity for social change, even at a time when such change was under way. It also reinforces the notions that women who pursue careers neglect their chil-dren, that mothering is the only appropriate activity for women, and that deviation from this norm will result in unhappiness for all involved. But we must look beyond the resolution to the conflict that precedes and necessitates it. The mere fact that the issue of women's work outside the home could inspire such a narrative conflict indicates its importance, and the appearance of various approaches to the issue exposes the society's lack of consensus. Although the resolution of *Imitation of Life* posits the abnormality of women working, the actions of the characters throughout the film contradict this position. Annie, of course, never questions that she will work, although her work is domestic. Lora wants to work; so does Sara Jane. A singular focus on racial inequality obfuscates the question that structures the film as well as the impossibility of individual solutions. The character Sara Jane, acting in accordance with an emergent notion of woman, uses the issue of race to reject her "destiny," but she strives for far more than recognition as a white. Like Lora, Sara Jane wants *more*. She wants the personal power that accompanies a successful career, and the sexual barrier that systematically blocks her progress is just as effective as the racial barrier. Both, surely, can be overcome only collectively. The film, in the tradition of the melodrama, privatizes the political and emphasizes

5.13

5.14

5.15

5.16

5.17

the power of the individual, a characteristically American move. As Chodorow pointed out, "Until the contemporary feminist movement, social
and psychological commentators put the burden of solution for these
problems onto the individual and did not recognize that anything was
systematically wrong."³⁰ Sara Jane's individual action will not open the
door to the glitter and the illusion, that imitation of life represented by the
trappings of opulence that surround Lora, and neither will her individual
moral decision to return for her mother's spectacular funeral, where glitter and glamour accompany the solemn ritual of humble people.

Long shots from inside the window of an antique shop show Annie's
mourners, marching with the horse-drawn hearse that carries Annie to the
mournful songs of a marching band. The shots curiously frame the artificiality and the sincerity of the pomp Annie has made her last request
(figure 5-13). Marina Heung suggested that these "objective" shots, the
outdoor setting (which contrasts with the indoor settings that dominate
most of the film), and the camera's panoramic, high angles that encom-
pass the procession lend the ending a "pseudo-documentary effect" (figure 5-14), as does the appearance of Mahalia Jackson, who—in a cameo—
sings at Annie's funeral (figure 5-15). For Heung, these strategies allow
the conservative thrust of the ending to predominate over Sirk's ironic
subtexts, and "we are all convinced" that, when Sara Jane reenters the

5.18

narrative, weeping over her mother's coffin in front of everybody (figure 5-16), "this time she is not performing." For Heung, though she admitted that the ironic subtext lurks not far from the surface, the drive toward closure is successful.[31] I suggest yet another reading: the excessive opulence of the funeral, the opulence of the funeral procession, and the heightened drama of Sara Jane's return serve as commentary on the ambiguities and contradictions that fueled the narrative; they call attention to the artificiality of happy endings. Even Heung, unbelieving, noted Sirk's opinion: "You don't believe the happy end, and you're not supposed to."[32] I don't.

What Sara Jane returns to is family, but even this is ambiguous. As Annie was a surrogate mother to and for Lora, Lora becomes at least momentarily a surrogate mother to Sara Jane. The final shots of Lora, Susie, Sara Jane, and Steve in a limousine place Lora as the source of strength for both "daughters" as she puts Sara Jane's head on her shoulder and holds Susie's hand (figure 5-17). In reaction shots, Steve gazes at the three women (figure 5-18).

Chodorow's theory of psychoanalysis encourages a reading that shows that Steve satisfies his "masculine" desire for a dyadic heterosexual relationship while Lora's "feminine" triadic model for relationships is also fulfilled, mothering reproduced. A Lacanian approach calls attention to the newly formed family that emerges as a result of Steve's provision of the masculine support for his and Lora's entry into the bourgeois adult social order. And analysis of the enunciative practices in this segment calls attention to his gaze and his physical separation from the group of women. Visually, he is distanced from Lora, Susie, and Sara Jane, and the unity of the family is placed in question.

As it tells its multiple stories, the film raises many questions and offers a variety of solutions. The film's ambiguous closure may privilege dominant ideologies, but it does not obliterate alternatives. The meaning of Steve's "look" is unclear. What does it really mean? Is he part of a family or outside the female collective? What does Sarah Jane's gesture of return really mean? Are issues of sexual identity, race, and social class in any way resolved? The narrative's structure focuses on the ambiguity that results from a skewed logic, and it highlights the delicacy of gender identity, family structure, and the value system in which they exist. The machinery of closure is there, but it is more than vaguely dissatisfying; it generates more questions than it answers. Although we must acknowledge the repressive elements within our culture's texts, we must also recognize the emancipatory elements that challenge them. In their interaction, we negotiate ourselves.

Epilogue: Reflections

The readings—of both theories and films—I present here respond to gaps in cultural studies and in feminist film studies, gaps that can be closed through mutual appropriation. Scholars in both arenas concentrate on the explication of power relations, and working in both areas, I am frustrated by the limitations of their overlap in the United States, especially when I think of the richness the two areas offer each other. Many cultural studies scholars seem satisfied by the discovery of polysemy and uninterested in examining how it works in texts, and the rigorous focus on textual analysis within feminist film studies can enrich cultural studies. Many feminists seem satisfied with the discovery of the cinematic mechanisms that contribute to women's oppression, and cultural studies offers theoretical and practical strategies for resisting oppression and intervening in the struggle over defining genders. However, our interventions must be rigorously considered because, as Stuart Hall argued, effects are never guaranteed, and we must choose our strategies carefully because, as Audre Lorde argued, "The master's tools will never dismantle the master's house."[1]

I harbor no fantasy that my readings are definitive, and even as I proffer them, I remain skeptical of the tools I have used in their construction. As I traced the ideological patterns within these mass-produced, mass-consumed film melodramas, I found that each of the various approaches I used illuminated certain "truths," that each provided a distinct way of looking at film narratives, and that each tempted me with satisfaction. But as surely as one approach gives answers, so do others, and I find none of them singularly sufficient. I find, in fact, that they raise as many questions as they answer: What has the epochal approach told us about the theories and films under consideration? Can we argue that melodrama is inherently conservative or subversive? What do these readings say about melodrama, the 1950s, and film melodrama in the 1950s? To what extent do critics' own ideological positions blind them to other approaches and lead them to predetermined conclusions? What is the effect of combining approaches in reading a film or a genre? And, to what extent are the approaches used determined by the very texts under consideration?

The analytic approaches I have examined—each focused on a different aspect of film texts—would seem to be applicable across the spectrum of film genres and useful for analyzing other audiovisual media as well, but certain texts seem to cry out for specific sorts of analyses. *Imitation of Life*, for instance, demands attention to the social problem of racial inequality, but exclusive attention to racial issues obscures questions of social class and even of women's work, a question that is at the heart of this narrative. Attention to race must be balanced by attention to class and, especially, to gender. To a certain extent, a film or genre may govern the degree to which one approach should be weighed against another; genre analysis itself privileges the study of narrative structure. Among the social problem films, the overwhelming similarity in the relationship of narrative structure to the representation of gender was impossible to ignore; as different as the films are, the relation of gender to narrative structures in *On the Waterfront* and *Come Back, Little Sheba* tells us the same thing: men act, women wait. On the other hand, the female-oriented melodramas have a similarly rigid relationship between the representation of gender and narrative structure, but in them, resolution is achieved through the action of female characters. Narrative structure, then, cannot be seen as inevitably tied to certain representations of gender.

Other films, genres, or subgenres might demand different priorities. Chodorow's theory of psychoanalysis seemed appropriate for the small group of female-oriented family melodramas I examined in chapter 4 because her description of female and male development resonates in the stories told by the films that compose this subgenre, stories constructed for consumption by a predominantly female audience. Her description, on the other hand, does not "fit" very well when applied to the male-oriented melodramas I discuss in chapter 5. Indeed, Freudian or Lacanian descriptions of the patriarchal family seem more appropriate for these films, as my reading of *Not as a Stranger* reveals. The point is not that one or another of these theories is superior but that none alone is sufficient; the theories help to explain different stories and stories told from distinctly different—and gendered—perspectives. The complexities of these theories of psychoanalysis have been of less concern to me here than their adequacies in explaining the struggle over gender in popular film texts. They do make it clear that melodramatic subgenres construct "reality" differently, with the male-oriented films presenting a dominant picture of "woman" and the female-oriented films allowing the expression of emergent and preemergent notions.

Combining approaches, as I did in my analysis of *Imitation of Life*, complicates the matter, calling attention to the ambiguities and contradictions that characterize mainstream texts, which are designed to appeal to broad audiences; such combination makes the desire for and possibility of clear-cut readings ridiculous. *Imitation of Life* examines a female community, focuses on the bonding between women, and places a strong female character in a position of power and independence, expressing a preemergent structure of feeling and appealing to women concerned with female friendships. At the same time, the film constructs race and class divisions that complicate the female relationships, and it drives toward a narrative closure that separates the women, resolving in favor of a heterosexual relationship and a newly constituted nuclear family. My claim that the message given by the bulk of the film—a message privileging female independence—overrides the ending, which also fails to convince because of its excessiveness, places me in opposition to Marina Heung, another feminist reader. Heung feels that the ending has a documentary feel that negates the jarring logical rupture and facilitates the leap of faith necessary to read the ending as convincing. Heung's and my readings, however, have in common an objection to the dominant ideology that refuses the compatibility of female independence in the public sphere with heterosexual romance (and mothering), privileging the latter as the only appropriate—even if unconvincing—closure. My reading says as much about my position as a critic struggling (in a friendly way) with other critics as it does about the film; in fact, it says quite a bit about both. In addition to our gaining knowledge about a film, addressing it from multiple perspectives allows us to understand the stakes involved in the construction of readings and the ways they are used in the construction of identity and of interpretive communities.

In fact, one of the major functions of textual analysis is the articulation of interpretive stances in the critical struggle over differing explanations of how we construct what we "know" to be "real." In and through this process, critics differentiate their own identities and align themselves with particular interpretive communities. In a fine article on the topic, Elizabeth Ellsworth analyzed published feminist responses to the 1982 film *Personal Best*, examining the way feminist communities constitute their social subjectivities despite and, in fact, partially through their interactions with Hollywood films.[2] Ellsworth showed how feminists produce discursive boundaries both between feminists and nonfeminists (to set themselves and their communities apart from the mainstream) and between their feminist community and other feminist communities (to position themselves as unique within the broader category "women involved in the feminist movement"). This is also the case, as I have shown, in the discursive distinctions feminists make in the struggles within the smaller sphere of academic feminist film studies. Ellsworth delineated several sorts of feminist reviewers (liberal, socialist, and lesbian), but for all her emphasis on discursive struggle, she finally argued that the text does not exert the primary limits on interpretation but that it simply provides the opportunity for discursive struggle. Such constraints are not, Ellsworth contended, textual but social; readings that challenge dominant meanings depend on an ability to reject and alter those very practices central to filmic representation—in the case of readings of *Personal Best*, for instance, the ability to ignore the film's conclusion.

Indeed, within feminist film studies, a fair amount of attention has been paid to conflicting approaches to the happy ending. Academic critics have differed significantly in the weight they give to an ending, as we have seen dramatically illustrated, in the pages of *Cinema Journal*, in the struggle among different feminist readings of *Stella Dallas*. Ellsworth's evidence suggests that readers fairly freely appropriate portions of the filmic text to create the reading they desire, a reading that aids in the creation and re-creation of their individual and communal identities. However, the published feminist reviews that Ellsworth examined took only limited liberties with the text; she noted, for instance, that even the most radical rewriters, the lesbian feminist reviewers, *did* stop short of rearranging the film's chronology or shifting the relations of actor to action. This suggests both that there exists a general consensus—perhaps a *limiting* consensus—on how film narratives are to be read and that, to be publishable, criticism cannot vary more significantly than the readings Ellsworth described. This indicates a hegemonic ideological process in which dominant notions of how to interpret conventional narrative and film forms are effectively taught and retaught not just within and through our "educational apparatus" but also through the mass media and, more implicitly, at home. Readers learn, for instance, the importance of the ending in traditional narratives and learn that they must address the ending even if they find it unbelievable. Readers also learn conventional ways of interpreting other narrative and enunciative patterns, though they are constrained to conformity only in public[ation]. With my readings, I address both the ways we have learned to interpret narrative and enunciative patterns and the possible ways of resisting the limitations that this learning places upon us.

Tania Modleski, in *The Women Who Knew Too Much*, sought to empower women's readings of Hitchcock's films, placing the knowledge of men's guilt in the oppression of women evidenced in these films "more securely than ever in the possession of women."[3] So too have my motives for undertaking this project guided my analyses of the various approaches I have considered and my readings of 1950s film melodramas. I wanted to show the complexities of this group of mainstream films, particularly those female-oriented films often denigrated as hopelessly simplistic, and I wanted to simultaneously provoke and empower readers by fine-tuning critical tools that can be turned on both theoretical and film texts. My political and philosophical proclivities have, of course, guided my critiques; we never do stand outside ideology, even as we attempt the critical distance necessary for discussing it. But I hope my predilections have not blinded me to the potential of those approaches I do not champion; I believe they have not predetermined my conclusions. For instance, I find that Freudian and Lacanian theories of psychoanalysis—which are founded on dominant notions of "woman"—are insufficient for explaining ideological change, the possibilities for feminist intervention, and the stories and the enunciative practices of female-oriented melodramas, but I do not deny that they offer powerful explanations of the majority of mainstream films. Because my aim is to provide tools for resisting those dominant notions of "woman" that have so constricted our lives, I have read these theories skeptically.

I have also read the film melodramas skeptically. Although melodrama originated as a subversive form, an examination of even such a limited group of melodramatic texts as this one shows that melodramatic forms have both conservative and subversive potential. Because mainstream texts are produced both to reinforce dominant ideologies and to appeal to large numbers of people, it is far from surprising that we see in them a tendency toward conservatism *and* the very emergent and preemergent (and sometimes residual) forces that challenge dominant ideologies; cultural texts are, after all, primary sites for ideological struggle. That struggle goes on not just within the texts but also in their readings. Even films that privilege resisting voices can be read as conservative, but a skeptical critical eye can often locate limited resistance to dominant notions of "woman" even in the most conservative of the films, as my readings of the social problem films of the 1950s indicate. Not surprisingly, resisting female voices are more noticeable in the small group of films oriented around female characters and women's concerns, some of them films that were addressed at a specifically female audience.

The epochal approach I borrowed from Raymond Williams has allowed me to trace ideological struggle both among (and within) particular approaches to textual analysis and within particular films and groups of films. The approach is implicit throughout all of my readings but becomes most explicit in chapter 5, where I focus on the struggle over ideologies of race, class, and gender within film melodramas of the late 1950s. Addressing groups of films in a roughly chronological order allowed me to show how the film melodramas of the late 1950s exhibited a more explicit attention to issues of class and race than was common earlier in the decade; still, however, preemergent issues concerning gender construction and sex roles remained implicit. This was not the only reason for combining a consideration of the representation of race, class, and gender with films from the late 1950s; it was not by accident that this approach dominated the last substantive chapter. The most exciting and, I feel, important contemporary feminist work concentrates precisely on the intersection of race, class, and gender, and in order to structurally privilege an approach to textual analysis that works to explain the tension between these categories in mainstream, mass-consumed texts, I placed this approach last. We are each of us limited *and* empowered by our own position in the matrices we individually and collectively use to define ourselves and others. Those of us who are outside of what Lorde called "the master's house"—and especially those of us who, in academe, tenuously inhabit it—must demand that our voices be heard. We must provide the spaces for others to speak and the tools for those who have difficulty articulating themselves. And we must deconstruct that house and build one with rooms for us all.

Notes

INTRODUCTION

1 Hartman, "The Family as Locus of Gender, Class, and Political Struggle," p. 371.
2 Modleski, *The Women Who Knew Too Much*, p. 15.
3 Kaplan delineated the distinctions between essentialist and antiessentialist feminisms in "Feminist Criticism and Television."
4 Robinson, *Sex, Class, and Culture*, p. 3.
5 Said, *The World, the Text, and the Critic*, p. 29.
6 Ibid., p. 26.
7 Robinson, *Sex, Class, and Culture*, p. xxiii.
8 Elshtain, "Feminist Discourse and Its Discontents." An extended version of the argument presented in this article is found in Elshtain's *Public Man, Private Woman*. For an additional analysis of the relation of gender to language and speech, see Kramarae, *Women and Men Speaking*.
9 Elshtain, "Feminist Discourse and Its Discontents," p. 621.
10 Gilligan, *In a Different Voice*, p. 1. Another example, in communication research: Kristin Langellier and Deanna Hall found that the research that has defined their field was done among men and in public settings, then was generalized as "normal" to the entire population. Not too surprisingly, they met with significant difficulty when they used these "norms" in trying to understand the data they had collected during their research on mother-daughter storytelling in intimate settings. See Hall and Langellier, "Storytelling Strategies in Mother-Daughter Communication."
11 Newton, *Women, Power, and Subversion*, p. xv.
12 I thank Stuart Hall for suggesting that I clarify my position on recuperation.
13 Newton, *Women, Power, and Subversion*, p. xviii.
14 Modleski, Introduction to *Studies in Entertainment*. Discussing the study of television, Raymond Williams also argued for additional textual analysis of mass cultural artifacts. See Stephen Heath and Gillian Skirrow, "An Interview with Raymond Williams," in Modleski, ed., *Studies in Entertainment*, pp. 14–15.
15 Polan, *Power and Paranoia*, p. 10.
16 My only exception to these admittedly arbitrary limits is the inclusion of two films that did not reach these annual lists but that are arguably sequels to films that did: (1) *Belles on Their Toes*, a contemporary melodrama never on the list,

was explicitly a sequel to *Cheaper by the Dozen* and a continuation of the story of a large and unique family, and (2) *All That Heaven Allows*, which, in certain terms, can be considered a sequel to the enormously successful *Magnificent Obsession*; in the wake of the latter's success, Universal Studios produced the next best thing to a sequel, combining the same producer (Ross Hunter), director (Douglas Sirk), cinematographer (Russell Metty), and cast (Jane Wyman, Rock Hudson, Agnes Moorehead) for a follow-up.

17 Schatz, *Hollywood Genres*, p. 226.

18 Gledhill, "The Melodramatic Field," p. 15. Gledhill's essay situates film melodrama and writing on melodrama more clearly and adequately than anything else yet produced.

19 Elsaesser, "Tales of Sound and Fury," pp. 2–3.

20 Brooks, *The Melodramatic Imagination*, pp. 15–16. The ideological process requires and takes different forms of representation in different situations. Although storytelling seems to be a cultural constant, the worldviews or Ideologies within which it functions are historically and culturally specific. Some literary scholars have persuasively argued (and have convincingly documented their arguments) that melodrama is a transhistorical theatrical form as are, they argue, tragedy and comedy. Smith, in *Melodrama*, and Heilman, in *Tragedy and Melodrama*, made this transhistorical argument that melodrama is an eternal theatrical form. In his history, Smith neglected the importance of the French Revolution in the development of melodrama, effectively attempting to depoliticize his critical practice, its object, and its product. Other scholars have—equally persuasively—argued that these modes are historically specific and variable. Williams, in *Modern Tragedy*, argued that tragedy, like other genres, has been appropriated and redefined by successive social formations, and in *The Melodramatic Imagination*, Brooks, of course, argued that melodrama was born of and was conditioned by the various historical situations in which it has found itself.

21 See all of chapter 1 in Brooks, *The Melodramatic Imagination*; this quotation comes from p. 21.

22 Neale, *Genre*, p. 22.

23 Gledhill, "The Melodramatic Field," p. 32.

24 Vardac, *Stage to Screen*, p. 66. Vardac's description of the transition of melodrama from stage to screen remains the classic account. In it he details techniques for presenting melodrama, showing how emphasis moved away from demonstrative performance and toward an increasingly complex cinematic *mise-en-scène* and, in addition, how the cinema's capacity for naturalistic photographic reproduction particularly suited it for adaptation of realist narratives.

25 Gledhill, "The Melodramatic Field," pp. 25–27 and 33–34.

26 For starters, see Heilman, "Tragedy and Melodrama," which formed the base for his book *Tragedy and Melodrama*; Corrigan and Rosenberg, eds., *The Context and Craft of Drama*; Corrigan, ed., *Tragedy*; Bentley, *The Life of the Drama*;

Booth, *English Melodrama*; Rahill, *The World of Melodrama*; Grimsted, *Melodrama Unveiled*; and Smith, *Melodrama*.

27 For a discussion of "historical" and "theoretical" genres, see Feuer, "Genre Study and Television."

28 For a more extensive discussion of writing on film melodrama during the 1970s, see Gledhill, ed., *Home Is Where the Heart Is*, pp. 5–13. I focus on understanding the ramifications of film criticism for an analysis of the representation of gender, but much of my argument in this section draws on Gledhill's analysis of writing on melodrama in the 1970s, included in her survey of melodrama in *Home Is Where the Heart Is* and in private correspondence.

29 Gledhill, ed., *Home Is Where the Heart Is*, p. 8. She noted that this antirealist critique began to emerge in a special issue of the British journal *Screen* (vol. 13, no. 1, Spring 1972). MacCabe proved influential in the formation of the "classic realist text." See MacCabe's "Realism and the Cinema" and *James Joyce and the Revolution of the Word*.

30 Indeed, one of the members of the editorial board, Ben Brewster, translated Althusser's *Lenin and Philosophy and Other Essays* into English. Particularly important was the essay "Ideology and Ideological State Apparatuses." The reliance on Althusser, Lacan, and then Metz led to the standard joke that the *Screen* theorists couldn't read anything that hadn't been written first in French.

31 In *The Films of the Fifties*, Dowdy reports Universal Studios' decision to produce an updated, 1950s version of the "weepy." To find Sirk's corroboration of *Screen*'s construction of his films, see Halliday, *Sirk on Sirk*. What was the man to say when questioned about his newfound brilliance?

32 Gledhill, ed., *Home Is Where the Heart Is*, pp. 11–12. This move also ignores the immense popularity of some of the "weepies." In "Notes on Sirk and Melodrama," Mulvey distinguished between Sirk's male-oriented and his female-oriented film melodramas, and this logic could be followed to account for the popularity of *Written on the Wind*, which she considers (problematically) male-oriented, but does not account for the popularity of the Sirk films she considers female-oriented, specifically *Magnificent Obsession* and *Imitation of Life*. These films reached *Variety*'s lists of Top Twenty Moneymakers, and it is doubtful that they did so solely on the strength of their female viewers.

33 Nowell-Smith, "Minnelli and Melodrama"; Mulvey, "Notes on Sirk and Melodrama." Both are reprinted in Gledhill, ed., *Home Is Where the Heart Is*.

34 A prime example of this trend was Kleinhans's "Notes on Melodrama and the Family under Capitalism."

35 Gledhill, ed., *Home Is Where the Heart Is*, p. 36.

36 There are, of course, arguments over the use of terms like *mode*, *form*, and *genre*. For an extensive treatment of the arguments as they are deployed in literary studies, see Fowler's *Kinds of Literature*.

37 Gledhill, "Dialogue," p. 45.

38 Gledhill, ed., *Home Is Where the Heart Is*, p. 31.

39 Smith, *Melodrama*, pp. 6–7, Thorburn, "Television Melodrama," and Baym, "Melodramas of Beset Manhood."

40 Thorburn, "Television Melodrama," pp. 538–39.

41 Brooks, *The Melodramatic Imagination*, p. 20. Also commenting on melodrama's base are Heilman, *Tragedy and Melodrama*; Corrigan, ed., *Tragedy*; and Smith, *Melodrama*. One reading of Smith would indicate that "we all" are at the mercy of social conflicts beyond our control—not an entirely inaccurate observation but a cynical one, at best, and one quite compatible with a structuralist perspective.

42 Neale, *Genre*, p. 22.

43 Mayne, "Feminist Film Theory and Criticism," p. 86.

CHAPTER ONE

1 Haskell, *From Reverence to Rape*, and Rosen, *Popcorn Venus*. Although both Haskell and Rosen catalogued Hollywood's inequitable treatments of women, they did occasionally acknowledge what they considered "positive" representations.

For other histories of feminist film criticism, see Camera Obscura Collective, "Chronology"; sections in Kuhn, *Women's Pictures*, pp. 69–80; the introduction to Doane, Mellencamp, and Williams, eds., *Re-vision*, pp. 1–17; and Gledhill, "Developments in Feminist Film Criticism." See also Mayne's review article, "Feminist Film Theory and Criticism," and Kaplan, "Feminist Film Criticism."

Some recent anthologies have gestured toward a writing of the history of feminist film theory and criticism. In her introduction to the anthology *Feminism and Film Theory*, Penley surveyed questions of concern to feminists who work within the tradition of Freudian and Lacanian theories of psychoanalysis, questions addressed by the various articles she chose to reprint in the volume. Mulvey introduced *Visual and Other Pleasures*, a collection of her own articles, by indicating the ways in which they are indicative of developments within feminist theory.

For histories of feminist filmmakers, see Rosenberg, *Women's Reflections* (on American feminist filmmakers in the 1960s and 1970s); Kuhn, *Women's Pictures*, pp. 131–96; Kaplan, *Women and Film*, pp. 83–199. Brunsdon's *Films for Women* provides numerous articles on feminist films made by European and American filmmakers.

2 In *Women's Reflections*, Rosenberg noted that in the United States during the 1960s and 1970s, female avant-garde filmmakers did not exhibit a feminist orientation.

3 Conversation with Christian Metz, spring 1981. His work on film "language" is included in a book aptly titled *Film Language*.

4 See, especially, Metz, *The Imaginary Signifier*. For an introduction, see Metz, "The Imaginary Signifier."

5 French feminists made rather different—but related—incursions into psycho-analysis. See Marks and de Courtivron, eds., *The New French Feminisms*.

6 For work in English on and by Raymond Bellour, most interesting are articles included in *Camera Obscura* 3/4 (Summer 1979): Bergstrom, "Enunciation and Sexual Difference (Part One)"; Bergstrom, "Alternation, Segmentation, Hypnosis"; Bellour, "Psychosis, Neurosis, Perversion"; and "Raymond Bellour: Selected Bibliography," pp. 133–34.

7 *Camera Obscura* was founded by Janet Bergstrom, Sandy Flitterman, Elizabeth Lyon, and Constance Penley.

8 The distinction between a "Semiotics 1" and a "Semiotics 2" became impor-tant. The former refers to an analysis of the structures of semiotic signs and codes, the latter to the *process* of meaning-making.

9 See chapters 10 and 11 of Kaplan's *Women and Film* for more on independent feminist films.

10 I address one example of such a dialogue, carried on through competing read-ings of the same film text, in chapter 4, when I discuss a dialogue contained in the following articles from *Cinema Journal*: Williams, "'Something Else Be-sides a Mother'" (Fall 1984); Kaplan, "Dialogue" (Winter 1985); Petro and Flinn, "Dialogue," and Kaplan's reply, "Dialogue" (Fall 1985); Gallagher's attack on both Williams and Modleski, followed by their brief responses to him, all in "Dialogue" (Winter 1986); and Gledhill's and Kaplan's separate contributions to "Dialogue" (Summer 1986).

11 Most psychoanalytically informed film theory is notoriously inaccessible, par-tially because of the jargon-ridden language in which it is written, which makes it almost as inaccessible as the Unconscious, the theoretical phenomenon on which it is based, and partially because the variety of psychoanalysis adopted by film theorists has certain important similarities to mysticism; most notable is that both require of their adherents a leap of faith.

12 De Lauretis's essay is entitled "Now and Nowhere: Roeg's *Bad Timing*" in both *Re-vision* and in her book, *Alice Doesn't*. The quote is found on p. 164 of *Re-vision* and was eliminated in the version in *Alice Doesn't*. The first essay in her book focuses on theories of classical semiology and of Lacanian psychoanalysis; she argued that both deny the status of "subject" to women and ignore any possible role women might have in the production of culture. The second essay recounts recent studies of perception in order to discuss the cinematic image in the production of subjectivity. The third and fourth essays discuss contempo-rary films in the context of issues currently dominant in film studies; the reading of Roeg's film is chapter 4. In the fifth essay, de Lauretis addressed

narrative theory, especially as it functions to create a "gendered subject." The final essay concerns the failure of semiotics and psychoanalysis to theorize experience, a failure that severely limits the usefulness of these theories for feminism. This book is undoubtedly the most ambitious and certainly the most interesting of the recent books that have emerged from feminist film studies.

13 De Lauretis, *Alice Doesn't*, pp. 7, 9.

14 Gledhill, "Developments in Feminist Film Criticism," in *Re-vision*, p. 18.

15 *The Spectatrix*, a special issue of *Camera Obscura* (20–21 [May–September 1989]), edited by Janet Bergstrom and Mary Ann Doane, is devoted to the question of female spectatorship, as are articles in two recently published anthologies: Pribram, ed., *Female Spectators*, and Marshment and Gamman, eds., *The Female Gaze*.

16 Kaplan, "Feminist Film Criticism," p. 18.

17 Modleski, *The Women Who Knew Too Much*, pp. 119, 121.

18 Gaines, "White Privilege and Looking Relations," pp. 59–60.

19 Gledhill, "Developments in Feminist Film Criticism," in *Re-vision*, pp. 41–43.

20 Kaplan, "Feminist Film Criticism," p. 18; Gaines, "White Privilege and Looking Relations," p. 79.

21 See the preface to Vogel's *Marxism and the Oppression of Women*, pp. ix–xi. In the book, Vogel reviewed the debate over the usefulness of Marxism for feminist theory, Marx's and Engel's writings on the "woman question," and socialist feminist reformulations of Marxist theory. She argued that "all too quickly, socialist feminism abandons the socialist tradition's revolutionary Marxist core" as she presented a review of socialist feminism's encounter with Marxism.

22 Ibid., p. 35.

23 Barrett's *Women's Oppression Today*—published originally in 1980 and again, with a new introduction, in 1988—directly addresses the encounter of Marxism and feminism, drawing on recent theorizing of the concept of ideology. In the new introduction, Barrett critiqued her own use of the concept of ideology but noted both that the controversy within Marxist theory over its use is unresolved in the book and elsewhere and that the concept is often replaced by the terms *discourse* and *subjectivity*, a slippery elision I often make myself.

24 Long, "Feminism and Cultural Studies," p. 427.

25 Long has noted that among articles that marginalize feminism's significance to cultural studies are two—by Alan O'Connor and Lawrence Grossberg—that appear in *Critical Studies in Mass Communication* with her article, "Feminism and Cultural Studies."

26 This list is neither inclusive nor definitive, and its order is consciously alphabetical to avoid the implication that some are more important or appeared earlier than others.

27 The hysterical reactions to challenges to the privileging of white, male, Western "culture" are most dramatically manifested in tracts by Allan Bloom, E. D. Hirsch, and William Bennett.

28 Carey is Dean of the College of Communications and is on the faculty of the Institute of Communications Research at the University of Illinois at Urbana-Champaign; Newcomb is on the faculty of the Department of Radio-Television-Film at the University of Texas at Austin. I use the distinction between "generations" of cultural studies scholars to indicate the direction in which the field is going. These categories, like most, are sloppy but useful. Newcomb, for instance, has been heard to utter the term *power*, and some scholars, like Larry Grossberg, have both studied with "first-generation" scholars (Carey, in Grossberg's case) and tutored other "second-generation" scholars; it is too early, I think, to speak of a "third generation" of American cultural studies scholars.

29 See Rowland, *The Politics of TV Violence*, and "Recreating the Past." See also Treichler and Wartella, "Interventions," especially pp. 5–6.

30 See particularly two articles by Carey: "Communication and Culture" and "Mass Communication and Cultural Studies."

31 Carey articulated these models in "A Cultural Approach to Communication."

32 Newcomb's early work, on literature, was influenced by Cawelti, who focused on popular formulaic literature (see *The Six Gun Mystique*). During the early 1970s, Newcomb carried this concern with formulaic entertainment texts into an analysis of television programming (see *TV: The Most Popular Art*); his work in the late 1970s and early 1980s focused on the argument that television operates as a "cultural forum" (see Newcomb and Hirsch, "Television as a Cultural Forum"). The quote in the text comes from an unpublished essay, "Symbolic Anthropology and the Study of Popular Culture."

For more on the notion of culture as developed by the symbolic anthropologists, see Turner, "Liminal to Liminoid"; Turner, "Process, System, and Symbol"; Geertz, *The Interpretation of Cultures*; Sahlins, *Culture and Practical Reason*; and Douglas, *Rules and Meanings*.

33 Garnham has argued that the segregated development of "film studies" and "media studies" in Great Britain has been less a problem for cultural studies than for film studies, the victim of its own institutional territoriality (see "Film and Media Studies"). Even within departments that include the study of both film and television (like those at the University of Wisconsin and the University of Iowa), overlap has been rare and still exists more as an exception than as a rule.

34 Elizabeth Long, "Feminism and Cultural Studies."

35 See Grossberg, "Cultural Studies Revisited and Revised." Grossberg compared the thought of John Dewey and Raymond Williams and then compared the work developed by Dewey and the Chicago School to the similar but distinct tradition that developed into British cultural studies. He argued that "despite its impeccable humanistic traditions," the American tradition seems "less fruitful" because it provides little direction for concrete and theoretical practice; because it celebrates epistemological relativism, ignoring power relations and undermining "coherent political critique"; and because it offers no explanation

for the process of meaning-making and its relation to material conditions. He ends the article with a call for a theory of culture that extends beyond "the meaningful" into the realms of power, pleasure, and desire.

In the article, Grossberg called the Chicago School tradition American *culturalism*, but Stuart Hall had already used the term to label the European tradition (deriving from the work of Raymond Williams) with which Grossberg contrasted the American tradition. In the interests of clarity, I apply the term only to the European tradition.

36 For specifically feminist work, see the special issue of *Communication* edited by Paula Treichler and Ellen Wartella and entitled "Feminist Critiques of Popular Culture" (vol. 9, no. 1 [1986]). In their introduction, Treichler and Wartella commented that they saw this special issue as an intervention "in the relationship between feminist theory and communication studies" and an effort to "advance research in feminist cultural studies" (p. 15).

37 This "ferment" is documented in a special 1983 issue—entitled "Ferment in the Field"—of the *Journal of Communication*. The quotes come from an article by Carey included in this special issue, "The Origins of the Radical Discourse on Cultural Studies in the United States." The 1985 conference of the journal's former sponsor, the International Communication Association, in Honolulu, was called "Paradigm Dialogues," and its members made efforts to clearly delineate opposing positions. Antagonism resulted. Struggle characterizes the amorphous arena of communication research.

Carey later undercut the claim that he deals significantly with ideology in the attack on the validity of the notion of "ideology" embodied in his critique of my paper "Ritual/Multiplicity/Power" at the 1986 meeting of the International Communication Association in Chicago.

38 See Hall, "Cultural Studies and the Centre," for a history of the activities of the Centre for Contemporary Cultural Studies at the University of Birmingham drafted in the late 1970s. In it, he reflected:

The search for origins is tempting but illusory. In intellectual matters absolute beginnings are exceedingly rare. We find, instead, continuities and breaks. New interventions reflect events outside a discipline but have effects within it. They most often work to reorganize a set of problems or a field of inquiry. They reconstitute existing knowledge under the sign of new questions. They dispose existing elements into new configurations, establish new points of departure. Cultural Studies, in its institutional manifestation, was the result of such a break in the 1960s (p. 16).

39 See Grossberg and Nelson, "Introduction: The Territory of Marxism," pp. 3–6, for a considerably expanded version of this history.

40 Hall, "Cultural Studies and the Centre," p. 17.

41 Johnson, "What Is Cultural Studies Anyway?," p. 38.

42 Feminist critiques of British cultural studies can be found in the CCCS Wom-

en's Study Group, *Women Take Issue*, and in the CCCS Stencilled Papers Series. In *Culture, Media, Language* (pp. 38–39), Hall called attention to the influence of feminism on the work of the CCCS, and in "What Is Cultural Studies, Anyway?" (pp. 38, 40), Johnson described the influence of feminism and the struggles against racism on British cultural studies.

43 For prime examples of CCCS theorizing on ideology, see the essays in the CCCS anthology *On Ideology*, and Hall et al., eds., *Culture, Media, Language*. See also Hall, "Signification, Representation, Ideology."

44 Johnson, "What Is Cultural Studies, Anyway?," pp. 39–40.

45 This is evidenced by attention to British cultural studies in American publications. In addition to Johnson's "What Is Cultural Studies Anyway?," see John Fiske's chapter, "British Cultural Studies and Television," in Allen, ed., *Channels of Discourse*.

46 See Williams, *Marxism and Literature*, particularly the chapters "Base and Superstructure" (pp. 75–82) and "Determination" (pp. 83–89). On page 78, Williams reminded us that, in light of classical ("vulgar") Marxism's reduction of the base-superstructure model,

> it is ironic to remember that the force of Marx's original criticism had been mainly directed against the *separation* of "areas" of thought and activity (as in the separation of consciousness from material production) and against the related evacuation of specific content—real human activities—by the imposition of abstract categories. The common abstraction of "the base" and "the superstructure" is thus a radical persistence of the modes of thought which he attacked.

47 Hall, lecture at the A. E. Havens Center for the Study of Social Structure and Social Change, Department of Sociology at the University of Wisconsin-Madison, September 9, 1985.

48 Hall, "Cultural Studies: Two Paradigms."

49 Borrowing from the continent was a major theoretical activity in both film and cultural studies during the 1970s; little attention was paid to the problems presented by what Said called "traveling theory" in his chapter by that name in *The World, the Text and the Critic*. Theories developed in a particular social and historical setting, because of and for specific circumstances, rarely travel without change. Marxism, of course, is not the same thing everywhere and at all times. For a discussion of the British importation of Althusserian Marxism, see Lovell, "Marxism and Cultural Studies."

50 Hall, "Signification, Representation, Ideology," p. 97.

51 Williams, *Marxism and Literature*, pp. 59–60; Althusser, "Ideology and Ideological State Apparatuses," in *Lenin and Philosophy and Other Essays*.

52 Barrett, *Women's Oppression Today*, p. xv.

53 Writing this in the wake of the simultaneous broadcast by all three major American commercial networks (ABC, CBS, and NBC), and by the Public

Broadcasting Service affiliates, of Ollie North's testimony to the combined Senate-House Iran-Contra investigating committee does make me hesitate to argue this point vigorously. Still, the links between ideological apparatuses and the state are, at least in the United States, more complex than Althusser posited.

54 Williams, *Marxism and Literature*, pp. 106–97.

55 Hall noted the influence of Paul Hirst on "post-modernism" in "Signification, Representation, Ideology," p. 94; Barrett, *Women's Oppression Today*, pp. 37–38. Post-modernist theories also draw heavily on Lacan's theory of psychoanalysis, Derrida's deconstructionism, and Foucault's discourse theory, altogether abandoning the culturalist emphasis on experience and the authority of the subject.

56 Gramsci is generally considered the grandad of this sort of theorizing. Much of his now published work was written in Italian prisons between 1927 and 1935, but newer is not necessarily better; many of his analyses were astute, and much of this theorizing is still convincing. His best-known work on ideology is scattered throughout *Selections from the Prison Notebooks* and *Selections from Cultural Writings*.

57 Of particular interest are Spivak, *In Other Worlds*; Said, *The World, the Text and the Critic*; Jameson, *The Political Unconscious*; Layoun, *Travels of a Genre*; and Kellner, "Ideology, Marxism, and Advanced Capitalism."

58 Williams, *Keywords*, pp. 40–43 ("Art"), 87–93 ("Culture"), and 153–57 ("Ideology"); also see Williams's short chapter "Ideology" in *Marxism and Literature*. Etymology is, for Williams, a kind of ideological analysis; we can see evidence of the increasing division of labor involved in aesthetic production—and academic discourses—in the parallel increase in the specialization of terminology that Williams chronicles.

59 Gitlin, "Prime Time Ideology."

60 In "Ideology, Marxism, and Advanced Capitalism" and in "TV, Ideology, and Emancipatory Popular Culture," Kellner has presented a description of ideology that is similar to mine. He considers ideologies "survival strategies" that provide us with "road maps" for everyday life.

61 Williams, *Marxism and Literature*, p. 122.

62 Ibid., p. 125.

63 Williams discussed the concept of "overdetermination," which—he noted—Althusser introduced to Marxism; however Althusser, Williams claimed, "failed to apply its most positive elements to his own work on ideology." Williams argued—as did Althusser—that the cultural, the social, the political, and the economic are relatively autonomous realms; Williams warned against categorically objectifying determined or overdetermined structures, since this would repeat "the basic error of 'economism' at a more serious level" by subsuming *all* human experience (ibid., pp. 88).

64 Williams, "Structures of Feeling," ibid., p. 128–35.

65 Ibid., p. 130, 132.

66 Benjamin, *Illuminations*, p. 227.

67 Ibid., p. 224.

68 Hall, "Encoding/Decoding," in Hall et al., eds., *Culture, Media, Language*, p. 137.

69 The textual analysis was published in Brunsdon and Morley, *Everyday Television*; the audience research was reported in Morley, *The "Nationwide" Audience*; and see Morley, *"The "Nationwide" Audience*: A Critical Postscript," for the auto-critique.

70 Johnson, "What Is Cultural Studies Anyway?," p. 45.

71 Williams, *Marxism and Literature*, pp. 113–14.

72 Elsaesser, "Tales of Sound and Fury," p. 4.

73 Williams, *Marxism and Literature*, pp. 119–20.

CHAPTER TWO

1 Rosen's book was reprinted in 1985, and a second edition of Haskell's book, published by the University of Chicago Press, adds a brief preface and a chapter on films in "the age of ambivalence," 1974–87.

2 Haskell, *From Reverence to Rape*, p. xviii; Rosen, *Popcorn Venus*, p. 9.

3 Kuhn, however, has described the method as "quasi-sociological," in *Women's Pictures*, p. 75. In light of Haskell's description, in *From Reverence to Rape*, of her own position as "a film critic first and a feminist second" (p. 38), Kuhn's derisive labeling becomes more understandable. Kuhn, herself a sociologist, must object to Haskell's clear preference for bringing everything down to the level of the personal and to her position that "art will always take precedence over sociology, the unique over the general" (p. 38). Although Haskell is considered a sociological critic—and she was clearly concerned with women as a sociological group—she argued for understanding "history and cinema and art in terms of individuals rather than groups" (pp. 39–40). In her preface to the second edition, Haskell maintained and defended her position, characterizing scholarly criticism as the "overly cerebral study of film in the laboratory." The danger in a movement or ideology, as she sees it, is "that it ceases to consider formal and aesthetic questions and concentrates on political ones. I've never wanted to overpoliticize the situation" (pp. viii–ix). Ironically, it was the very move toward formalism among scholars and Haskell's steadfast refusal to see the aesthetic as also political that caused academic feminist film theorists and critics to reject her work.

4 Haskell, "Introduction," *From Reverence to Rape*, pp. vii–xiv; Rosen, "Preface," *Popcorn Venus*, pp. 7–10.

5 For more on interpretive communities, see Ellsworth, "Illicit Pleasures"; Fish,

Is There a Text in This Class?; and Radway, *Reading the Romance*. The concept is fertile, and work based in it is beginning to abound.

6 Doane, Mellencamp, and Williams, eds., *Re-vision*, p. 5.

7 Gledhill, "Developments in Feminist Film Criticism," in ibid., p. 44.

8 Doane, Mellencamp, and Williams, eds., *Re-vision*, pp. 5–6.

9 French, *On the Verge of Revolt*, pp. xxii–xxiii. In this book, French presented analyses of thirteen films: *Sunset Boulevard*; *The Quiet Man*; *The Marrying Kind*; *Shane*; *From Here to Eternity*; *The Country Girl*; *The Tender Trap*; *Marty*; *All That Heaven Allows*; *Picnic*; *Heaven Knows, Mr. Allison*; *The Nun's Story*; and *Some Like It Hot*.

10 Ibid., p. xxi.

11 Ibid., p. xv.

12 Perkins, "Rethinking Stereotypes," p. 135. See also Seiter, "Stereotypes and the Media." Seiter presented Perkins's theoretical advances in her argument that American communications scholars must rethink the concept in order to refine quantitative and qualitative studies of the media and to improve pedagogical methodology.

13 Haskell, *From Reverence to Rape*, p. 30.

14 Perkins, "Rethinking Stereotypes," p. 155.

15 Ibid., p. 156.

16 Ibid., p. 143.

17 Ibid., p. 139.

18 *WKRP in Cincinnati* premiered September 18, 1978, on CBS. After eight weeks, production—by MTM Enterprises—was suspended, but the show returned to the network's schedule the following fall and ran until September 20, 1982; it is now constantly in syndication in local markets. Created and produced by Hugh Wilson, *WKRP* was a half-hour situation comedy set at an ailing radio station. It featured Loni Anderson as the voluptuous and intelligent and very blonde secretary Jennifer Marlowe; Gary Sandy as Andy Travers, the program director, who was hired to turn the station around; Gordon Jump as Arthur Carlson, the inept station manager (who had the hots for Jennifer); Richard Sanders as Les Nessman, the station's news, weather, and agriculture department; Frank Bonner as Herb Tarlek, the sales manager (and king of the polyester leisure suit); Jan Smithers as Bailey Quarters, program assistant (attractive, but pale next to Jennifer); Howard Hesseman as the lively but sometimes spaced-out disc jockey Johnny Caravella, whose on-the-air pseudonym was Dr. Johnny Fever; and Tim Reid as Venus Flytrap, another flamboyant (and, conveniently, black) disc jockey.

19 Perkins, "Rethinking Stereotypes," p. 146.

20 Ibid., p. 154. In "Developments in Feminist Film Criticism," Gledhill also called attention to this example; I gained my first awareness of this exceptional "rethinking" from this article. For that—and for other insights—I am grateful to Christine Gledhill.

21 Rosen, *Popcorn Venus*, p. 269.

22 Haskell, *From Reverence to Rape*, p. 94.

23 In the premiere episode of the short-lived 1988 television series *Baby Boom*, the youthful version of the female protagonist watches Rosalind Russell dictate to her secretary as the adult version (played by Kate Jackson) tells us in a voice-over that it was from characters like this that she received her inspiration to become a career woman.

24 Haskell, *From Reverence to Rape*, pp. 174–75.

25 Rosen, *Popcorn Venus*, pp. 269, 271.

26 Perkins, "Rethinking Stereotypes," p. 148.

27 U.S. Department of Commerce, *Historical Statistics*, p. 133.

28 Periodization is always difficult and always sloppy. What we generally consider "the 1950s" seems to have begun at the end of World War II and ended sometime in the early 1960s. The films I write about, however, were all popular in the period 1950–59.

29 French, *On the Verge of Revolt*, pp. xiii, xxiv.

30 Goldman, *The Crucial Decade*, p. v.

31 May, *Homeward Bound*, p. 23. For more-extended examinations of the fear of atomic warfare in the 1950s, see Paul Boyer, *By the Bomb's Early Light*, and Robert J. Lifton, *The Broken Connection*.

32 May, *Homeward Bound*, p. 13.

33 Ibid., chapter 2 (pp. 37–57).

34 Walsh has pointed out, in *Women's Films* (pp. 51–52), that in the early part of the war, women were encouraged to volunteer services and that it wasn't until mid-1942 that government and industry needed large numbers of additional reliable workers to fill production quotas and began to actively encourage women to "get a war job" (the title of a 1942–43 government campaign).

35 Chafe, *The American Woman*, pp. 135–39; Anderson, *Wartime Women*; Banner, *Women in Modern America*; Milkman, *Gender at Work*; May, *Homeward Bound*; Hartmann, *The Home Front and Beyond*; Walsh, *Women's Films*, pp. 74–75.

36 Anderson, *Wartime Women*, pp. 172–73. Walsh, in *Women's Films* (p. 79, n. 8), pointed out that the description of women as a "reserve army" of labor, in the classical Marxist sense, is not entirely unproblematic. She directs us to articles in *The Political Economy of Women: Review of Radical Political Economics* 4, no. 3 (July 1972) for a discussion of this issue.

37 Kaledin, *Mothers and More*, p. 68.

38 Kerber argued that the idea of separate spheres is a rhetorical trope and that its continued usage denies the reciprocity between gender and society and imposes a static model on dynamic relationships. See her article "Separate Spheres, Female Worlds, Woman's Place."

39 Rothman, *Woman's Proper Place*, p. 224; Kaledin, *Mothers and More*, p. 66; Walsh, *Women's Films*, p. 78. The pattern continues; in 1988, of workers earn-

ing the minimum wage, 61.4 percent were women.

40 Perkins, "Rethinking Stereotypes," p. 154.

41 Zinn, *Postwar America*, pp. 29–36.

42 Walsh, *Women's Films*, p. 79.

43 Anderson, *Wartime Women*, pp. 172–73; Kaledin, *Mothers and More*, p. 64. That women's employment is related to socioeconomic status would seem to still hold true. A Roper Organization poll, reported in February 1988, revealed that the percentage of upper-class and upper-middle-class women (47%) and lower-middle-class women (48%) who worked full-time was higher than that of working-class women (36%). The highest percentage of women who did not work outside the home, by class, was in the working class (33%, as opposed to 24% in each of the other categories).

44 May, *Homeward Bound*, chapter 6 (pp. 162–82).

45 Kaledin, *Mothers and More*, p. 69. In 1988, nearly three-fourths of American children had mothers who worked outside the home, either part-time or full-time. Forty-six percent had mothers who worked full-time, and 25 percent had mothers who worked part-time. This broke down by class: 74 percent of children from upper-income and upper-middle-income families had mothers who worked, compared with 58 percent of children from lower-income families (Roper Organization survey).

46 May, *Homeward Bound*, p. 9.

47 Chafe, *The American Woman*, pp. 221–23.

48 Green and Melnick, "What Has Happened to the Feminist Movement?," pp. 283, 300.

49 Farnham and Lundberg, *Modern Woman*. See particularly the last chapter, "Ways to a Happier End," pp. 355–77.

50 Spock, *The Common Sense Book*. These quotes come from a section called "The Working Mother," under "Special Problems," pp. 484–89.

51 Green and Melnick, "What Has Happened to the Feminist Movement?," p. 300. They noted, however, that Stern issued "no new call to arms, resigning herself to women's conservatism" and that she saw little possibility of a housewives' rebellion.

52 Ibid., p. 302.

53 Kaledin, in *Mothers and More*, pp. 73–74, gave an account of this interchange, including this quote from Hoff's January 22, 1956, letter.

54 May, *Homeward Bound*, pp. 25–26.

55 See Fornatale and Mills, *Radio in the Television Age*, for a detailed picture of the transition of radio technology, programming, and usage during this period.

56 McNeil, *Total Television*, pp. 41–42.

57 For additional information on the decline of the studio system and the rise of independent production, see Cook, *A History of Narrative Film*, pp. 531–34; Sklar, *Movie-Made America*, pp. 269–85; Conant, "The Impact of the Paramount Decrees"; and Bordwell, Staiger, and Thompson, *The Classical Hollywood Cinema*, pp. 330–37.

58 On changes in technology during the period, see Cook, *A History of Narrative Film*, pp. 480–505; Sklar, *Movie-Made America*, pp. 283–85; Bordwell, Staiger, and Thompson, *The Classical Hollywood Cinema*, pp. 339–64; and Jowett, *Film*, pp. 356–60.

59 On the decline of the influence of the Legion of Decency and the Production Code, see Cook, *A History of Narrative Film*, pp. 535–37; Sklar, *Movie-Made America*, pp. 295–300; Conant, "The Impact of the Paramount Decrees," p. 349; Jowett, *Film*, pp. 365–69, and Dowdy, *The Films of the Fifties*, pp. 204–20.

60 Sklar, *Movie-Made America*, pp. 282–83.

61 See Dowdy, *The Films of the Fifties*, p. 183. Universal, in fact, produced three of the four female-oriented family melodramas included in *Variety*'s annual Top Twenty Moneymakers lists during the 1950s.

62 Arnold, *Flashback!*, pp. 3, 86–92.

63 Many of *Harvard Lampoon*'s "worst awards" were given to these films, indicative of their status in the eyes of the intelligentsia.

64 Hackett and Burke, *80 Years of Bestsellers*.

65 See U.S. Department of Commerce, *Historical Statistics*, p. 9. In fact, women had begun to outnumber men in the United States as early as 1946; the popular realization of the implication of this demographic change trailed only slightly behind the actuality.

In 1986, a report indicated that women waiting until their thirties to marry may never do so. Newspaper accounts at the time seemed to be engendering a similar (controlled) hysteria by pointing out that women who "wait too long" have as good a chance of getting married as they do of being attacked by a terrorist in an airport. At least one feminist comedienne commented, in her routine, that the latter option might, indeed, be preferable.

66 Kaledin, *Mothers and More*, pp. 74–77, 204. Kaledin noted that in the early 1950s, the number of women in engineering was in decline but that, by the mid-1950s, the trend had reversed. In 1952, the Society of Women Engineers had fewer than sixty members; by 1955, however, it had several hundred more members.

67 Haskell, *From Reverence to Rape*, p. 181.

68 In the chapter entitled "The Woman's Film," Haskell outlined the primary themes of the subgenre: sacrifice, affliction, choice, and competition (ibid., p. 163).

69 Rosen, *Popcorn Venus*, p. 264. Other films in which Taylor played the doting wife were *The Conspirator* (1949), *Giant* (1956), and *Cat on a Hot Tin Roof* (1958).

70 Degler, *At Odds*, pp. 439–40.

71 Hartmann, "The Family as Locus of Gender, Class, and Political Struggle," p. 268.

72 U.S. Department of Commerce, *Historical Statistics*, p. 133.

73 Haskell, *From Reverence to Rape*, p. ix.

74 Shipley, *The Crown Guide to the World's Great Plays.*

75 Peter Biskind, in *Seeing Is Believing*, commented that, in films from a variety of genres in the 1950s, ambitious women were punished for their independence: "the scarlet letter stood for ambition, not adultery" (p. 263).

CHAPTER THREE

1 In *Narration in the Fiction Film*, Bordwell reported finding, in one hundred randomly selected Hollywood films, that over sixty ended "with a display of the united romantic couple. . . .Thus an extrinsic norm, the need to resolve a plot in a way that yields 'poetic justice,' provides a structural constant" (p. 159). Bordwell, however, failed to note the ideological dimension of narrative.

2 Gledhill, "Dialogue," p. 46.

3 Kuhn, *Women's Pictures*, pp. 31–35. Haralovich's paper was written in 1979, when she was a graduate student, as part of an independent study project with Jeanne Allen. The other study, by Dalton, was published as "Women at Work: Warners in the Thirties," in *Velvet Light Trap*, no. 6, pp. 15–20.

4 Fischer, "Two-Faced Women"; Waldman, "'At Last I Can Tell It to Someone!'"; Williams, "'Something Else Besides a Mother.'" See chapter 4 for an account of the controversy generated by Williams's article.

5 Brooks, *Reading for the Plot*, p. 94.

6 Ibid., pp. 101–2.

7 Ibid., p. 22.

8 Ibid., p. 109; Peter Brooks, "The Mark of the Beast: Prostitution, Serialization, and Narrative," chapter 6 in ibid., pp. 143–70. I acknowledge that this is a truly reductive reading of a complex analysis, but it is not unjustifiable.

9 Chodorow, *The Reproduction of Mothering*; Gilligan, *In a Different Voice*. See chapter 4 for an extended discussion of the relevance of their work to textual analysis of 1950s film melodramas.

10 Brooks, *Reading for the Plot*, pp. 39, 330. He refers to Miller, *The Heroine's Text.*

11 DuPlessis, *Writing beyond the Ending*, pp. ix, xi. Other feminist literary critics who have focused on the relation of narrative structure and gender include Miller, *The Heroine's Text*; Gilbert and Gubar, *The Madwoman in the Attic*; and Newton, *Women, Power, and Subversion.*

12 DuPlessis, *Writing beyond the Ending*, p. 1. Writing to directly confront the values reinforced by this model, twentieth-century women writers have used the strategies of reparenting, woman-to-woman and brother-to-sister bonds, and forms of the communal protagonist.

13 Ibid., p. 3.

14 Jowett, *Film*, p. 368.

15 Ibid., p. 368.

16 Halberstam, *The Powers That Be*, p. 579; Cole, *Television Today*, pp. 94–95.

17 Wood, *America in the Movies*, pp. 131, 135.

18 Ray, *A Certain Tendency of the Hollywood Cinema, 1930–1980*, p. 153.

19 Neale, *Genre*, p. 16; Schatz, *Hollywood Genres*, p. 12.

CHAPTER FOUR

1 Neale, *Genre*, p. 22.

2 Elsaesser, "Tales of Sound and Fury," p. 6.

3 Schatz, *Hollywood Genres*, p. 223.

4 Here I use the "big I" Ideology to refer to a configuration of "little i" ideologies that concern such areas as race, gender, sex, law, etc.

5 Mulvey, "Notes on Sirk and Melodrama," p. 56.

6 Ibid.

7 Bakhtin, *The Dialogic Imagination*.

8 See Moi, *Sexual/Textual Politics*, pp. 27–29; Millett, *Sexual Politics*; and Mitchell, *Psychoanalysis and Criticism*. Moi noted that this aversion to psychoanalysis was not shared by French feminists, who "took it for granted that psychoanalysis could provide an emancipatory theory of the personal and a path to the exploration of the unconscious, both of vital importance to the analysis of the oppression of women in patriarchal society" (p. 96). Feminist film theory and criticism, however, was initially dominated by the English-speaking.

9 Mulvey, "Visual Pleasure and Narrative Cinema," p. 7. For a description of *Screen*'s participation in this endeavor, 1971 to 1977, see Rosen, "*Screen* and the Marxist Project in Film Criticism."

10 In conversations, the sociologist Stanley Aronowitz has claimed the incommensurability of Marxism and psychoanalysis, and the philosopher Nancy Fraser has also expressed serious doubts concerning the adequacy of (any theory of) psychoanalysis as an explanatory social theory.

11 Gallop, *The Daughter's Seduction*, p. 144.

12 Altman traced these two strains of psychoanalytic film analysis, as they were pursued by the French theoretical avant-garde, in his review of volume 23 of the French journal *Communications*, a special issue on psychoanalysis and the cinema edited by Christian Metz, Thierry Kuntzel, and Raymond Bellour. See Altman, "Psychoanalysis and Cinema."

13 Heath and Nowell-Smith, "A Note on 'Family Romance,'" p. 119.

14 Mulvey, "Visual Pleasure and Narrative Cinema" and "Afterthoughts on 'Visual Pleasure and Narrative Cinema.'" Quote from "Afterthoughts," in *Visual and Other Pleasures*, p. 31.

15 Mulvey, "Afterthoughts on 'Visual Pleasure and Narrative Cinema,'" pp. 12–15.

16 Researchers in numerous areas have found that the theories on which they

based their analysis were themselves the problem. See the quote from Gilligan's *In a Different Voice* in my introduction; she noted the difficulties she encountered when trying to explain female experiences with theories based on research on males. Researchers in interpersonal communication have met with a similar problem. Puzzled by their difficulty in interpreting data collected in their research on storytelling—data collected from women—Deanna Hall and Kristin Langellier realized "that research on storytelling has focused on stories gathered primarily from male subjects, and this research has analyzed stories from a 'male-as-norm' perspective." Women's communication experience had not previously been considered worthy of study, and women's storytelling had been described as deviant or deficient in comparison to male models. Such research implies that women cannot tell stories "right" and that what women tell are not "real" stories. In fact, the authors' problem was that data had repeatedly been collected on men's storytelling, usually in public places, and generalized to the entire speech community. As a result, the structures, purposes, styles, strategies, and functions of women's storytelling have—until recently—been inadequately understood. (Quotes are from "Storytelling Strategies in Mother-Daughter Communication," a paper delivered at the International Communication Association annual conference, Chicago, May 1986.)

17 In "On Narcissism," the sociologist Aronowitz argued that the sense of autonomy gained from a self-affirmative narcissism is necessary for sexual and political liberation. This radical departure from the negative attitude toward narcissism evidenced by Freud is also found in the French psychoanalyst Kofman's article "The Narcissistic Woman." In this article, Kofman presented a thorough reading of Freud's essay "On Narcissism," one of the few points in the body of his work where he opens up in a less negative direction for studying the female.

18 For a description and analysis of this debate in the Lacanian camp, see David-Menard, "Lacanians against Lacan."

19 Rose, "Introduction—II," p. 57.

20 Hall, "Recent Developments in Theories of Language and Ideology," in Hall et al., eds., *Culture, Media, Language*, p. 160.

21 I make this argument, as it pertains to television, in "Reading Feminine Discourse: Prime-Time Television in the U.S." and, in terms of both film and television, in "Gazes/Voices/Power." In the second article, I include summaries of the analyses, presented here, of *All That Heaven Allows* and *Picnic*, as well as an analysis of a male-oriented melodrama, *Not as a Stranger*; the latter analysis shows how a Lacanian approach does help to explain male-oriented films.

22 This compliment by Jessica Benjamin comes from a review of Chodorow's book, published with reviews by Mary Brown Parlee and Carol Nadelson in Leila Lerner, ed., "Special Book Review." For a review of the influence of feminist theories of psychoanalysis, including Chodorow's, on literary criticism, see Gardiner, "Mind Mother."

23 Chodorow, *The Reproduction of Mothering*, p. 218.

24 Rich, "Compulsory Heterosexuality and Lesbian Existence," pp. 635–37; Raymond, *A Passion for Friends*, pp. 49–55.

25 Rich, "Compulsory Heterosexuality and Lesbian Existence," pp. 635, 637.

26 Raymond, *A Passion for Friends*, p. 55.

27 Rich, "Compulsory Heterosexuality and Lesbian Existence," p. 637.

28 See Hoagland, *Lesbian Ethics*. Hoagland's thesis is built around understanding precisely the possibilities of agency under oppression.

29 Gilligan, "The Conquistador and the Dark Continent," p. 88. See also Gilligan's *In a Different Voice*.

30 Tronto, in "Beyond Gender Difference to a Theory of Care," p. 646. Tronto feels that although an ethic of care is an important intellectual concern for feminists, it should be phrased in terms not of gender difference but of the ethic's adequacy as a moral theory.

31 Card, "Women's Voices and Ethical Ideals."

32 This expansion allows us to consider intervention in both the social and the biological arenas.

33 Dowdy, *The Films of the Fifties*, p. 183.

34 Nowell-Smith, "Minnelli and Melodrama," p. 118.

35 Neale, *Genre*, p. 59.

36 See Radway, *Reading the Romance*.

37 Chodorow, *The Reproduction of Mothering*, p. 200.

38 See Schatz, *Hollywood Genres*, for descriptions of the intruder-redeemer in the masculine genres.

39 Radway, *Reading the Romance*, p. 147.

40 A few film theorists reject the use of a linguistic analogy in describing cinematic signifying processes. See, for instance, Bordwell, *Narration in the Fiction Film*, pp. 21–26. Bordwell has acknowledged that enunciation theory has "set cinephiles thinking about narration in more sophisticated ways," but because he finds a lack of equivalence between cinematic signification and verbal enunciation, he has suggested "that we abandon the enunciative account." But most film theorists—among them most mainstream feminist film theorists—consider enunciative theory crucial, and Bordwell's objections do not seem to have swayed them.

41 Augst, "The *Défilement* into the Look." *Camera Obscura* has published translations of articles by Raymond Bellour, Thierry Kuntzel, and their cohorts in the French theoretical avant-garde; it has also published articles and interviews on their work. See particularly the double volume 3/4.

42 Lacan, "Le stade du miroir." Cowie's analysis of *Coma* is particularly interesting and helpful.

43 See Jean-Louis Baudry, "The Ideological Effects of the Basic Cinematographic Apparatus," and Christian Metz, *The Imaginary Signifier*, p. 97.

44 See Oudart, "Cinema and Suture."

45 See Bellour, "*Les Oiseaux*," or Bergstrom, "Enunciation and Sexual Difference (Part One)."

46 Mulvey, "Visual Pleasure and Narrative Cinema," p. 11.

47 Bergstrom, "Alternation, Segmentation, Hypnosis," p. 93.

48 Neale, *Genre*, p. 59.

49 Ibid., p. 60.

50 Mulvey, "Afterthoughts on 'Visual Pleasure and Narrative Cinema.'"

51 Kuhn, *Women's Pictures*, p. 77.

52 Morley, "Texts, Readers, Subjects," p. 167.

53 Kaplan, *Women and Film*, pp. 7, 30.

54 Ibid., pp. 31, 33. See particularly her arguments in chapter 1 and in chapter 15, her conclusion.

55 Ibid., p. 4.

56 Doane, Mellencamp, and Williams, eds., *Re-vision*, p. 14.

57 Silverman, "Disembodying the Female Voice," p. 131.

58 Doane, "The 'Woman's Film,'" pp. 68, 69, 80.

59 Williams, "When the Woman Looks," p. 90.

60 Ibid., pp. 96, 97.

61 Williams, "'Something Else Besides a Mother,'" pp. 5, 7–8, 9.

62 Ibid., p. 17.

63 Kaplan, "Dialogue" (Winter 1985), p. 42.

64 Bordwell, in *Narration in the Fiction Film*, argued that multiplicity of point of view is a standard feature of melodramatic style, though some melodramas still manage to encourage identification with a single character.

65 Kaplan, "Dialogue" (Fall 1985), pp. 52, 53.

66 Gledhill, "Dialogue" (Summer 1986), pp. 45, 46. One other episode does not merit much attention: in the Winter 1986 issue of *Cinema Journal*, the sexist film "appreciator" (contrast that with "theorist" or "critic") Gallagher attacked Williams's article and one by Modleski for "raping" film texts by "reducing art to example." They, briefly, responded.

67 Gledhill, "Developments in Feminist Film Criticism," in Doane, Mellencamp, and Williams, eds., *Re-vision*, p. 45.

68 Kaplan, "Dialogue" (Summer 1986), p. 51.

CHAPTER FIVE

1 The theoretical avant-garde of this trend has been found—as has frequently been the case—in literary studies, and writers (critics, theorists, novelists, poets) concerned with race and class have extended their publication efforts beyond the academic world to the popular press and television. For instance, Michelle Wallace has published—even on film—in the *Village Voice* and has appeared on *The Phil Donahue Show*.

2 Gaines, "The *Scar of Shame*," p. 3.

3 Constance Penley's new anthology, *Feminism and Film Theory*, is dramatic evidence of the lack of attention to race and class in the mainstream of feminist film studies.

4 The editorial board for this socialist feminist series included Michele Barrett, Annette Kuhn, Anne Phillips, and Ann Rosalind Jones. In addition to the articles by Bobo (*"The Color Purple"*) and Larkin ("Black Women Film-makers Defining Ourselves"), the anthology includes articles by Linda Williams, Jeanne Allen, Michelle Citron, E. Ann Kaplan, Teresa de Lauretis, Christine Gledhill (who is British but who has periodically taught in the United States), and me.

5 Most theory and criticism influenced by Althusser has been remarkably formalist, with little attention to film content.

6 Steeves, "Feminist Theories and Media Studies," p. 106. See Jaggar, *Feminist Politics and Human Nature*; Elshtain, *Public Man, Private Woman*.

7 Kaplan, "Feminist Criticism and Television," pp. 215–17.

8 The further distinction between feminist radical separatists (who advocate the separation of women from men) and lesbian radical separatists (who work from within a lesbian context) has recently complicated the category "radical feminism" and merits attention. It does not, however, contribute to the argument I am developing here.

9 Raymond, *A Passion for Friends*, p. 21.

10 Ellsworth, "Illicit Pleasures."

11 In "Feminist Theories and Media Studies," pp. 97–100, Steeves noted radical feminist writing on pornography but argued that it has been primarily polemical rather than analytic. For a article on lesbian filmmaking, see Hammer's analysis of her own filmmaking practices in "Lesbian Filmmaking."

12 Steeves did note recent liberal feminist challenges to male-biased research methods; see her note no. 8, on Gaye Tuchman, in "Feminist Theories and Media Studies."

13 Jaggar, *Feminist Politics and Human Nature*, p. 52.

14 Gaines, "In the Service of Ideology"; Gaines, "White Privilege and Looking Relations," pp. 62–63.

15 In "The Hegemonic Female Fantasy," Lesage presented analyses of the dominant version of the fantasy, presented in *An Unmarried Woman*, and challenges to that fantasy presented in Dorothy Arzner's *Craig's Wife*; the quote comes from p. 83 of that article. Lesage is part of the editorial board of *Jump Cut*, which has consistently maintained an overt concern with the relation of the cinema to race, class, and gender.

16 Lesage, "Women's Rage," in Nelson and Grossberg, *Marxism and the Interpretation of Culture*, pp. 426–28. See also Fanon, *The Wretched of the Earth*.

17 For a statement of this position, see Horkheimer and Adorno, "The Culture Industry: Enlightenment as Mass Deception," in their book *Dialectic of Enlightenment*, pp. 120–67.

18 *Giant*, directed by George Stevens, was adapted from Edna Ferber's novel of the same name. All of the films discussed in this chapter were, in fact, adaptations. *Written on the Wind* was adapted from a novel by Robert Wilder. *Cat on a Hot Tin Roof* was originally a play by Tennessee Williams. *The Long, Hot Summer* combined William Faulkner's novel *The Hamlet* with two of his short stories, "Barn Burning" and "Spotted Horses." *East of Eden* was an adaptation of John Steinbeck's biblical allegory. *A Place in the Sun* was based on Theodore Dreiser's *American Tragedy*. *From Here to Eternity* came from a novel by James Jones, as did *Some Came Running. A Streetcar Named Desire* came, of course, from Tennessee Williams's famous play. A novel by Morton Thompson provided the base for *Not as a Stranger*, and *God's Little Acre* was adapted from a famous novel by Erskine Caldwell. *Imitation of Life* was a remake of a 1934 adaptation of a novel by Fanny Hurst.

19 Stern, "Interview," p. 32.

20 Newcomb, "Appalachia on Television," p. 158.

21 Kuhn, "Structures of Patriarchy and Capital in the Family," in Kuhn and Wolpe, eds., *Feminism and Materialism*, p. 65.

22 Fannie Hurst's novel was first published serially under the title *Sugar House*; copyrighted in 1932–33, it was published in its entirety as *Imitation of Life* (New York: F. P. Collier and Son, 1932–33), Broadway edition.

23 Handzo, "Imitations of Lifelessness"; Steinberg, *Reel Facts*, p. 22.

24 Halliday, *Sirk on Sirk*, p. 129.

25 Heung, "'What's the Matter with Sara Jane?,'" pp. 28–29.

26 Halliday, *Sirk on Sirk*, p. 21.

27 Chodorow, *The Reproduction of Mothering*, p. 206.

28 Heung, "'What's the Matter with Sara Jane?,'" has proposed a subversive reading that reveals Sara Jane as the central disturbance in the film "because she has the catalytic ability to activate the themes that are otherwise suppressed in the film" (p. 31).

29 Crowther, "*Imitation of Life*."

30 Chodorow, *The Reproduction of Mothering*, p. 214.

31 Heung, "'What's the Matter with Sara Jane?,'" pp. 35–38.

32 Halliday, *Sirk on Sirk*, p. 132.

EPILOGUE

1 Hall, "Signification, Representation, Ideology"; Lorde, "The Master's Tools."

2 Ellsworth, "Illicit Pleasures." Released by Warner Brothers in 1982, *Personal Best* chronicles the meeting and the subsequent love affair, cohabitation, and separation of two female athletes, Chris Cahill (Mariel Hemingway) and Tory Skinner (Patrice Donnelly). Initially, they meet at the 1976 Olympic Track

Trials, but when their coach places them in competition with each other and suggests that Tory is sabotaging Chris's progress, they separate. Chris, predictably, becomes involved with another athlete—a male swimmer. Chris and Tory meet again at the 1980 Olympic Track Trials and, despite the coach's intervention, renew their friendship; both, in the "happy ending," win berths on the ill-fated 1980 U.S. Olympic team, though Chris is still involved with the swimmer.

3 Modleski, *The Women Who Knew Too Much*, p. 121.

Bibliography

Allen, Robert C., ed. *Channels of Discourse: Television and Contemporary Criticism*. Chapel Hill: University of North Carolina Press, 1987.

Althusser, Louis. *Lenin and Philosophy and Other Essays*. Translated by Ben Brewster. New York: Monthly Review Press, 1971.

Altman, Charles F. "Psychoanalysis and Cinema: The Imaginary Discourse." *Quarterly Review of Film Studies* 11, no. 3 (August 1977): 257–72.

Anderson, Karen. *Wartime Women: Sex Roles, Family Relations, and the Status of Women during World War II*. Westport, Conn.: Greenwood Press, 1981.

Arnold, Eve. *Flashback! The 50's*. New York: Alfred A. Knopf, 1978.

Aronowitz, Stanley. "On Narcissism." *Telos* 44 (Summer 1980): 65–74.

Augst, Bertrand. "The *Défilement* into the Look." *Camera Obscura* 2 (Fall 1977): 95–103.

Bakhtin, M. M. *The Dialogic Imagination*. Translated by Caryl Emerson and Michael Holquist. Austin: University of Texas Press, 1981.

Balio, Tino, ed. *The American Film Industry*. Madison: University of Wisconsin Press, 1976.

Banner, Lois W. *Women in Modern America: A Brief History*. New York: Harcourt Brace Jovanovich, 1974.

Barrett, Michele. *Women's Oppression Today: The Marxist/Feminist Encounter*. 1980. Rev. ed. London: Verso, 1988.

Barrett, Michele, et al., eds., *Ideology and Cultural Production*. London: Croom Helm, 1979.

Barthes, Roland. *Elements of Semiology*. Translated by Annette Lavers and Colin Smith. New York: Hill and Wang, 1967.

———. *S/Z*. Translated by Richard Miller. New York: Hill and Wang, 1974.

Baudry, Jean-Louis. "Cinéma: Effets idéologiques produits par l'appareil de base." *Cinétique* 7/8 (1970). Translated as "The Ideological Effects of the Cinematographic Apparatus." *Film Quarterly* 28, no. 2 (Winter 1974/75): 39–47.

Baym, Nina. "Melodramas of Beset Manhood: How Theories of American Fiction Exclude Women Authors." *American Quarterly* 33, no. 2 (Summer 1981): 123–39.

Bellour, Raymond. "*Les Oiseaux*: Analyse d'une sequence" ("*The Birds*: Analysis of a Sequence"). *Cahier du Cinema* 219 (1969). Available in mimeographed form from the British Film Institute, Educational Advisory Service.

_____. "Psychosis, Neurosis, Perversion." *Camera Obscura* 3/4 (Summer 1979): 105–32.

Benjamin, Jessica. "Special Book Review: Chodorow's *Reproduction of Mothering*." Published with reviews by Mary Brown Parlee and Carol Nadelson. Edited by Leila Lerner. *Psychoanalytic Review* 69, no. 1 (Spring 1982): 151–62.

Benjamin, Walter. *Illuminations*. Translated by Harry Zohn. New York: Schocken Books, 1969.

Bentley, Eric. *The Life of the Drama*. New York: Atheneum, 1965.

Bergstrom, Janet. "Alternation, Segmentation, Hypnosis: Interview with Raymond Bellour." *Camera Obscura* 3/4 (Summer 1979): 71–103.

_____. "Enunciation and Sexual Difference (Part One)." *Camera Obscura* 3/4 (Summer 1979): 32–69.

Biskind, Peter. *Seeing Is Believing: How Hollywood Taught Us to Stop Worrying and Love the Fifties*. New York: Pantheon, 1983.

Bobo, Jacqueline. "*The Color Purple*: Black Women as Cultural Readers." In Pribram, ed., *Female Spectators*, pp. 90–109.

Booth, Michael. *English Melodrama*. London: Herbert Jenkins, 1965.

Bordwell, David. *Narration in the Fiction Film*. Madison: University of Wisconsin Press, 1985.

Bordwell, David, Janet Staiger, and Kristin Thompson. *The Classical Hollywood Cinema: Film Style and Mode of Production to 1960*. New York: Columbia University Press, 1985.

Boyer, Paul S. *By the Bomb's Early Light: American Thought and Culture at the Dawn of the Atomic Age*. New York: Pantheon, 1985.

Brooks, Peter. *The Melodramatic Imagination*. New Haven: Yale University Press, 1976.

_____. *Reading for the Plot: Design and Intention in Narratives*. New York: Vintage Books, 1984.

Brunsdon, Charlotte, and David Morley. *Everyday Television: "Nationwide."* London: British Film Institute, 1980.

_____, ed. *Films for Women*. London: British Film Institute, 1986.

Byars, Jackie. "Gazes/Voices/Power: Expanding Psychoanalysis for Feminist Film and Television Theory." In Pribram, ed., *Female Spectators*, pp. 110–31.

_____. "Gender Representation in American Family Melodramas of the Nineteen-fifties." Ph.D. diss., University of Texas at Austin, 1983.

_____. "Reading Feminine Discourse: Prime-Time Television in the U.S." *Communication* 9, no. 3–4 (1987): 289–304.

Camera Obscura Collective. "Chronology." *Camera Obscura* 3/4 (Summer 1979): 5–13.

Card, Claudia. "Women's Voices and Ethical Ideals: Must We Mean What We Say?" *Ethics* 99 (October 1988): 125–35.

Carey, James W. "Communication and Culture." *Communication Research* 2 (1975): 173–91.

_____. *Communication as Culture: Essays on Media and Society*. Boston: Unwin Hyman, 1989.

_____. "A Cultural Approach to Communication." *Communication* 2, no. 1 (1975): 1–22.

_____. "Mass Communication and Cultural Studies: An American View." In Curran, Gurevitch, and Woollacott, eds., *Mass Communication and Society*, pp. 409–26.

_____. "The Origins of the Radical Discourse on Cultural Studies in the United States." *Journal of Communication* 33, no. 3 (Summer 1983): 311–13.

Cawelti, John. *The Six Gun Mystique*. Bowling Green, Ohio: Bowling Green University Press, 1970.

Centre for Contemporary Cultural Studies. *On Ideology*. London: Hutchinson, 1978.

_____. Women's Study Group. *Women Take Issue: Aspects of Women's Subordination*. London: Hutchinson, 1978.

Chafe, William. *The American Woman: Her Changing Social, Economic, and Political Roles, 1920–1970*. New York: Oxford University Press, 1972.

_____. *Women and Equality: Changing Patterns in American Culture*. New York: Oxford University Press, 1977.

Chodorow, Nancy. *The Reproduction of Mothering: Psychoanalysis and the Sociology of Gender*. Berkeley: University of California Press, 1978.

Cole, Barry. *Television Today*. New York: Oxford University Press, 1981.

Conant, Michael. "The Impact of the Paramount Decrees." In Tino Balio, ed., *The American Film Industry*, pp. 348–54.

Cook, David A. *A History of Narrative Film*. 2d ed. New York: W. W. Norton and Co., 1990.

Corrigan, Robert W., ed. *Tragedy: Vision and Form*. San Francisco: Chandler Publishing Co., 1965.

Corrigan, Robert W., and James L. Rosenberg, eds. *The Content and Craft of Drama*. San Francisco: Chandler Publishing Co., 1964.

Cowie, Elizabeth. "Discussion of *Coma*—Part 2." *m/f* 4 (1980): 57–69.

Crowther, Bosley. "*Imitation of Life*." *New York Times*, April 18, 1959, p. 18.

Curran, James, Michael Gurevitch, and Janet Woollacott, eds. *Mass Communication and Society*. London: Edward Arnold, 1977.

David-Menard, Monique. "Lacanians against Lacan." *Social Text* 6 (Fall 1982): 86–111.

Degler, Carl N. *At Odds: Women and Family in America from the Revolution to the Present*. New York: Oxford University Press, 1980.

De Lauretis, Teresa. *Alice Doesn't: Feminism, Semiotics, Cinema*. Bloomington: Indiana University Press, 1984.

Doane, Mary Ann. "The 'Woman's Film': Possession and Address." In Doane, Mellencamp, and Williams, eds., *Re-vision*, pp. 67–82.

Doane, Mary Ann, Patricia Mellencamp, and Linda Williams, eds. *Re-vision*.

Frederick, Md.: University Publications of America, 1984.

Douglas, Mary. *Rules and Meanings*. Harmondsworth, Middlesex: Penguin Books, 1973.

Dowdy, Andrew. *The Films of the Fifties: The American State of Mind*. New York: William Morrow and Co., 1973.

DuPlessis, Rachel Blau. *Writing beyond the Ending: Narrative Strategies of Twentieth-Century Women Writers*. Bloomington: Indiana University Press, 1985.

Ellsworth, Elizabeth. "Illicit Pleasures: Feminist Spectators and *Personal Best*." *Wide Angle* 8, no. 2 (1986): 45–56.

Elsaesser, Thomas. "Tales of Sound and Fury: Observations on the Family Melodrama." *Monogram* 4 (1975): 1–15. Reprinted in Gledhill, ed., *Home Is Where the Heart Is*.

Elshtain, Jean Bethke. "Feminist Discourse and Its Discontents: Language, Power, and Meaning." *Signs* 7, no. 3 (Spring 1982): 603–21.

———. *Public Man, Private Woman: Women in Social and Political Thought*. Princeton: Princeton University Press, 1981.

Fanon, Frantz. *The Wretched of the Earth*. Translated by Constance Farrington. New York: Grove Press, 1964.

Farnham, Marynia, and Ferdinand Lundberg. *Modern Woman: The Lost Sex*. New York: Harper and Brothers, 1947.

"Ferment in the Field." *Journal of Communication* 33, no. 3 (Summer 1983). A special issue.

Feuer, Jane. "Genre Study and Television." In Allen, ed., *Channels of Discourse*, pp. 113–33.

———. *The Hollywood Musical*. London: Macmillan, 1982.

Fischer, Lucy. "Two-Faced Women: The 'Double' in Women's Melodrama of the 1940s." *Cinema Journal* 23, no. 2 (Winter 1983): 24–43.

Fish, Stanley. *Is There a Text in This Class?: The Authority of Interpretive Communities*. Cambridge: Harvard University Press, 1980.

Flinn, Carol. "The 'Problem' of Femininity in Theories of Film Music." *Screen* 27, no. 6 (November–December 1986): 56–72.

Fornatale, Peter, and Joshua E. Mills. *Radio in the Television Age*. Woodstock, N.Y.: Overlook Press, 1980.

Fowler, Alastair. *Kinds of Literature: An Introduction to the Theory of Genres and Modes*. Cambridge: Harvard University Press, 1982.

French, Brandon. *On the Verge of Revolt: Women in American Films of the Fifties*. New York: Frederick Ungar Publishing Co., 1978.

Friday, Nancy. *My Mother, My Self*. New York: Dell Publishing Co., 1977.

Friedman, Jean E., and William Shade, eds. *Our American Sisters: Women in American Life and Thought*. Boston: Allyn and Bacon, 1973.

Gaines, Jane. "In the Service of Ideology: How Betty Grable's Legs Won the War." *Film Reader* 5 (1982): 47–59.

_____. "The *Scar of Shame*: Skin Color and Caste in Black Silent Melodrama," *Cinema Journal* 26, no. 4 (Summer 1987): 3–21.

_____. "White Privilege and Looking Relations." *Cultural Critique* 4 (Fall 1986): 59–79.

Gallagher, Tag. "Dialogue." *Cinema Journal* 25, no. 2 (Winter 1986): 65–66.

Gallop, Jane. *The Daughter's Seduction: Feminism and Psychoanalysis*. Ithaca, N.Y.: Cornell University Press, 1982.

Gardiner, Judith Kegan. "Mind Mother: Psychoanalysis and Feminism." In Greene and Kahn, eds., *Making a Difference*, pp. 113–45.

Garnham, Nicholas. "Film and Media Studies: Reconstructing the Subject." *Film Reader* 5 (1982): 177–83.

Geertz, Clifford. *The Interpretation of Cultures*. New York: Basic Books, 1973.

Gilbert, Sandra M., and Susan Gubar. *The Madwoman in the Attic: The Woman Writer and the Nineteenth-Century Literary Imagination*. New Haven: Yale University Press, 1979.

Gilligan, Carol. "The Conquistador and the Dark Continent: Reflections on the Psychology of Love." *Daedalus* 113, no. 3 (Summer 1984): 75–95.

_____. *In a Different Voice: Psychological Theory and Women's Development*. Cambridge: Harvard University Press, 1982.

Gilligan, Carol, Janie Victoria Ward, and Jill McLean Taylor, with Betty Bardige, eds. *Mapping the Moral Domain: A Contribution to Women's Thinking to Psychological Theory and Education*. Cambridge: Harvard University Press, 1989.

Gitlin, Todd. "Prime Time Ideology: The Hegemonic Process in Television Entertainment." *Social Problems* 26, no. 3 (February 1979): 251–66. Reprinted in Newcomb, ed., *Television*.

Gledhill, Christine. "Developments in Feminist Film Criticism." *Quarterly Review of Film Studies* 3, no. 4 (1978): 458–93. Also included in a revised form in Doane, Mellencamp, and Williams, eds., *Re-vision*, pp. 18–48.

_____. "Dialogue." *Cinema Journal* 25, no. 4 (Summer 1986): 44–48.

_____. "The Melodramatic Field: An Investigation." In Gledhill, ed., *Home Is Where the Heart Is*, pp. 5–39.

_____, ed. *Home Is Where the Heart Is: Studies in Melodrama and the Woman's Film*. London: British Film Institute, 1987.

Goldman, Eric F. *The Crucial Decade: America, 1945–1955*. New York: Alfred A. Knopf, 1956.

Gouldner, Alvin W., ed. *Studies in Leadership and Democratic Action*. New York: Harper and Brothers, 1950.

Gramsci, Antonio. *Selections from Cultural Writings*. Edited by David Forgacs and Geoffrey Nowell-Smith. Translated by William Boelhower. Cambridge: Harvard University Press, 1985.

_____. *Selections from the Prison Notebooks*. Edited and translated by Quentin Hoare and Geoffrey Nowell-Smith. New York: International Publishers, 1971.

Green, Arnold W., and Eleanor Melnick. "What Has Happened to the Feminist Movement?" In Gouldner, ed., *Studies in Leadership and Democratic Action*, pp. 277–302.

Greene, Gayle, and Coppélia Kahn, eds., *Making a Difference: Feminist Literary Criticism*. New York: Methuen, 1985.

Grimsted, David. *Melodrama Unveiled: American Theater and Culture, 1800–1850*. Chicago: University of Chicago Press, 1968.

Grossberg, Lawrence. "Cultural Studies Revisited and Revised." In Mander, ed., *Communications in Transition*, pp. 39–70.

Grossberg, Lawrence, and Cary Nelson. "Introduction: The Territory of Marxism." In Nelson and Grossberg, eds., *Marxism and the Interpretation of Culture*, pp. 1–13.

———, eds. *Marxism and the Interpretation of Culture*. Urbana: University of Illinois Press, 1988.

Hackett, Alice P., and James H. Burke. *80 Years of Bestsellers: 1895–1975*. New York: R. R. Bowker Co., 1977.

Halberstam, David. *The Powers That Be*. New York: Dell Publishing Co., 1979.

Hall, Deanna L., and Kristin M. Langellier. "Storytelling Strategies in Mother-Daughter Communication." International Communication Association, Chicago, Illinois, May 1986.

Hall, Stuart. "Cultural Studies: Two Paradigms." *Media, Culture, and Society* 2 (1980): 57–72.

———. "Cultural Studies and the Centre: Some Problematics and Problems." In Hall et al., eds., *Culture, Media, Language*, pp. 15–47.

———. "Encoding and Decoding in Television Discourse." Centre for Contemporary Cultural Studies Stencilled Paper No. 7. An edited extract appears as "Encoding/Decoding" in Hall et al., eds., *Culture, Media, Language*, pp. 128–38.

———. "Recent Developments in Theories of Language and Ideology: A Critical Note." In Hall et al., eds., *Culture, Media, Language*, pp. 157–62.

———. "Signification, Representation, Ideology: Althusser and the Post-Structuralist Debates." *Critical Studies in Mass Communication* 2 (1985): 91–114.

Hall, Stuart, Dorothy Hobson, Andrew Lowe, and Paul Willis, eds. *Culture, Media, Language*. London: Hutchinson, 1980.

Halliday, Jon. *Sirk on Sirk*. New York: Viking Press, 1972.

Hammer, Barbara. "Lesbian Filmmaking: Self-Birthing." *Film Reader* 5 (1982): 60–66.

Handzo, Stephen. "Imitations of Lifelessness: Sirk's Ironic Tearjerker." *Bright Lights* 2, no. 2 (Winter 1977–78): 20–22 and 34.

Hartmann, Heidi. "The Family as Locus of Gender, Class, and Political Struggle: The Example of Housework." *Signs* 6, no. 3 (Spring 1980): 266–94.

Hartmann, Susan M. *The Home Front and Beyond: American Women in the 1940s.* Boston: Twayne Publishers, 1982.

Haskell, Molly. *From Reverence to Rape: The Treatment of Women in the Movies.* 2d ed. Chicago: University of Chicago Press, 1987.

Heath, Stephen, and Geoffrey Nowell-Smith. "A Note on 'Family Romance.'" *Screen* 18, no. 2 (Summer 1977): 118–19.

Heilman, Robert B. *Tragedy and Melodrama.* Seattle: University of Washington Press, 1968.

————. "Tragedy and Melodrama: Speculations on Generic Form." *Texas Quarterly* 3 (Summer 1960): 36–50.

Heung, Marina. "'What's the Matter with Sara Jane?': Daughters and Mothers in Douglas Sirk's *Imitation of Life*." *Cinema Journal* 26, no. 3 (Spring 1987): 21–43.

Hoagland, Sarah Lucia. *Lesbian Ethics: Toward New Value.* Palo Alto: Institute of Lesbian Studies, 1988.

Horkheimer, Max, and Theodore Adorno. *Dialectic of Enlightenment.* Translated by John Cumming. New York: Seabury Press, 1972.

Hurst, Fannie. *Imitation of Life.* Broadway ed. New York: F. P. Collier and Son, 1932–33. First published serially under the title *Sugar House.*

Jaggar, Alison M. *Feminist Politics and Human Nature.* Sussex: Rowman and Allanhad/Harvester Press, 1983.

Jameson, Fredric. *The Political Unconscious: Narrative as a Socially Symbolic Act.* Ithaca: Cornell University Press, 1983.

Johnson, Richard. "What Is Cultural Studies Anyway?" *Social Text* 16 (Winter 1986–87): 38–80.

Jowett, Garth. *Film: The Democratic Art.* Boston: Little, Brown and Co., 1973.

Kaledin, Eugenia. *Mothers and More: American Women in the 1950s.* Boston: Twayne Publishers, 1984.

Kaplan, E. Ann. "Dialogue." *Cinema Journal* 24, no. 2 (Winter 1985): 40–43.

————. "Dialogue." *Cinema Journal* 25, no. 1 (Fall 1985): 52–54.

————. "Dialogue." *Cinema Journal* 25, no. 4 (Summer 1986): 49–53.

————. "Feminist Criticism and Television." In Allen, ed., *Channels of Discourse*, pp. 211–53.

————. "Feminist Film Criticism: Current Issues and Problems." *Studies in the Literary Imagination* 19, no. 1 (Spring 1986): 7–20.

————. *Women and Film: Both Sides of the Camera.* New York: Methuen, 1983.

Kellner, Douglas. "Ideology, Marxism, and Advanced Capitalism." *Socialist Review* 8, no. 6 (November–December 1978): 37–65.

————. "TV, Ideology, and Emancipatory Popular Culture." *Socialist Review* 45 (May–June 1979). Reprinted in Newcomb, ed., *Television*, pp. 386–421.

Kerber, Linda. "Separate Spheres, Female Worlds, Woman's Place: The Rhetoric of Women's History." *Journal of American History* 75, no. 1 (June 1988): 9–39.

Kinneavy, James L. *A Theory of Discourse*. New York: W. W. Norton and Co., 1971.

Kleinhans, Chuck. "Notes on Melodrama and the Family under Capitalism." *Film Reader* 3 (1978): 40–47.

Kofman, Sarah. "The Narcissistic Woman: Freud and Girard." *Diacritics* 10, no. 3 (Fall 1980): 36–45.

Kramarae, Cheris. *Women and Men Speaking*. Rowley, Mass.: Newbury House, 1981.

Kuhn, Annette. *Women's Pictures: Feminism and Cinema*. London: Routledge and Kegan Paul, 1982.

Kuhn, Annette, and Ann Marie Wolpe, eds. *Feminism and Materialism*. London: Routledge and Kegan Paul, 1978.

Lacan, Jacques. *Feminine Sexuality*. Translated by Jacqueline Rose. Edited by Juliet Mitchell and Jacqueline Rose. New York: W. W. Norton and Co., 1982.

————. *The Four Fundamental Concepts of Psycho-Analysis*. Translated by Alan Sheridan. Edited by Jacques-Alain Miller. New York: W. W. Norton and Co., 1978.

————. "Le stade du miroir comme formateur de la fonction de Je." *Ecrits I*, pp. 89–97. Paris: Editions du Seuil, 1966.

Larkin, Alile Sharon. "Black Women Film-makers Defining Ourselves: Feminism in Our Own Voice." In Pribram, ed., *Female Spectators*, pp. 157–73.

Layoun, Mary N. *Travels of a Genre: Ideology and the Modern Novel*. Princeton: Princeton University Press, 1989.

Lerner, Gerda. "The Grimké Sisters: Women and the Abolition Movement." In Friedman and Shade, eds. *Our American Sisters*, pp. 183–94.

————. "The Lady and the Mill Girl: Changes in the Status of Women in the Age of Jackson." In Friedman and Shade, eds., *Our American Sisters*, pp. 82–95.

Lesage, Julia. "The Hegemonic Female Fantasy in *An Unmarried Woman* and *Craig's Wife*." *Film Reader* 5 (1982): 83–94.

————. "Women's Rage." In Nelson and Grossberg, eds., *Marxism and the Interpretation of Culture*, pp. 419–28.

Lifton, Robert J. *The Broken Connection: On Death and the Continuity of Life*. New York: Basic Books, 1983.

Long, Elizabeth. "Feminism and Cultural Studies: Britain and America." *Critical Studies in Mass Communication* 6, no. 4 (December 1989): 427–35.

Lorde, Audre. "The Master's Tools Will Never Dismantle the Master's House." In Moraga and Anzaldua, eds., *This Bridge Called My Back*, pp. 98–101.

Lovell, Terry. "Marxism and Cultural Studies." *Film Reader* 5 (1982): 184–91.

MacCabe, Colin. *James Joyce and the Revolution of the Word*. London: Macmillan, 1978.

————. "Realism and the Cinema: Notes on Some Brechtian Theses." *Screen* 15, no. 2 (Summer 1974): 7–27.

McDonough, Roison. "Ideology as False Consciousness." In Centre for Contemporary Cultural Studies, *On Ideology*, pp. 33–44.

McLennon, Gregor, Victor Molina, and Roy Peters. "Althusser's Theory of Ideology." In Centre for Contemporary Cultural Studies, *On Ideology*, pp. 77–105.

McNeil, Alex. *Total Television: A Comprehensive Guide to Programming from 1948 to 1980.* New York: Penguin Books, 1980.

McRobbie, Angela. "*Jackie*: An Ideology of Adolescent Femininity." In Bernard Waites et al., eds., *Popular Culture: Past and Present*, pp. 263–83.

Mander, M., ed. *Communications in Transition.* New York: Praeger, 1983.

Marks, Elaine, and Isabel de Courtivron, eds. *The New French Feminisms.* New York: Schocken Books, 1981.

Marshment, Margaret, and Lorraine Gamman, eds. *The Female Gaze.* London: Women's Press, 1988.

May, Elaine Tyler. *Homeward Bound: American Families in the Cold War Era.* New York: Basic Books, 1988.

Mayne, Judith. "Feminist Film Theory and Criticism." *Signs* 11, no. 1 (Autumn 1985): 81–100.

Mead, Margaret. *Culture and Commitment: A Study of the Generation Gap.* New York: Doubleday, 1970.

Metz, Christian. *Film Language: A Semiotics of the Cinema.* Translated by Michael Taylor. New York: Oxford University Press, 1974. Published originally in French as *Essais sur la Signification au Cinema, Tome I.* Paris: Editions Klincksieck, 1968.

————. "The Imaginary Signifier." *Screen* 16, no. 2 (Summer 1975): 14–76.

————. *The Imaginary Signifier: Psychoanalysis and the Cinema.* Translated by Celia Britton, Annwyl Williams, Ben Brewster, and Alfred Guzzetti. Bloomington: Indiana University Press, 1982. Published originally as *Le Signifiant Imaginaire.* Paris: Union General d'Editions, 1977.

Milkman, Ruth. *Gender at Work: The Dynamics of Job Segregation by Sex during World War II.* Urbana: University of Illinois Press, 1987.

Miller, Nancy K. *The Heroine's Text: Readings in the French and English Novel, 1722–1782.* New York: Columbia University Press, 1980.

Millett, Kate. *Sexual Politics.* New York: Avon/Hearst, 1970.

Mitchell, Juliet. *Psychoanalysis and Criticism.* Harmondsworth: Penguin, 1974.

————. *Psychoanalysis and Feminism.* Harmondsworth: Penguin, 1974.

Modleski, Tania. "Dialogue." *Cinema Journal* 25, no. 2 (Winter 1986): 66.

————. *Loving with a Vengeance: Mass-produced Fantasies for Women.* New York: Methuen, 1982.

————. *The Women Who Knew Too Much.* New York: Methuen, 1988.

————, ed. *Studies in Entertainment: Critical Approaches to Mass Culture.*

Bloomington: Indiana University Press, 1986.

Moi, Toril. *Sexual/Textual Politics: Feminist Literary Theory.* New York: Methuen, 1985.

Moraga, Cherrie, and Gloria Anzaldua, eds. *This Bridge Called My Back: Writings by Radical Women of Color.* Watertown, Mass.: Persephone Press, 1981.

Morley, David. *The "Nationwide" Audience.* London: British Film Institute, 1980.

———. *"The 'Nationwide' Audience*: A Critical Postscript." *Screen Education* 39 (Summer 1981): 3–14.

———. "Reconceptualizing the Media Audience." Centre for Contemporary Cultural Studies Stencilled Paper No. 9.

———. "Texts, Readers, Subjects." In Hall et al., eds., *Culture, Media, Language,* pp. 163–73.

Mulvey, Laura. "Afterthoughts on 'Visual Pleasure and Narrative Cinema' Inspired by *Duel in the Sun* (King Vidor, 1946)." *Framework* 15–16–17 (Summer 1981): 12–15. Reprinted in Mulvey, *Visual and Other Pleasures.*

———. "Notes on Sirk and Melodrama." *Movie* 25 (1977): 53–56. Reprinted in Gledhill, ed., *Home Is Where the Heart Is.*

———. *Visual and Other Pleasures.* Bloomington: Indiana University Press, 1989.

———. "Visual Pleasure and Narrative Cinema." *Screen* 16, no. 3 (Autumn 1975): 6–18.

Neale, Stephen. *Genre.* London: British Film Institute, 1980.

———. "Melodrama and Tears." *Screen* 27, no. 6 (November–December 1986): 6–22. Special issue on melodrama.

Nelson, Cary, and Lawrence Grossberg, eds. *Marxism and the Interpretation of Culture.* Urbana: University of Illinois Press, 1988.

Newcomb, Horace. "Appalachia on Television: Region as Symbol in American Popular Culture." *Appalachian Journal* 7, no. 1–2 (Autumn–Winter 1979–80): 155–64.

———. "Symbolic Anthropology and the Study of Popular Culture." Paper delivered to the Popular Culture Association, Detroit, 1980.

———. *TV: The Most Popular Art.* Garden City, N.Y.: Anchor Books, 1974.

———, ed. *Television: The Critical View.* 4th ed. New York: Oxford University Press, 1987.

Newcomb, Horace, and Paul Hirsch. "Television as a Cultural Forum." In Newcomb, ed., *Television: The Critical View,* pp. 455–70.

Newton, Judith Lowder. *Women, Power, and Subversion: Social Strategies in British Fiction, 1778–1860.* Athens: University of Georgia Press, 1981.

Nowell-Smith, Geoffrey. "Minnelli and Melodrama." *Screen* 18, no. 2 (Summer 1977): 113–18. Reprinted in Gledhill, ed., *Home Is Where the Heart Is.*

Oudart, Jean-Pierre. "Cinema and Suture." *Screen* 18, no. 4 (Winter 1977–78): 35–47.

Penley, Constance, ed. *Feminism and Film Theory.* New York: Routledge, 1988.

Perkins, T. E. "Rethinking Stereotypes." In Barrett et al., eds., *Ideology and Cultural Production*, pp. 135–59.

Petro, Patrice, and Carol Flinn. "Dialogue." *Cinema Journal* 25, no. 1 (Fall 1985): 50–52.

Polan, Dana. *Power and Paranoia: History, Narrative, and the American Cinema, 1940–1950*. New York: Columbia University Press, 1986.

Pollock, Griselda. "Report on the Weekend School." In "Dossier on Melodrama." *Screen* 18, no. 2 (Summer 1977): 105–13.

Pribram, E. Deidre, ed. *Female Spectators: Looking at Film and Television*. New York: Verso, 1988.

Radway, Janice. "Identifying Ideological Seams: Mass Culture, Analytic Method, and Political Practice." *Communication* 9, no. 1 (1986): 93–123.

———. *Reading the Romance: Women, Patriarchy, and Popular Literature*. Chapel Hill: University of North Carolina Press, 1984.

Rahill, Frank. *The World of Melodrama*. University Park: Pennsylvania State University Press, 1967.

Ray, Robert B. *A Certain Tendency of the Hollywood Cinema, 1930–1980*. Princeton: Princeton University Press, 1985.

Raymond, Janice G. *A Passion for Friends: Toward a Philosophy of Female Affection*. Boston: Beacon Press, 1986.

Rich, Adrienne. "Compulsory Heterosexuality and Lesbian Existence." *Signs* 5, no. 4 (Summer 1980): 631–60.

Robinson, Lillian. *Sex, Class, and Culture*. Bloomington: Indiana University Press, 1978. Reprint. New York: Methuen, 1986.

Rose, Jacqueline. "Introduction—II." In Jacques Lacan, *Feminine Sexuality*, translated by Jacqueline Rose and edited by Juliet Mitchell and Jacqueline Rose, pp. 27–57.

Rosen, Marjorie. *Popcorn Venus: Women, Movies and the American Dream*. New York: Coward, McCann and Geoghegan, 1973.

Rosen, Philip. "*Screen* and the Marxist Project in Film Criticism." *Quarterly Review of Film Studies* 2, no. 3 (August 1977): 273–87.

Rosenberg, Jan. *Women's Reflections: The Feminist Film Movement*. Studies in Cinema, no. 22. Ann Arbor: UMI Research Press, 1983.

Rothman, Sheila. *Woman's Proper Place: A History of Changing Ideas and Practices, 1870 to the Present*. New York: Basic Books, 1978.

Rowland, Willard. *The Politics of TV Violence*. Beverly Hills: Sage, 1983.

———. "Recreating the Past: Problems in Rewriting the Early History of American Communications Research." Paper presented to the International Association of Mass Communication Research Conference, Prague, 1984.

Sahlins, Marshall. *Culture and Practical Reason*. Chicago: University of Chicago Press, 1976.

Said, Edward. *The World, the Text, and the Critic*. Cambridge: Harvard University Press, 1983.

Schatz, Thomas. *Hollywood Genres: Formulas, Filmmaking and the Studio System.* New York: Random House, 1981.

Seiter, Ellen. "Stereotypes and the Media: A Re-evaluation." *Journal of Communication* 36, no. 2 (Spring 1986): 14–26.

Shipley, Joseph Twadell. *The Crown Guide to the World's Great Plays.* New York: Crown Publishers, 1984.

Silverman, Kaja. "Disembodying the Female Voice." In Doane, Mellencamp, and Williams, eds., *Re-vision*, pp. 131–49.

Sklar, Robert. *Movie-Made America: A Cultural History of American Movies.* New York: Vintage Books, 1975.

Sloan, Kay. *The Loud Silents.* Urbana: University of Illinois Press, 1988.

Smith, James L. *Melodrama.* London: Methuen, 1973.

Sontag, Susan. *On Photography.* New York: Farrar, Straus and Giroux, 1973.

Spivak, Gayatri C. *In Other Worlds: Essays in Cultural Politics.* New York: Methuen, 1987.

Spock, Benjamin. *The Common Sense Book of Baby and Child Care.* New York: Duell, Sloane and Pearce, 1945.

Steeves, H. Leslie. "Feminist Theories and Media Studies." *Critical Studies in Mass Communication* 4, no. 2 (June 1987): 95–135.

Steinberg, Cobbett. *Reel Facts.* New York: Vintage Books, 1981.

Stern, Michael. "Interview." *Bright Lights* 2, no. 2 (Winter 1977–78): 29–34.

Thorburn, David. "Television Melodrama." In Newcomb, ed., *Television: The Critical View*, pp. 628–44.

Treichler, Paula, and Ellen Wartella. "Interventions: Feminist Theory and Communication Studies." *Communication* 9, no. 1 (1986): 1–18.

Tronto, Joan C. "Beyond Gender Difference to a Theory of Care." *Signs* 12, no. 4 (Summer 1987): 644–63.

Turner, Victor. "Liminal to Liminoid in Play, Flow, and Ritual: An Essay in Comparative Symbology." *Rice University Studies* 60, no. 3 (1974): 53–92.

―――. "Process, System, and Symbol: A New Anthropological Synthesis." *Daedalus* 106, no. 3 (Summer 1977): 61–80.

U.S. Department of Commerce. *Historical Statistics of the United States.* Washington, D.C.: U.S. Bureau of the Census, 1975.

Vardac, Nicholas A. *Stage to Screen: Theatrical Method from Garrick to Griffith.* Cambridge: Harvard University Press, 1949.

Vogel, Lise. *Marxism and the Oppression of Women: Toward a Unitary Theory.* New Brunswick, N.J.: Rutgers University Press, 1983.

Waites, Bernard, et al., eds. *Popular Culture: Past and Present.* London: Croom Helm, 1982.

Waldman, Diane. "'At Last I Can Tell It to Someone!': Feminine Point of View and Subjectivity in the Gothic Romance Film of the 1940s." *Cinema Journal* 23, no. 2 (Winter 1983): 29–40.

Walsh, Andrea S. *Women's Films and Female Experience, 1940 to 1950.* New York: Praeger, 1984.

Welter, Barbara. "The Cult of True Womanhood: 1820–1860." In Friedman and Shade, eds., *Our American Sisters*, pp. 96–123.

Willemen, Paul. "Presentation." In Neale, *Genre*, pp. 1–4.

Williams, Linda. "Dialogue." *Cinema Journal* 25, no. 2 (Winter 1986): 66–67.

———. "'Something Else Besides a Mother': *Stella Dallas* and the Maternal Melodrama." *Cinema Journal* 24, no. 1 (Fall 1984): 2–27.

———. "When the Woman Looks." In Doane, Mellencamp, and Williams, eds., *Re-vision*, pp. 83–99.

Williams, Raymond. *Keywords.* New York: Oxford University Press, 1983.

———. *Marxism and Literature.* New York: Oxford University Press, 1977.

———. *Modern Tragedy.* London: Chatto and Windus, 1966.

Wood, Michael. *America in the Movies.* New York: Basic Books, 1975.

Zinn, Howard. *Postwar America: 1945–1971.* Indianapolis: Bobbs-Merrill, 1973.

Filmography

All That Heaven Allows

Rel. 1955, color, 89 min. Universal-International
Prod: Ross Hunter; Dir: Douglas Sirk; Screenplay: Peg Fenwick, based on an
original story by Edna Lee and Harry Lee; Cine: Russell Metty; Ed: Frank
Gross. Did not appear on *Variety*'s Top Twenty Moneymaker list.

CAST:

Cary Scott	Jane Wyman
Ron Kirby	Rock Hudson
Sara Warren	Agnes Moorehead
Harvey	Conrad Nagel
Alida Anderson	Virginia Grey
Kay Scott	Gloria Talbott
Ned Scott	William Reynolds
Mona Plash	Jacqueline de Wit
Mick Anderson	Charles Drake
Howard Hoffer	Donald Curtis

(Ref: *Magill's*)

Belles on Their Toes

Rel. 1952, color, 88 min. Twentieth Century-Fox
Prod: Samuel G. Engel; Dir: Henry Levin; Screenplay: Phoebe and Henry
Ephron, based on a book by Frank B. Gilbreth, Jr., and Ernestine Gilbreth
Carey; Cine: Arthur E. Arling; Ed: Robert Fritch; Music Dir: Lionel Newman.
Did not appear on *Variety*'s Top Twenty Moneymaker list.

CAST:

Ann Gilbreth	Jeanne Crain
Mrs. Gilbreth	Myrna Loy
Martha	Debra Paget
Dr. Bob Grayson	Jeffrey Hunter
Sam Harper	Edward Arnold
Tom Bracken	Hoagy Carmichael
Ernestine Gilbreth	Barbara Bates

(Ref: *Motion Picture Guide*)

Cat on a Hot Tin Roof

Rel. 1958, color, 108 min. Metro-Goldwyn-Mayer
Prod: Lawrence Weingarten; Dir: Richard Brooks; Screenplay: Richard Brooks
and James Poe, based on a play by Tennessee Williams; Cine: William Daniels;
Ed: Ferris Webster; Art Dir: William A. Horning and Urie McCleary; Set
Decoration: Henry Grace and Robert Priestley. Position #8 on *Variety*'s Top
Twenty Moneymaker list for 1958.

CAST:

Maggie	Elizabeth Taylor
Brick	Paul Newman
Big Daddy	Burl Ives
Gooper	Jack Carson
Big Mama	Judith Anderson
Mae	Madeleine Sherwood

(Ref: *Magill's*)

Cheaper by the Dozen

Rel. 1950, color, 85 min. Twentieth Century-Fox
Prod: Lamar Trotti; Dir: Walter Lang; Screenplay: Lamar Trotti, based on the
novel by Frank B. Gilbreth, Jr., and Ernestine Gilbreth Carey; Cine: Leon
Shamroy: Ed: J. Watson Webb, Jr.; Music Dir: Lionel Newman; Art Dir: Lyle
Wheeler. Position #4 on *Variety*'s Top Twenty Moneymaker list for 1950.

CAST:

Frank Bunker Gilbreth	Clifton Webb
Ann Gilbreth	Jeanne Crain
Mrs. Lillian Gilbreth	Myrna Loy
Libby Lancaster	Betty Lynn
Dr. Burton	Edgar Buchanan
Ernestine Gilbreth	Barbara Bates
Mrs. Mebane	Mildred Natwick
Mrs. Monahan	Sara Allgood
Fred Gilbreth	Anthony Sydes
Jack Gilbreth	Roddy McCaskill
Frank Gilbreth, Jr.	Norman Ollestad
Martha Gilbreth	Patti Brady
Lillie Gilbreth	Carole Nugent
William Gilbreth	Jimmy Hunt
Dan Gilbreth	Teddy Driver
Mary Gilbreth	Betty Barker

(Ref: *American Movies*)

Come Back, Little Sheba

Rel. 1952, B&W, 99 min. Paramount Pictures Corp.
Prod: Hal B. Wallis; Dir: Daniel Mann; Screenplay: Ketti Frings, based on the play by William Inge; Cine: James Wong Howe; Ed: Warren Low. Tied for position #13 on *Variety*'s Top Twenty Moneymaker list for 1953.

CAST:

Doc Delaney	Burt Lancaster
Lola Delaney	Shirley Booth
Marie Buckholder	Terry Moore
Turk Fisher	Richard Jaeckel
Ed Anderson	Philip Ober
Mrs. Coffman	Liza Golm
Bruce	Walter Kelley

(Ref: *Magill's*)

The Country Girl

Rel. 1954, B&W, 104 min. Paramount Pictures Corp.
Prod: William Perlberg and George Seaton; Dir: George Seaton; Screenplay: George Seaton, based on the play "Winter Journey" by Clifford Odets; Cine: John F. Warren; Ed: Ellsworth Hoagland. Position #6 on *Variety*'s Top Twenty Moneymaker list for 1955.

CAST:

Frank Elgin	Bing Crosby
Georgie Elgin	Grace Kelly
Bernie Dodd	William Holden

(Ref: *Magill's*)

East of Eden

Rel. 1955, color, 115 min. Warner Brothers Pictures, Inc., and First National Prod. and Dir: Elia Kazan; Screenplay: Paul Osborn; Dialogue: Guy Tomajean, based on the novel by John Steinbeck; Cine: Ted McCord; Ed: Owen Marks. Tied for position #13 on *Variety*'s Top Twenty Moneymaker list for 1955.

CAST:

Cal Trask	James Dean
Abra	Julie Harris
Adam Trask	Raymond Massey
Aron Trask	Richard Davalos
Kate	Jo Van Fleet
Sam Cooper	Burl Ives
Will Hamilton	Albert Dekker
Ann	Lois Smith

Mr. Albrecht	Harold Gordon
Joe	Timothy Carey
Piscora	Mario Siletti
Roy Turner	Lonny Chapman
Rantany	Nick Dennis

(Ref: *International Dictionary*)

Father of the Bride

Rel. 1950, B&W, 93 min. Metro-Goldwyn-Mayer
Prod: Pandro S. Berman; Dir: Vincente Minnelli; Screenplay: Frances Goodrich and Albert Hackett, based on the novel by Edward Streeter; Cine: John Alton; Ed: Ferris Webster. Tied for position #6 on *Variety*'s Top Twenty Moneymaker list for 1950.

CAST:

Stanley Banks	Spencer Tracy
Ellie Banks	Joan Bennett
Kay Banks	Elizabeth Taylor
Buckley Dunstan	Don Taylor
Doris Dunstan	Billie Burke
Herbert Dunstan	Moroni Olsen

(Ref: *Magill's*)

Father's Little Dividend

Rel. 1951, B&W, 82 min. Metro-Goldwyn-Mayer
Prod: Pandro S. Berman; Dir: Vincente Minnelli; Screenplay: Albert Hackett and Frances Goodrich; Cine: John Alton; Ed: Ferris Webster. Position #10 on *Variety*'s Top Twenty Moneymaker list for 1951.

CAST:

Stanley Banks	Spencer Tracy
Ellie Banks	Joan Bennett
Kay Dunstan	Elizabeth Taylor
Buckley Dunstan	Don Taylor
Doris Dunstan	Billie Burke
Herbert Dunstan	Moroni Olsen

(Ref: *American Movies*)

From Here to Eternity

Rel. 1953, B&W, 118 min. Columbia Pictures Corp.
Prod: Buddy Adler; Exec. Prod: Harry Cohn; Dir: Fred Zinnemann; Screenplay: Daniel Taradash, based on the novel by James Jones; Cine: Burnett Guffey; Ed: William A. Lyon. Filmed in Hawaii at the Schofield Barracks. Position #2 on *Variety*'s Top Twenty Moneymaker list for 1953.

CAST:

Sergeant Milton Warden	Burt Lancaster
Robert E. Lee "Prew" Prewitt	Montgomery Clift
Karen Holmes	Deborah Kerr
Angelo Maggio	Frank Sinatra
Alma "Lorene" Burke	Donna Reed
Captain Dana Holmes	Philip Ober
Sergeant "Fatso" Judson	Ernest Borgnine

(Ref: *International Dictionary*)

Giant

Rel. 1956, color, 198 min. Warner Brothers Pictures, Inc.
Prod: George Stevens and Henry Ginsberg; Dir: George Stevens; Screenplay: Fred Guiol and Ivan Moffat, based on the novel by Edna Ferber; Cine: William C. Mellor and Edwin DuPar; Ed: William Hornbeck, Philip W. Anderson, and Fred Bohanen. Filmed in Texas. Position #3 on *Variety*'s Top Twenty Moneymaker list for 1957.

CAST:

Leslie Lynnton Benedict	Elizabeth Taylor
Jordan "Bick" Benedict	Rock Hudson
Jett Rink	James Dean
Luz Benedict (older)	Mercedes McCambridge
Vashti Snythe	Jane Withers
Uncle Bawley Benedict	Chill Wills
Luz Benedict (younger)	Carroll Baker
Jordan Benedict III	Dennis Hopper
Juana Benedict	Elsa Cardenas
Judy Benedict	Fran Bennett
Angel	Sal Mineo

(Ref: *International Dictionary*)

God's Little Acre

Rel. 1958, B&W, 110 min. United Artists
Prod: Sidney Harmon; Dir: Anthony Mann; Screenplay: Philip Yordan, based on the novel by Erskine Caldwell; Cine: Ernest Haller; Musical Dir: Elmer Bernstein; Ed: Richard C. Meyer; Asst Dir: Louis Brandt; Costumes: Sophia Stutz. A Security Pictures Production. Tied for position #17 on *Variety*'s Top Twenty Moneymaker list for 1958.

CAST:

Ty Ty Walden	Robert Ryan
Bill Thompson	Aldo Ray
Griselda	Tina Louise

Pluto	Buddy Hackett
Buck Walden	Jack Lord
Darlin' Jill	Fay Spain
Shaw Walden	Vic Morrow
Rosamund	Helen Westcott
Jim Leslie	Lance Fuller
Uncle Felix	Rex Ingram
Dave Dawson	Michael Landon
(Ref: *American Movies*)	

Imitation of Life

Rel. 1959, color, 124 min. Universal-International
Prod: Ross Hunter; Dir: Douglas Sirk; Screenplay: Eleanore Griffin and Allan Scott, based on the novel by Fannie Hurst; Cine: Russell Metty; Ed: Milton Carruth. Position #4 on *Variety*'s Top Twenty Moneymaker list for 1959.

CAST:

Lora Meredith	Lana Turner
Steve Archer	John Gavin
Allen Loomis	Robert Alda
Susie (older)	Sandra Dee
Sara Jane (older)	Susan Kohner
Annie Johnson	Juanita Moore
Susie (younger)	Terry Burhan
Sara Jane (younger)	Karen Dicker
David Edwards	Dan O'Herlihy
Frankie	Troy Donahue
(Ref: *Magill's*)	

The Long, Hot Summer

Rel. 1958, color, 115 min. Twentieth Century-Fox
Prod: Jerry Wald; Dir: Martin Ritt; Screenplay: Irving Ravetch and Harriet Frank, Jr., based on the short stories "Barn Burning" and "Spotted Horses" and part of the novel *The Hamlet* by William Faulkner; Cine: Joseph LaShelle; Ed: Louis R. Loeffler. Tied for position #17 on *Variety*'s Top Twenty Moneymaker list for 1958.

CAST:

Ben Quick	Paul Newman
Clara Varner	Joanne Woodward
Jody Varner	Anthony Franciosa
Will Varner	Orson Welles
Eula Varner	Lee Remick

Minnie Littlejohn	Angela Lansbury
Alan Stewart	Richard Anderson

(Ref: *Magill's*)

Magnificent Obsession

Rel. 1954, color, 107 min. Universal-International
Prod: Ross Hunter; Dir: Douglas Sirk; Screenplay: Robert Blees, based on the
novel by Lloyd C. Douglas and Wells Root's adaptation of a screen story by
Sarah Mason and Victor Heermen; Cine: Russell Metty; Ed: Milton Carruth.
Tied for position #7 on *Variety*'s Top Twenty Moneymaker list for 1954.

CAST:

Helen Phillips	Jane Wyman
Bob Merrick	Rock Hudson
Joyce Phillips	Barbara Rush
Nancy Ashford	Agnes Moorehead
Randolph	Otto Kruger

(Ref: *Magill's*)

The Man with the Golden Arm

Rel. 1955, B&W, 119 min. United Artists
Prod and Dir: Otto Preminger; Screenplay: Walter Newman and Lewis Meltzer,
based on the novel by Nelson Algren; Cine: Sam Leavitt; Ed: Louis R. Loeffler.
Tied for position #13 on *Variety*'s Top Twenty Moneymaker list for 1956.

CAST:

Frankie Machine	Frank Sinatra
Zasha	Eleanor Parker
Molly	Kim Novak
Sparrow	Arnold Stang
Louie	Darren McGavin
Schwiefka	Robert Strauss
Drunky	John Conti
Vi	Doro Merande
Markette	George E. Stone
Williams	George Mathews
Dominowski	Leonid Kinskey

(Ref: *American Movies*)

Not as a Stranger

Rel. 1955, B&W, 135 min. United Artists
Prod and Dir: Stanley Kramer; Screenplay: Edna and Edward Anhalt, based on
the novel by Morton Thompson; Cine: Franz Planer; Music: George Antheil;

Ed: Frederick Knudtson. Position #5 on *Variety*'s Top Twenty Moneymaker list for 1955.

CAST:

Kristina Hedvigson	Olivia de Havilland
Lucas Marsh	Robert Mitchum
Alfred Boone	Frank Sinatra
Harriet Lang	Gloria Grahame
Dr. Aarons	Broderick Crawford
Dr. Runkleman	Charles Bickford
Dr. Snider	Myron McCormick
Job Marsh	Lon Chaney
Ben Cosgrove	Jesse White
Oley	Harry Morgan
Brundage	Lee Marvin
Bruni	Virginia Christine
Dr. Dietrich	Whit Bissell
Dr. Lettering	Jack Raine
Miss O'Dell	Mae Clarke

(Ref: *American Movies*)

On the Waterfront

Rel. 1954, B&W, 108 min. Horizon Productions
Released by Columbia Pictures Corp.
Prod: Sam Spiegel; Dir: Elia Kazan; Screenplay: Budd Schulberg, based on an original story by Budd Schulberg, suggested by a series of newspaper articles by Malcolm Johnson; Cine: Boris Kaufman; Ed: Gene Milford; Music Score: Leonard Bernstein. Filmed in New York and Hoboken, N.J. Position #15 on *Variety*'s Top Twenty Moneymaker list for 1954.

CAST:

Terry Malloy	Marlon Brando
Edie Doyle	Eva Marie Saint
Father Barry	Karl Malden
Johnny Friendly	Lee J. Cobb
Charley Malloy	Rod Steiger
"Pop" Doyle	John Hamilton
"Kayo" Dugan	Pat Henning
Big Mac	James Westerfield
Glover	Leif Erickson
Gilette	Martin Balsam

(Ref: *International Dictionary*)

Peyton Place

Rel. 1957, color, 162 min. Twentieth Century-Fox
Prod: Jerry Wald; Dir: Mark Robson; Screenplay: John Michael Hayes, based on
the novel by Grace Metalious; Cine: William C. Mellor; Ed: David Bretherton.
Position #2 on *Variety*'s Top Twenty Moneymaker list for 1958.

CAST:

Constance MacKenzie	Lana Turner
Selena Cross	Hope Lange
Michael Rossi	Lee Philips
Dr. Swain	Lloyd Nolan
Lucas Cross	Arthur Kennedy
Norman Page	Russ Tamblyn
Alison MacKenzie	Diane Varsi
Betty Anderson	Terry Moore
Rodney Harrington	Barry Coe
Nellie Cross	Betty Field
Ted Carter	David Nelson
Mr. Harrington	Leon Ames
Paul Cross	Bill Lundmark
(Ref: *Magill's*)	

Picnic

Rel. 1955, color, 115 min. Columbia Pictures Corp.
Prod: Fred Kohlmar; Dir: Joshua Logan; Screenplay: Daniel Taradash, based on
the play by William Inge; Cine: James Wong Howe; Ed: Charles Nelson and
William A. Lyon; Art Dir: William Flannery and Jo Meilziner; Set Decoration:
Robert Priestley. Position #6 on *Variety*'s Top Twenty Moneymaker list for 1956.

CAST:

Hal Carter	William Holden
Madge Owens	Kim Novak
Rosemary Sidney	Rosalind Russell
Millie Owens	Susan Strasberg
Flo Owens	Betty Field
Alan Benson	Cliff Robertson
Howard Bevans	Arthur O'Connell
Mrs. Potts	Verna Felton
(Ref: *Magill's*)	

A Place in the Sun

Rel. 1951, B&W, 122 min. Paramount Pictures Corp.
Prod and Dir: George Stevens; Screenplay: Harry Brown and Michael Wilson,
based on the novel *An American Tragedy* by Theodore Dreiser; Cine: William C.

Mellor; Ed: William Hornbeck; Music: Franz Waxman; Costumes: Edith Head. Position #8 on *Variety*'s Top Twenty Moneymaker list for 1951.

CAST:

George Eastman	Montgomery Clift
Angela Vickers	Elizabeth Taylor
Alice Tripp	Shelley Winters
Hannah Eastman	Anne Revere
Anthony Vickers	Shepperd Strudwick
Mrs. Vickers	Frieda Inescort
Earl Eastman	Keefe Brasselle
Bellows	Fred Clark
Frank Marlowe	Raymond Burr

(Ref: *International Dictionary*)

Rebel without a Cause

Rel. 1955, color, 111 min. Warner Brothers Pictures, Inc.
Prod: David Weisbart; Dir: Nicholas Ray; Screenplay: Stewart Stern, from an adaptation by Irving Shulman of a story by Nicholas Ray inspired from the story "The Blind Run," title from a book by Dr. Robert M. Lindner (1944); Cine: Ernest Haller; Ed: William Ziegler; Production Design: William Wallace; Music: Leonard Rosenman. Filmed in nine weeks. Tied for position #11 on *Variety*'s Top Twenty Moneymaker list for 1956.

CAST:

Jim Stark	James Dean
Judy	Natalie Wood
Jim's Father	Jim Backus
Jim's Mother	Ann Doran
Judy's Mother	Rochelle Hudson
Judy's Father	William Hopper
Plato	Sal Mineo
Buzz	Corey Allen
Goon	Dennis Hopper
Ray	Edward Platt
Mil	Steffi Sydney
Plato's Nursemaid	Marietta Canty
Jim's Grandmother	Virginia Brissac

(Ref: *International Dictionary*)

Some Came Running
Rel. 1958, color, 127 min. Metro-Goldwyn-Mayer
Prod: Sol C. Siegel; Dir: Vincente Minnelli; Screenplay: John Patrick and Arthur
Sheekman, based on the novel by James Jones; Cine: William Daniels; Ed:
Adrienne Fazan; Music: Elmer Bernstein. Position #10 on *Variety*'s Top Twenty
Moneymaker list for 1959.

CAST:

Dave Hirsh	Frank Sinatra
Bama Dillert	Dean Martin
Ginny Moorhead	Shirley MacLaine
Gwen French	Martha Hyer
Frank Hirsh	Arthur Kennedy
Raymond Lanchak	Steven Peck
Agnes Hirsh	Leora Dana

(Ref: *Magill's*)

A Streetcar Named Desire
Rel. 1951, B&W, 125 min. Warner Brothers Pictures, Inc.
Prod: Charles K. Feldman; Dir: Elia Kazan; Screenplay: Tennessee Williams,
based on Oscar Saul's adaptation of the play by Tennessee Williams; Cine: Harry
Stradling; Ed: David Weisbart; Art Dir: Richard Day; Set Decoration: George
James Hopkins; Music: Alex North. Position #5 on *Variety*'s Top Twenty
Moneymaker list for 1951.

CAST:

Blanche DuBois	Vivien Leigh
Stanley Kowalski	Marlon Brando
Stella Kowalski	Kim Hunter
Mitch	Karl Malden

(Ref: *International Dictionary*)

Written on the Wind
Rel. 1956, color, 99 min. Universal-International
Prod: Albert Zugsmith; Dir: Douglas Sirk; Screenplay: George Zuckerman,
from the novel by Robert Wilder; Cine: Russell Metty; Ed: Russell Schoengarth.
Filmed Nov. 1955 through Jan. 1956. Position #11 on *Variety*'s Top Twenty
Moneymaker list for 1957.

CAST:

Mitch Wayne	Rock Hudson
Lucy Moore Hadley	Lauren Bacall
Kyle Hadley	Robert Stack
Marylee Hadley	Dorothy Malone

Jasper Hadley   Robert Keith
Biff Miley   Grant Williams
Hoak Wayne   Harry Shannon
Dan Willis   Robert J. Wilke
Dr. Cochran   Edward Platt
(Ref: *International Dictionary*)

REFERENCES

Magill's Survey of Cinema, edited by Frank N. Magill. Englewood Cliffs, N.J.:
Salem Press, 1980.
American Movies Reference Book, edited by Paul Michael. Englewood Cliffs, N.J.:
Prentice-Hall, 1969.
The Motion Picture Guide, edited by Jay Robert Nash and Stanley Ralph Ross.
Chicago: Cinebooks, 1985.
The International Dictionary of Films and Filmmakers, edited by Christopher Lyon.
Chicago: St. James Press, 1984.

Index